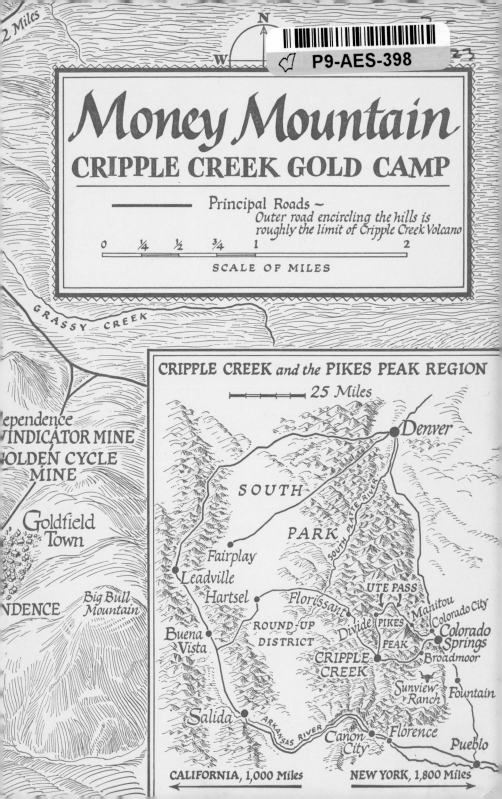

Money Mountain
CRIPPLE CREEK GOLD CAMP

Principal Roads ~
*Outer road encircling the hills is
roughly the limit of Cripple Creek Volcano*

0   ¼   ½   ¾   1   2

SCALE OF MILES

GRASSY CREEK

ependence
VINDICATOR MINE
OLDEN CYCLE
MINE

Goldfield
Town

NDENCE   Big Bull
Mountain

CRIPPLE CREEK *and the* PIKES PEAK REGION

25 Miles

Denver

SOUTH

PARK

SOUTH PLATTE RIVER

Fairplay
Leadville
Hartsel

UTE PASS

Florissant   Manitou
Divide   PIKES   Colorado City
ROUND-UP   PEAK   Colorado
DISTRICT   Springs
Buena   Broadmoor
Vista   CRIPPLE
CREEK
Sunview
Ranch   Fountain

Salida   ARKANSAS RIVER   Florence

Canon   Pueblo
City

CALIFORNIA, 1,000 Miles   NEW YORK, 1,800 Miles

By Marshall Sprague

THE BUSINESS OF GETTING WELL

MONEY MOUNTAIN

MONEY MOUNTAIN

Photo by Knutson-Bowers

It is a beautiful drive of an hour or so from Colorado Springs up to Cripple Creek. As you approach the great old gold town from above, you can see beyond it the crests of the Sangre de Cristos and the snow-capped Continental Divide.

MONEY MOUNTAIN

The Story of Cripple Creek Gold

By MARSHALL SPRAGUE

WITH ILLUSTRATIONS

Little, Brown and Company · *Boston*

For

EDNA JANE

One man's bonanza

Foreword

IF YOU EVER VISIT the Pikes Peak region you should spend an hour or so going up to Cripple Creek. It is one of the loveliest drives in Colorado and it won't curl your hair even though you climb from 6000 feet at Colorado Springs to 10,000 feet near Cripple. The Ute Pass road meanders around the north slope of Pikes Peak to Divide and dips south along the placid old mountain. There comes a final ascent and a leveling out in wild country where the ravens frown at you as they float overhead in the deep blue sky. The air has a bite to it and the top of Pikes Peak seems very near. Fifty miles south are the lacy crests of the Sangre de Cristos. To the west is the Continental Divide. Then your road skirts the rim of a depression which contains the last thing you would expect, a large red-and-white town spreading up the hillside toward the spruce-capped cone of Mount Pisgah.

This is Cripple Creek, capital of the Cripple Creek Mining District, once the world's greatest gold camp. The town is a quiet, dilapidated place today and there is something pathetic about the traffic light at Second and Bennett blinking hour after hour for a trickle of cars. It is not a ghost town, though gold production is a tenth of what it was in the late Nineties and early 1900s. All around are low, grassy hills spotted with tan, gray, purple and orange mine dumps.

Aspen and spruce groves cap some of the hills and spill down the gulches. Weathered gallows-frames rise above clusters of unpainted mine-shaft buildings. The gold camp as a whole, hemmed in by higher hills, is the size of a small cattle ranch, barely ten thousand acres. Nobody writes odes to it and yet it has an odd bleak beauty, like the profile of William S. Hart.

But our story is about the past, about the sad or comic events, the often frantic events, that occurred when a peaceful alpine pasture was found to overlay one of the great treasures of history. The main use of gold is emotional, not material; it is something everybody has yearned for since the time of Adam and Eve. Kings and dictators and money experts have tried to suppress the craving but it has remained with us always, as anyone will tell you who is familiar with today's enormous international black market. No small spot on earth has satisfied this gold craving so completely for so many people over so long a period as Cripple Creek, Colorado. During its first quarter century, 1891 to 1916, Cripple's production reached $340,000,000. Another $90,000,000 has been found in the years of decline, making a grand total to 1952 of $432,000,000. The gold total, weighing 20,000,000 ounces, or 625 tons, is figured mostly at the gold price of $20.67 an ounce which prevailed up to 1934. At today's official gold price of $35 an ounce the grand total would be $700,000,000.

This is a terrible amount of wealth with which to stimulate the greed of men. The South African Rand has produced far more, but the Rand is a vast region, not a gold camp measured in acres. Australia's famous camps, Bendigo and Kalgoorlie, have produced gold worth $425,000,000 each. The epic Mother Lode of the Forty-Niners produced a little more than half as much gold as Cripple. The Comstock Lode's production, two-thirds silver and one-third gold, was $380,-000,000. Shortlived gold camps like Dawson (Klondike), Nome and Fairbanks were far behind Cripple. Today's great producers — the Homestake Mine in South Dakota and the booming Ontario districts, Porcupine and Kirkland Lake — didn't catch up with Cripple until the late 1930s, twenty years after Cripple's good days were ended. Homestake, Porcupine and Kirkland Lake are not free gold camps at all, but giant corporations like General Motors. Cripple was the last of the free gold camps, the likes of which are not apt to be seen again.

It was in 1890 that Bob Womack, a part-time cowboy, ended his long search for pay dirt by striking the El Paso Lode near what became Cripple Creek town. Two years later, the tenderfeet wired Senator Teller to stop worrying about the national debt: Cripple's gold would pay it. Between '91 and 1900, Cripple's population increased from fifteen people to 50,000; its monthly payroll from $50 to $1,000,000; its annual production from $2000 worth of calves to $20,000,000 worth of gold bricks. In '99, a carload of Cripple Creek ore brought $219,040.92, an all-time record. Winfield Scott Stratton, a three-dollar-a-day Colorado Springs carpenter, sold his Independence Mine for $10,000,000, the highest price ever paid for a single bonanza.

Cripple's story from the time of Bob Womack's strike through a decade of growth ending with Stratton's death in 1902 and on to the big business period dominated by A. E. Carlton is a capsule history of the United States from country bumpkin to world power. The camp's prosperity helped the nation through the Panic of '93. Its gold routed the forces of Populism in '94 and helped to ruin the political ambitions of William Jennings Bryan. It had a great deal to do with making Colorado what it is today.

But Cripple never had a good press agent. Virginia City had Mark Twain, Lucius Beebe and many others. The Klondike had Jack London and Robert W. Service. All Cripple had was Julian Street and his belated essay about sporting life on Myers Avenue. Maybe writers avoided Cripple because it did not conform to gold camp tradition. The boom did not start in a wilderness but in well-established cow country. Cripple was accessible from the beginning — only eighteen miles as the crow flies from Colorado Springs which was served in 1891 by six railroads. By '95, two railroads reached Cripple itself, and honeymooners from Denver took the de luxe sleeper "Eleven Come Seven" just for the beauty and comfort of the trip. In 1901 a third railroad climbed up to the camp.

It is almost impossible now to picture Bennett Avenue as it once was: swarming with gamblers in sharp shoes, Upper Tens (mine owners, supers and such), tourists peering warily into wine rooms to see sights they wouldn't see back home. There were mule-skinners, ministers, railroaders, hammersmen and drillers, tram-men and skippers, timbermen and hoisters. Now and then an unshaven prospector would amble by with his burro, coffeepot and pick. Men in city clothes were mostly lawyers or brokers or pimps or politicians or assayers or labor union leaders or bunco steerers. Ladies in Paris gowns and floppy hats might be Upper Tens or sporting women up to shop. The sporting women lived on Myers Avenue, a happy sin belt 433 yards long — dance halls, parlor houses, pawnshops, drug mills and one-girl cribs with talent of every color from the hook shops of the world.

Above Bennett were churches, schools and social clubs

carrying the torch for conventional morality — on the surface at least. These upper towners were not snide about the sporting life below them. On the contrary, they were proud of it. They were proud, for instance, that any woman could walk anywhere in Cripple at any time without being molested. It wasn't a matter of good policing. It was just a code. Of course it wasn't wise to walk down Myers during gunplay, fist fights or hair pullings. Harm that came to a lady under such circumstances was really her own fault.

Somewhere in the milling mob you could have noticed a tall, shabby fellow in his late forties, a bit unsteady on his feet and a grin on his pleasant pudding of a face. That would have been Bob Womack, but you wouldn't have paid any attention to him.

He only discovered the place.

Contents

List of Illustrations

PART ONE

Womack & Company

CHAPTER I

Kentucky Goes West

THE WOMACK FAMILY had the gold idea built into their bones. Samuel Redd Womack, Bob's father, was born somewhere in the Deep South, in 1820, four years after the English started modern times with a scheme which they called "going on the gold standard." This meant that they would give one English pound to anybody from anywhere, in exchange for .2354 ounces of gold.

As a youngster, Sam Womack moved north to Kentucky, became an ardent Jackson Democrat, and said "Amen" when Andrew Jackson proposed that the value of the dollar, in relation to the English pound, be fixed at $4.8665. In 1837, the United States Treasury began to pay $20.67 for an ounce of gold.

Sam acquired a farm in Jefferson County, Kentucky, about nine miles from Louisville. He married a gentle creature from the neighborhood, named Corella Booker, who loved Sam because of his distinguished bearing, his scholarly mind, his chivalrous manners, and his neat goatee. Sam was subject to minor ailments and Corella decided that he did not have long to live. She applied herself to the task of making life easy for him. When the children arrived Corella didn't ask Sam to help with their care. Bob Womack, who one day would discover Cripple Creek, was the first child, born in

1844.[1] Maggie Booker was born in 1846; Eliza G. in 1848; and William W. in 1851.

During the 1840s Sam had observed that the English gold standard was being accepted by most countries. But, as world trade expanded, he heard complaints that the small existing gold supply and the existing tiny production of new gold were not meeting the demand for the metal in its role as the official world-wide standard of value.

And then came the historic event that solved the gold shortage and changed the destinies of the Womack family, plus a billion other people. On January 24, 1848, James Wilson Marshall spotted pure gold gleaming in the sands of Sutter's Mill, on the American River, California.

Of all the forces making our modern world, none appears to have been more effective than the chain reaction set off by the observant Marshall. Between 1849 and 1859 the existing world gold supply (which had accumulated during the previous fifty centuries) had doubled. World credit burgeoned like those breakfast foods blown many times their natural size. The American West was the chief beneficiary of the fantastic outpouring of gold-created capital and credit. But even the Javanese noticed people were eating more coconuts.

When the year 1849 began, Sam Womack was spending half his time reading Louisville papers and everything else which carried stories about gold in California. As the Forty-Niners started their conquest of the Far West, Sam longed to join the rush. But his children were small, and he refused to desert his family as many of his neighbors were doing. So he stayed home to watch the growth of an immense industry that set men to digging up the landscape all over the world. In 1851 he read of the discovery of gold at Bendigo in Australia. He read about gold at Antioquia in Colombia, and gold at Morro Velho in Brazil. Word reached him about the silver-and-gold Comstock Lode at a spot to be called Virginia City, Nevada. He heard that thousands were flocking from the exhausted California placers to the Fraser River in British Columbia.

These discoveries were exciting but what thrilled Sam most was news of the so-called Pikes Peak Gold Rush, the biggest and most dramatic since the migration to California. The Pikes Peak Rush never got within sixty miles of Pikes Peak. It began in '58, at Cherry Creek, on the eastern edge of the Rockies. A town named Denver was established there and swarms of gold-seekers were moving into the mountains just west of Denver where gold and silver could be picked up, somebody said, by the bucketful. The size of the Pikes Peak Rush reflected the desperation of people suffering from the Panic of '57.

Sam discovered that Louisville was only 1200 miles from Denver. He had friends in Denver. George and David Griffith were there, Kentuckians who would find a bonanza soon and would stake out as a homestead the future mining center of Georgetown, Colorado. Sam's youngest child, William, was now almost nine years old and Sam's family could manage on the farm without him for a while. Sam's wife, Corella, was not much of a manager but she could lean on eleven-year-old Eliza G., a stolid little person who exhibited already a conviction that two plus two equals four. And still Sam hesitated about leaving for Colorado. Like many others in the border state of Kentucky, he was confused by the partisan struggle preceding the Civil War. Most of his friends and neighbors were Unionists. Sam regarded himself as a true Southerner, stressing his Deep South origin by referring to his farm as a "plantation."

Perhaps Sam thought that he could help keep Kentucky in the South. But when Beauregard attacked Fort Sumter Sam realized that Kentucky was lost. And he feared that seventeen-year-old Bob would be called into the Union Army unless Bob got away from Kentucky. Bob was a big boy now. He weighed 180 pounds and was almost six feet tall. He was shy, docile and clumsy. He liked to hunt for birds' nests or for egrets. He liked to hunt for things.

Before the end of April, 1861, Sam decided to head West and to take Bob with him. They could duck any Union draft in the wilds of Colorado. Sam and Bob took the usual route — by rail to St. Joe, Missouri, and a little farther, to Atchison, Kansas, and then on to Denver by ox team, along the Platte River. Bob was in the awkward age and he could never get enough to eat. He got pretty tired on the trip, so Sam left him in Denver to rest up. Sam continued a short distance into the mountains to Idaho Springs.

Bob took a decrepit stage to join Sam and was frightened by the terrifying ride up Clear Creek Canyon. He arrived at Idaho Springs in a fearful temper, one of the few times in his life when he really got mad. The stage, Bob told his father, had rattled his leg bones out of line and he swore he would never ride one of the damned things again. Sam replied that this was nonsense. The stage may not have been like a railway coach back East but no finer transportation could be found in Colorado. Quite an argument ensued, the upshot of which was that Bob packed his grip and announced his immediate departure on foot back to God's country, Kentucky.

Sam was involved in mining projects around Idaho Springs, so he let the boy go while he stabilized his own affairs. Bob would be safe enough. The trail from Denver to Atchison,

Kansas, was crowded with travelers. Late in June, Sam took a fast stage to catch Bob. It was a long chase. As Sam entered the railhead at Atchison there was Bob trudging along barefoot. He had been walking steadily for thirty-nine days.

But Sam wasn't going to abandon Colorado's mines just because his son didn't like the Idaho Springs stage. From Atchison to Louisville, Sam talked to Bob about the wonderful silver and gold gulches around Idaho Springs and Central City. Bit by bit Bob lost his antipathy for the mountains and started to dream of finding a bonanza. Back on the plantation Sam talked to Corella and the children about the glories of Colorado. Some weeks later Sam sold the plantation, and all six Womacks — father, mother, two boys and two girls — made the long trip to Idaho Springs.

During the next few years, Sam and Bob and the youngest boy, William, tackled every phase of gold and silver mining — placers, lodes, an early stamp mill on Clear Creek, stock promotion. They learned how to detect salted prospect holes, and how to take assays of unlikely holes in such a way as to make the holes look promising to a tenderfoot. Sam found a rich silver streak on a Georgetown claim that became a part of Lee R. Seaton's $500,000 bonanza.

By 1867 Sam had piled up a considerable fortune, $10,000 or more. But he conceived a notion that mountains and mining were having a terrible effect on his health. Sam's frailty, which Corella had coddled for twenty years, had stood the rugged conditions of mountain life surprisingly well. But once again he and Corella felt that his days were numbered.[2]

Bob Womack was twenty-three years old now and strong as an ox. William Womack was sixteen and a willing worker. Sam figured that what he needed was a cattle ranch on the plains where his two sons could do the chores, and he could be waited on by Corella, Eliza G., and Maggie. In this way he figured that he could hang on to the slender thread of his life a little longer. For a month he toured the plains north of Denver, but found no good ranch land that was unoccupied. Then he journeyed south of Denver seventy-five miles to Colorado City, at the foot of Pikes Peak.

He ran into a smart lad named Irving Howbert, who knew everything about the Pikes Peak region.[3] Howbert told him that most of the land on Monument and Fountain Creeks was taken, but that there was vacant land twelve miles south on Rock Creek or on Little Fountain Creek. Howbert warned Sam not to be discouraged by the inhospitable aspect of this land. Its sparse brown grass was very nourishing to cattle even in winter.

On Little Fountain Creek Sam found a picturesque acreage close up to the Front Range foothills near Deadman Canyon. For the next quarter century this acreage, which Sam called Sunview Ranch, would be headquarters for the Womack family. From the beginning, Sam's position at Sunview was like that of the feudal lords of Europe. He did no work, and his word was law. The ranch's operating boss was not Bob or William, but Sam's eldest daughter, Eliza G., who served also as legal adviser and fiscal agent. Eliza already was a confirmed spinster. She was by no means an unattractive girl, but she was as far as she could be from the cuddly type. Her sex appeal suffered further from the fact that she had a fine brain. The average male was afraid of her. From her teens on she was addressed respectfully as "Miss Lida."

In 1869, Irving Howbert became clerk of El Paso County, which encompassed the Pikes Peak area. Miss Lida made a habit of dropping in on him for advice on land matters once a week. One day Howbert tipped her off that a big promotion was on the way. A man named General William J. Palmer was planning a railroad down from Denver, and would found a town, Colorado Springs, three miles east of Colorado City. Irving advised her to get a firm legal grip on Sunview Ranch.

Miss Lida knew the dodges by which men took more land from the government than they were entitled to. She could have picked up thousands of acres around Sunview by using dummy names and paying a bribe here and there. She was incapable of fraud, though she believed in taking full advantage of the law. Carefully she charted the course of Little Fountain Creek, and then asked for land patents at strategic points along the stream. Pre-emption patents of 160 acres each, at $1.25 per acre, went to Bob and William Womack. Miss Lida and Sam Womack received free 160-acre homesteads. Miss Lida selected these four bits of land so wisely in relation to Little Fountain that Sunview Ranch and its water controlled an area six miles square. On it the family could run a herd of a thousand beef cattle.

For a while Miss Lida tried hard to make a rancher out of Bob. In most respects he failed her. However, he did like the riding part of ranch work. He was a graceful, expert rider, drunk or sober, and many tales went over El Paso County about his horsemanship. People said that he rode a horse up the stairs of the first parlor house in Colorado City. He could lean from the saddle and snatch a bottle of bourbon from the ground with his teeth. He could shoot out a street lamp at a full gallop. He could guide his horse safely at a canter any dark night along the rough road from Colorado City southward to Sunview Ranch.

These feats were not of a sort that encouraged the Pikes Peak community to take Bob seriously. Yet he was admired for his knowledge of fishing streams, of bear and elk terrain, of old Indian trails, of gravel beds that might contain placer gold. Bob panned Little Fountain Creek mile by mile up the foothills of Pikes Peak almost to its source near St. Peter's Dome in the blue-green forests high above Colorado City. He searched the sands of nearby Rock Creek, following it northwesterly to the slopes of Vigil Peak.

In 1871 Bob and the other Womacks heard interesting news. Some friends of theirs, the Welty family, were leaving their plains ranch north of Colorado Springs, and were moving to a high valley on the southwest side of Pikes Peak. Water for their stock up there would come from a stream which the Weltys called Cripple Creek.

CHAPTER II

They Called It Cripple

LEVI WELTY and his four children came to Colorado from Ohio to find a gold mine, and then took up ranching near Pikes Peak shortly before the Womacks settled at Sunview. All went well with the Weltys until General Palmer turned up with his railroad and his new town of Colorado Springs. These developments multiplied the population of the plains around Pikes Peak tenfold in a single year. Levi Welty found himself in continual squabbles over water rights. There was some cattle rustling. The grass was becoming overgrazed.

The Weltys decided to investigate the sparsely populated country west of Pikes Peak. In '71 Levi Welty and his three boys rode up Ute Pass and across the hills thirty-five miles to Judge Castello's Ute trading post, which the Judge called Florissant after his home town near St. Louis. Castello told the Weltys to look over the land south of Florissant. A nine-mile ride brought them to a stream junction southeast of which the terrain rose in forested foothills culminating in the cone of Mount Pisgah. The Weltys pushed up the ravines around the north side of Pisgah, and saw below them a park-like valley watered by a winding stream. The valley's sides seemed steep enough to contain cattle.

The four men went to work in that valley and built a log cabin near a spring which was the source of the winding stream. Soon Welty cattle from the plains were grazing in the valley and on the low grassy hills around it. One day the Weltys built a shack over the spring to keep the deer and elk from fouling it. While building the shack a log got away from one of the boys and rolled hard against his brother, injuring him slightly. In the excitement Levi Welty discharged his gun and a piece of buckshot nipped the flesh of his hand. A pet calf then tried to hightail it out of there by jumping the stream, breaking its leg in the process.

When order was restored, Levi Welty remarked, "Well, boys, this sure is some cripple creek!" And that's how the place which was to become the world's greatest gold camp got its name.[1]

Though Bob Womack had never visited Cripple Creek, he knew exactly where it was. A number of times he had chased bear or elk from the slopes of Vigil Peak, westward across a ridge or two to Middle Beaver, and down Middle Beaver to its junction with West Beaver. West Beaver formed the eastern boundary of the Cripple Creek area which was six miles wide from east to west. Its average altitude was around 10,000 feet. Beyond it westward the West Pikes Peak country was 1000 feet lower, stretching for sixty miles across South Park to the Upper Arkansas River and the Big Divide.

A favorite route West used by the Forty-Niners and the Fifty-Niners was along the Arkansas to the Rockies and northerly past Pikes Peak. Many paused at this scenic spot to prospect. No luck. They panned the Fountain up Ute Pass, but they did not push far enough around the peak to reach Cripple Creek. During the Sixties, miners by the thousands crossed and recrossed the West Pikes Peak country. A mere handful had settled down there to ranch up to the time of the arrival of the Welty family at Cripple Creek. The West Pikes Peak country had fine grazing land but it had not been surveyed and was not open for homesteading.

In July of '73, Miss Lida Womack sent Brother Bob east of Sunview a few miles to Uncle Ben Requa's general store and restaurant at Fountain, Colorado, to buy some thread. Ben's store catered to travelers between Denver and Santa Fé. Bob found a dozen men eating lunch at Requa's, one of the group being a sort of relative of his, Colonel Theodore Lowe. Lowe was just Bob's age, twenty-nine. He was born in Kentucky not far from the old Womack place, and was a cousin of Emery Lowe, who had married Bob's sister, Maggie Womack.

Theodore Lowe was a great fixer, which may explain how he got to be a Union colonel at the age of nineteen. After the Civil War he studied engineering in Kentucky, coming to Idaho Springs in 1867, at Sam Womack's urging, to set up as a mining expert, notary public, and anything else that might turn a dollar in a mining camp. During the next five years he acquired a wife and a solid reputation in Denver mining circles.

Theodore told Bob that the gang in the restaurant was there for the United States Geological and Geographical Survey of the Territories and that he himself had come down with them from Denver as an adviser. The fellow at the head of the table who was eating the most was Ferdinand Vandeveer Hayden, boss of the survey.[2] The party's present objective was to chart the West Pikes Peak country so that it could be opened legally for settlement. Theodore took Bob across the room and introduced him to Hayden. For thirty minutes Bob described to Hayden the various streams and trails which led over the Pikes Peak range to the rolling country beyond.

The surveyors visited the Cripple Creek area a week later,

but Hayden himself stayed in Fountain to correct Lieutenant Pike's faulty triangulations of Pikes Peak and to eat Uncle Ben Requa's good food. Later in the summer, Theodore Lowe told Bob that geologists in the party had called the Cripple Creek area a volcanic formation composed of "trachorheite." Some of them had become quite excited over some small chunks of dirty-gray rock which they had picked up in the gulches.

Just a year after Bob's meeting with the survey party, Irving Howbert sent word asking him to drop in at the County Clerk's office in Colorado Springs. When Bob got there, a man was talking to Irving, a man named H. T. Wood, who said he had been with the Government surveyors in '73. Wood declared that there was gold in Cripple's volcanic rock. He wanted to form a party to drive a tunnel at Cripple, and he wanted a guide. Bob said no guide was necessary if the party went in by way of Ute Pass and Florissant. The road to the Welty ranch at Cripple Creek source was well marked.

Irving Howbert couldn't find any gold-seekers for Wood in Colorado Springs. Uncle Ben Requa did much better down at Fountain. He collected nearly a hundred men. Miss Lida gave Bob a day off and he went with the party to the Welty cabin in Cripple Creek valley at the east base of Mount Pisgah. From there Wood led the group southeasterly along the base of the round hills, to a ravine now known as Eclipse Gulch. A tunnel of a hundred feet was blasted in a dike of decomposed, greenish basalt. Aspens cut from the slopes of Lone Tree Hill (today's Raven Hill) provided the timbering.

On September 17, 1874, the Wood-Requa party gave its Lone Tree Prospect Tunnel an official air by naming the area "the Mount Pisgah Mining District." When County Clerk Howbert made out the location certificate for the tunnel he listed as locators the names of Wood, Requa, Clayton J. Croft, H. N. Brown, M. E. Jones, and R. H. Magee. But they found no gold in the tunnel, only a gray stuff which Wood said was "white iron." Probably it was sylvanite, Cripple's characteristic gold ore. The tunnel lay in the heart of what would become, in twenty years, the richest part of Cripple Creek.[3]

Bob Womack stayed in Cripple only briefly on his first trip. Most of that time he visited with the Weltys — old Levi and his boys, George, Frank and Alonzo. Levi thought the Wood-Requa party was a joke. He knew gold ore when he saw it. If Cripple had any he would have found it long ago. He told Bob that he would be glad when Wood and Requa called off the search. The Weltys did not relish this influx of gold-crazy people scaring the cattle with dynamite and otherwise disturbing the peace of the range. Levi said, though, that he would welcome a few more ranchers. It was pretty lonely.

During 1875 the Womacks often discussed Cripple Creek. Bob and William took Sam up Rock Creek and on to West Beaver to show him that cattle from Sunview Ranch could be driven to Cripple's high pastures. The Womacks were beginning to feel the same population pressure that the Weltys had felt north of Colorado Springs five years earlier. Big sheep operators like J. F. Seldomridge were taking up all the land they could find along the edge of the mountains in El Paso County and were bringing their flocks from New Mexico. The grasshoppers were very bad that summer. If the Womacks didn't find additional range soon, they would have to reduce their stock.

William Womack made a trip to Kentucky in '76 and returned with a wife, the former Ida Van Dyck, who was related distantly to both the Womacks and to Theodore Lowe. Miss Lida Womack and William Womack's bride learned in a day or two that Sunview was not big enough for two strong-minded females. This threat of warfare disturbed Sam so profoundly that he sent the boys off the very next week to find a spot at Cripple Creek where William and Ida could have their own home.

Bob and William reached the Welty log cabin at a propitious time. The Weltys were about to abandon Cripple Creek because they planned to qualify for homesteads on the lower west side of Mount Pisgah, in the rich Four-Mile Valley. Levi Welty offered the Womacks his squatter's rights to the 160 acres around Cripple Creek spring, plus the log dwelling, corral and springhouse, for $500 and two pigs. The Womack boys returned to Sunview and put the proposition before Miss Lida and Ida, both of whom were delighted at the prospect of getting rid of each other.

Miss Lida went scurrying to Irving Howbert. Irving said that the Welty deal looked good to him. He suggested that William Womack apply for the Cripple Creek spring homestead and that Bob apply for a second homestead nearby, if one could be found with water on it. Bob examined the ground south of the Welty cabin and picked 160 acres around a stream two miles south of Cripple Creek spring in a place called Arequa Gulch. The "A" in Arequa got thrown in somehow — the name was supposed to honor Uncle Ben Requa whose pioneer Lone Tree Tunnel was in the next gulch to the south.

Ida and William Womack trundled their belongings happily up Ute Pass to Florissant and southerly to Cripple Creek.

Ida got pregnant and settled down to a life of high-altitude bliss. Bob Womack drove Womack cattle back and forth between Cripple Creek and Sunview, as required by grazing conditions. For a time he had a room in the Welty cabin of the William Womacks. From there it was only a short walk to the pool below the springhouse where Bob concealed his whiskey from Ida's disapproving eyes. Then Ida gave birth to the first of a series of daughters. The domesticity stifled Bob and he built a shack at the foot of the gulch nearest the Welty cabin. Bob called this "Poverty Gulch," a common mining name in the West.

One day Bob bought a white colt. The colt poked his nose into a bee's nest and got stung. The swelling made the colt whistle as he breathed, so Bob called him Whistler. Bob's daily routine at Cripple Creek was to ride Whistler from Poverty Gulch southward along Cripple Creek to Arequa Gulch and northward again to the top of the ridge above Poverty Gulch. From old habit developed at Idaho Springs, Bob watched the ground as he rode, looking for outcroppings. He had a good eye for quartz outcroppings, a common clue to gold or silver veins. But he saw no quartz outcroppings at Cripple, or anything else that seemed familiar to him.

There were boulders, gravel and sandstone. Bob knew that the gravel contained placer gold as is the case on any Colorado stream. But it wasn't worth washing. Besides, Bob had the hard-rock miner's scorn of placer ground. He knew that sand was a secondary source of gold. The sand caught tiny grains of gold that came from the top of a gold-filled vein in solid rock somewhere — tiny grains broken off by erosion and washed down the stream to the sand bed. Even sand beds rich in gold were exhausted soon because they were shallow, ending at bedrock.

But gold imbedded in a crack in solid rock was apt to be a real bonanza. The gold-filled crack could extend downward all the way to China. It could extend horizontally for hundreds of yards. Placer beds were for short-term miners. What Bob wanted was to find a gold-filled crack or vein or lode — all three terms mean the same thing — in hard rock. Such a vein might produce wealth for generations.

One morning in May of '78, Bob was watering Whistler below the old Welty springhouse. His glance fell on a piece of gray stuff about nine inches long and three inches wide. He dismounted and picked up the rock and examined it. It was as light as wood, but Bob knew it to be a kind of rock called "float." Float is rock broken off of an outcrop by erosion, then carried downward by flood water. Exposure to air makes the float lighter than the outcrop from which it came, just as wood gets light when no longer a part of the living tree.

Holding the float in his hand, Bob turned his eyes upstream, hoping to spot the outcrop from which the float had broken. He knew there was no visible outcropping because he had covered the stream's drainage area hundreds of times. And yet the outcrop had to exist, buried, perhaps, under shallow wash. The float might be from a vein in the outcrop and the vein might contain gold. If it did contain gold, the float in Bob's hand would contain gold, too.

Bob pocketed the float and, on his next trip to Colorado Springs, mailed the specimen to Theodore Lowe in Denver, asking him to have an assay made. Lowe showed the float to an assayer, who promptly said it wasn't worth spending thirty-five cents on; it was just plain old rotten rock.

Lowe insisted, and the assayer went ahead. Bob's piece of float turned out to be gold-bearing ore worth $200 a ton.

Theodore Lowe hurried up to Cripple Creek to tell Bob about the assay. It meant that if Bob could find the gold-bearing vein from which his float had broken, each ton of ore from that vein could be sold to the smelters for $200, less smelting and transportation charges of 15 per cent. Bob and Theodore Lowe began to hunt for the gold vein. Their method was the same that they had used above Clear Creek at Idaho Springs. They stood at the spot where Bob had seen the float first, and they tried to pick out the routes that water took in flowing down from the slopes and gulches. Then they moved slowly up the possible routes looking for more telltale float.

They knew that as long as pieces of float could be found, the original vein from which the pieces had broken had to be still higher. When the float trail petered out then the gold vein itself must be near. They discovered that following the float was going to be a long-drawn-out business. Theodore Lowe gave up soon and returned to Denver.

One big difficulty was in the concealed nature of Cripple Creek outcrops. In ages past, Cripple's gold-bearing veins had come to the ground's surface, allowing erosion by wind and water to do its work of breaking off bits of vein and scattering these bits below. But subsequently these exposed veins had been covered by dirt and gravel to a depth of several feet, exactly as Bob had surmised.

Another trouble was that no two pieces of float assayed the same, or looked the same, due to surface alteration. At one point in the float trail the float might be gray. A few yards higher another piece of float might be brown or purple.

This confusion required constant assays, and neither Bob nor Theodore Lowe had the cash for enough of them.

Nevertheless, in the course of three years, Bob worked up his float trail for nearly two miles, reaching a point east of the Welty cabin on the west side of Poverty Gulch. All the while he punched cows in an abstracted manner, losing so many calves that Miss Lida often refused to pay him his wages. She had no faith in Bob's prospecting, and she worried about his increasing tendency, when he did have any money, to pass days at a time playing faro and soaking up bad whiskey in Colorado City.

Bob's carousing probably did him no harm, because it was counteracted by his outdoor life. What his carousing did harm was the reputation of Cripple Creek as a prospect area. On Colorado City sprees Bob bragged of his as yet undiscovered bonanza in Poverty Gulch. Transient prospectors who might have followed him to Cripple gave up the idea when they heard him declaiming in his cups. Only one miner, a Cornishman from Central City named Henry Cocking, joined Bob in this period. Cocking staked a claim in 1881 at the highest point of Bob's float trail in Poverty Gulch, and drove a short tunnel in iron-stained rock. He found nothing. He stopped two feet short of a vein that later produced $3,000,000.

There was still another reason why people around Pikes Peak were sour on Cripple's gold. Everybody knew and respected Major Demary, a mining man with important holdings at the South Park gold camps of Alma and Fairplay. Demary was an odd duck, who owned a vacation shack at Cripple Creek, in a hollow on the southeast side of Bull Hill, two miles southeast of Poverty Gulch.

Demary teased Bob about almost everything he did. He

made jokes about Bob's riding, his clothes, his drinking, his Cripple Creek gold mine. Especially his gold mine. The Major would drive Bob almost crazy with sarcastic questions about this dream mine. And then, down in Colorado Springs, Demary would imitate Bob's speech, always certain of a big laugh. Demary told Irving Howbert and other Springs leaders that Bob's float trail didn't mean much. Bob's assayer was probably faking the assays. There was no resemblance between Cripple's grassy hills and any gold field with which Major Demary was familiar. And what gold field was there with which he was not familiar?

Major Demary's opinion constituted the sort of irony that gives spice to so much mining history. His Bull Hill shack, where he sat for weeks speculating on where to find a great gold mine and thinking up gibes to make Bob Womack squirm, was located on top of the future $27,000,000 Vindicator mine.

The Major was one of many trials that Bob had to bear, trials that he weathered with the help of whiskey. His faith in Cripple did not waver, but the float trail was always getting lost, and he realized that if and when he came to the end of the float trail he would still have to locate the gold-bearing vein buried in the dirt. After he found the vein he would have to find money to blast a shaft downward. Hard-rock mining was altogether different from placer mining, where a fellow simply picked up gold pure enough to put in his teeth. Though hard-rock mines were richer than placers they required capital for development.

But the worst trial for Bob was still ahead. It happened in the spring of 1884.

CHAPTER III

Hoax at "Mount Pisgah"

THE WINTER of '84 was tough for gold and silver miners throughout Colorado. The previous ten years had brought them continuous prosperity with rich strikes occurring regularly in the San Juans, in the mountains north of Gunnison, at Leadville and at Aspen. Then a lull came. New discoveries were rare and the great Leadville activity began to contract. A large population of idle miners piled into Denver to wash dishes and to shovel snow.

Early in April, when the mountain bluebirds were starting to nest all over the West Pikes Peak country, two untidy men wearing slouch hats and plaid shirts arrived in Canon City by rail from Leadville and bought an impressive array of supplies for a prospecting trip, With two burros they moved up the steep stage road along Currant Creek. They left it near the southeast edge of South Park and ambled down West Four-Mile to the homestead of Captain H. B. Grose.

Grose's place was thirteen miles west of the two Womack homesteads at Cripple Creek. It was seven miles from the three Welty homesteads at the west foot of Mount Pisgah. Grose was a miner and a rancher who maintained an assay office across South Park at Alma. He received the two strangers and had a long talk with them. Then they left him and moved two miles up a valley which passed along the east side of Mount McIntyre. This valley was government land which Grose used for grazing.

The two men picked a spot on the gentle slope of the Mount McIntyre valley. In a few hours they dug a hole eighteen feet deep in the rich grassy loam. The spectacular thing about this hole was its unimpressiveness as a source of gold. The men stuck a post in the dirt pile which had been removed from the hole and on top of the post they nailed a smooth board. On this board they announced to the world: TELLER PLACER, TWENTY ACRES. S. J. BRADLEY, LOCATOR: DISCOVERED APRIL 5, 1884. SURVEYED BY D. G. MILLER, M. E., APRIL 7, 1884. They repacked their outfit, including a small bag of the black loam, and trekked back, forty-five miles, to Canon City.

After their departure Captain Grose mounted his horse and pulled a metallurgical Paul Revere act, alerting his neighbors on West Four-Mile that gold had been discovered at Mount McIntyre. The Piggs and the Witchers and the Witherspoons and the Covers and the Dells heard about it and passed the news northward on Four-Mile to the Weltys and Faulkners and the Marcotts and the Riggs and the Fackerells who, in turn, told the Castellos and the Bells and Captain Hensley, and the Copelands, at Florissant. In twenty-four hours, ranchers throughout the West Pikes Peak country believed that they were in on a tremendous thing. Most of them threw packs together and rushed for Mount McIntyre. Not far behind them were people from Leadville and Fairplay and Alma.

Meanwhile the two prospectors, Locator Bradley and Surveyor Miller, arrived in Canon City full of smiles. They did not object, when they had their black loam assayed, to public announcement of the results — $2000 worth of gold to the ton! The wonderful word spread over Canon City and raced beyond to Salida and Pueblo and Denver. The Denver & Rio Grande Railroad agent called a meeting of Canon City merchants and freighters. Contributions were collected to help Bradley and Miller in developing their bonanza. More money was given to them to make it worth their while to reveal the site of their treasure. The D. & R. G. agent wired his Denver superiors that a gold rush was about to occur, with Canon City as a supply point. The D. & R. G. high command filled the Denver papers with ads offering excursion rates to "the great new gold camp at Mount Pisgah, near Canon City." As we have seen, Teller Placer was at Mount McIntyre, thirteen miles west of Mount Pisgah. Nobody knows who was responsible for the error in names.

Locator Bradley hardly had time to hurry back up Currant Creek to his prospect hole before the gold rush was in full flood. The Denver & Rio Grande press agent reported in the papers that "all the country is excited over an alleged gold discovery at Mount Pisgah, near Pikes Peak. Crowds from neighboring towns are flocking in. Passenger and freight transportation lines are operating from Canon City, Fairplay, and Leadville. Grocery and outfitting stocks are on the way. The mineral is a carbonate assaying one hundred ounces in gold."

Hackmen from Salida and Pueblo hurried to Canon City to help haul men to the "Mount Pisgah" gold field, at five dollars a head. Canon City merchants piled their wares on the sidewalks to save the time of the prospectors. The D. & R. G. ran frequent trains from Denver to Canon City, at $6.40 each way. Soon the Currant Creek stage road and the trails leading from it to Mount McIntyre were jammed with old and young miners, clerks and ranchers, bums and bankers. They walked or they rode in wagons, carts and hacks, on mules, burros and horses. They were loaded down with picks, shovels, tents, frying pans, coffeepots, beveled gold pans, whiskey barrels, beer kegs, hams and groceries. At Mount McIntyre everything was in turmoil. Three square miles of gramma grass pasture surrounding "Teller Placer" were staked out.

Bob Womack heard about the discovery soon after Captain Grose began spreading the news. Frank Welty had a pet buffalo calf and Bob had gone down to the Welty ranch to examine it. Bob's notion was that Ida Womack's small daughter, aged four, needed a playmate. A two-hundred-pound buffalo calf, he figured, would be just the thing. While he was discussing the matter with Frank, Grose came hurrying over with his gold story.

Grose had souped it up considerably, and right away Bob scented a rat. He had been all over the West Four-Mile area, from the gulches of Cover and Witcher Mountains around McIntyre and the Castle to Saddle Mountain. Only a week earlier he and Bob Witherspoon and some others had driven Old Mose, the famous grizzly, from hibernation and chased him past McIntyre and Saddle until they lost him in Eleven-Mile Canyon, on the South Platte.[1] Mount McIntyre, Bob decided, was a good place for grizzly bears, but it couldn't be a placer gold area. To make certain, Bob left the Weltys and rode Whistler south along Four-Mile to Kittridge's Ranch, and due west along West Four-Mile for five miles. Here on his right there was a gate in the fence. Beyond the gate up the valley beside Mount McIntyre were hundreds of men wandering about on their new placer claims, among their horses, tents, carts, and mining equipment.

As Bob rode toward Teller Placer he noted that the slopes of McIntyre had been stripped of pine and aspen which were used for temporary shelters. Several large corrals had been built. A big tent contained a general store. Somebody was stringing lines in an attempt to lay out a townsite. A saloon man from Alma had customers lined up for yards. If they wanted whiskey he made them drink a bottle of beer first so that he could fill the beer bottle from his whiskey keg.

At the Teller shaft, Bob found Locator Bradley seated placidly on his black loam pile, chewing cut-plug and guarding his bonanza with a shotgun. Bob ran a handful of the dump dirt through his fingers. It seemed much too heavy, too gooey to be placer-ground. He circulated around camp, talking to some of the old-timers — Tim Hussey, the Houghton boys, Pat Walsh. They said that Bradley and Miller had salted the Teller shaft with gold dust from South Park. One of them maintained that Bradley was an employee of the Leadville mine salter, Chicken Bill Lovell.[2] The Teller Placer salters stood to gain only a couple of hundred dollars paid to them by Canon City merchants for creating the gold rush. But that was a lot of money in 1884.

Bob Womack rode the thirteen miles from Mount McIntyre back to Mount Pisgah and his Poverty Gulch shack in Cripple Creek. He was not disturbed as yet by the fact that the Mount McIntyre hoax was mislabeled "Mount Pisgah." When he went down to Colorado Springs a week later he found the town boiling with excitement about the "Mount Pisgah" rush. As he walked along Tejon Street he was stopped a dozen times by friends who assumed that the rush was taking place right near his Cripple Creek shack on the east slopes of Mount Pisgah. The news that the rush was fake as well as mislabeled had not penetrated to the Springs. Bob

was never an articulate man, and now he was almost tongue-
tied, as it dawned on him that his beloved Mount Pisgah
was about to get a terrible black eye. The more he stammered
and stuttered trying to explain the difference between Pisgah
and McIntyre, the surer people were that Pisgah was the
place.

Whenever he was worried, Bob went to Irving Howbert.
Irving told him that he had been saying for days that gold at
"Mount Pisgah" must exist largely in the imaginations of rail
officials and Canon City merchants. However, Irving explained, nobody could stop a gold rush, even if it was a
hoax, and nobody could change the name of one. Irving was
always right. On April 18, Bob found the "Mount Pisgah"
story spread over the front page of the *Colorado Springs
Gazette.*

On that day Denver & Rio Grande trains passing through
the Springs on their way to Canon City were still jammed
with gold-seekers. Tejon Street merchants stood in groups
discussing the sales they were losing because the Argonauts
were buying their supplies at Canon City. At last the merchants called a town meeting to draw up a program to cash
in on the gold rush.

Bob attended the meeting at which Captain W. F. Wilder
(wool grower) presided. Some time was spent trying to figure
out if D. J. Martin (dry goods) was president of the Board
of Trade. Martin said that the Board of Trade no longer
existed, whereupon a demand was made for the money that
had been in its treasury before it died. At this tense moment,
Captain Marcellin L. DeCoursey (real estate) rose and declared, "To hell with the Board of Trade! The matter at
issue is the great Pisgah gold field! Action!"

Captain DeCoursey was an important man, being one of

that sacred band who had served through the Civil War under General Palmer, founder of Colorado Springs. De-Coursey was a man of ideas and a man of action. This gold rush seemed to him a chance for the kind of excitement he had known during the Civil War.

After DeCoursey's electrifying repudiation of the Board of Trade, Bob heard him propose five Mount Pisgah Gold Field Committees —"Advertising, Finance, Transportation, Correspondence and Examining." Since nobody had an inkling as to the duties of these committees, it was easy for DeCoursey to assume control of all of them, thereby attaining his objective — a free trip to the gold field to investigate.

DeCoursey left town next day in a spring-wagon up Ute Pass accompanied by four other eager scouts. That afternoon Bob Womack met two prospectors, just back from McIntyre, with ten specimens of so-called ore. He took the stuff to Henry Lamb, a new metallurgy man at Colorado College. Excerpts from Lamb's assay report read:

> Specimen No. Three, from claim twenty-five feet south of Teller Shaft. Gold, none; silver, none. Specimen No. Seven, C. C. Rickard's claim, one quarter mile from Teller Shaft. Gold, none; silver, three-tenths of an ounce. Specimen Number Two, one-and-a-half miles from Teller Shaft. Gold, one-tenth of an ounce.

These assays simply meant that there was nothing around Teller Placer that couldn't be found anywhere in the Rocky Mountains.

Long before DeCoursey reached McIntyre he learned from disgusted travelers that the gold rush was a hoax. But it was a beautiful trip through the rolling hills, and he wasn't going to miss it just because the question was settled. On return-

ing to the Springs, he told the Board of Trade how the hoax
was exposed. "For a time," DeCoursey said, "this mine salter,
Bradley, was able to keep the curious away from his bonanza
but suspicion of him became so widespread that he pulled
out of camp. Next day a large group of men dug a hole
in the loam, a few feet from Teller Placer. At the proper
depth, a placer miner went down to investigate. General
silence prevailed among the men packed around the top
of the hole. Then the miner's head appeared. He glanced
once around the crowd and said, 'We should-a hung the
bastard.' "

For some days after DeCoursey's return from McIntyre,
the *Gazette* ran editorials on the perfidy of those who had
created the "Mount Pisgah" hoax in the interests of that
"convict town, Canon City." But elsewhere in the *Gazette*
were bits of comment indicating that Springs merchants
weren't so terribly upset, after all, by the low business morality of their neighbors. What really burned them up was
that they hadn't got in on the gravy themselves.

"Five thousand men," the *Gazette* complained, "on Mr.
Bradley's invitation spent $30 each on transportation alone
— $150,000.00. How much of that went to Canon City?
The Denver papers boomed Mount Pisgah for the D. & R. G.
Railroad. Thousands followed their advice and paid $6.40
each way to Canon City and back. Canon City stage men
took them to the mines for $5.00. Colorado Springs could
have got them there for half as much."

Nobody — neither the *Gazette* nor DeCoursey nor even
Irving Howbert — perceived the true significance of the
"Mount Pisgah" hoax. Nobody excepting Bob Womack.

In all the news stories Bob read about the hoax, never
once was Mount McIntyre mentioned. Always the hoax was

referred to as occurring at "Mount Pisgah." Some accounts
used the phrase, "on the east slopes of Mount Pisgah" —
which is Cripple Creek. Bob knew that the story of the
"Mount Pisgah" hoax had gone all over Colorado, all over
the United States. It was a good story. It made people laugh
wryly. This ridicule was bound to injure Cripple because of
its close association with Mount Pisgah.

Major Demary had done a good job of making Bob's faith
in Cripple seem ridiculous. And Bob was unable to create
confidence in Cripple's prospects because he was such a
heavy drinker, and such a blowhard in his cups. But the
"Mount Pisgah" hoax would be the worst handicap of all.
If Bob struck a million tons of pure gold at Cripple now, he
would have the devil's own time persuading anybody to take
stock in it.

Cow Path to Golconda

ABOUT THE TIME of the "Mount Pisgah" hoax Ida Womack announced to William Womack that she was pregnant again. She went on to say that she had spent seven years in the Welty cabin at Cripple Creek and had given birth to two daughters. It was no fun being pregnant at 9500 feet. The more she thought about it the more she yearned for the green hills, the soft rains, the windless privies, the numerous relatives of her native Shelby County, Kentucky.

William Womack told Bob how Ida felt and Bob told Miss Lida and Miss Lida told old Sam. There were some family conferences during which it was decided that William and Ida would return east with their daughters. The William Womack homestead around the source of Cripple Creek would be sold and so would the Bob Womack homestead at Arequa Gulch. At the same time, Miss Lida would begin the slow liquidation of Sunview Ranch.

Ida's pregnancy was only one of many reasons why the Womacks elected to reduce their cattle operation. Corella Womack, Sam's wife, had died quietly in 1879, in the midst of her accustomed task of keeping Sam alive. With Corella gone, Sam seemed to lose interest in Sunview and talked of moving to Colorado Springs. Miss Lida encouraged him in this and she approved especially of selling the two Cripple

Creek homesteads. Neither Bob nor William had the kind of personalities that make for profitable ranching. William was a sober, steady, plodding man, and he had worked hard at Cripple. But his disposition was more suited to urban life than to chasing cows around Cripple's bleak hills. Bob had never been able to put more than one tenth of his mind on ranch work. The other nine tenths was absorbed in his search for his bonanza.

So the William Womacks left the mountains and went back to Kentucky. Miss Lida wrote to Theodore Lowe in Denver, and told him to find someone who would pay $5000 for the two 160-acre Womack homesteads. By this time Cripple's merits for cattle grazing were well known. The Womack homesteads had acquired a value ten times higher than a decade earlier. Cripple's population, of course, was small compared with that of the lower, more fertile Four-Mile and West Four-Mile valleys on the west side of Mount Pisgah. Even so the Cripple Creek district contained a half dozen squatters like Major Demary and eight or nine homesteaders, each holding 160 acres along strategic water fronts. About one tenth of the Cripple Creek district was privately owned. The rest was free range used by all the ranchers in common.

It didn't take Theodore Lowe long to unload the Womack homesteads for Miss Lida at $5000.[1] The purchaser named on the deeds was Frank Anderson, acting for a Denver family named Thompson. Fred Thompson had a secondhand furniture store on Lawrence Street, Denver. A. N. Thompson and George N. Thompson were in the auction business on Larimer Street. While selling Anderson the Womack homesteads, Theodore Lowe also sold him the Allen Gullion place eastward from the Womacks over Bull Hill on Gassy Creek.

The name "Gassy" had been given to Gullion's creek by lumber crews because that was the sort of digestive system old Allen had. Anderson complained that the name was unattractive, so Lowe changed it to "Grassy."

Frank Anderson and the three Thompsons took these three homesteads, plus a fourth on the east slopes of Mount Pisgah, and formed an outfit called the Pikes Peak Land and Cattle Company. The company owned only 640 acres but they controlled water sources which gave the firm exclusive use of most of the free range on the east side of the Cripple Creek district. In theory, anybody could use that free range, but it was useless to do so without access to the water of Cripple Creek stream.

Somehow the three Thompsons met a wealthy glove manufacturer from Gloversville, New York, named Phillip Ellsworth. The Thompsons explained to him the advantages of their water setup. They claimed that Cripple Creek water controlled the entire west side of Pikes Peak and would soon be essential to the growth of Colorado Springs. They pointed out that Cripple's scenic beauty was so great that the district would become the site of a great resort hotel. Ellsworth concluded that Cripple was a veritable gold mine. He gave the Thompsons $75,000 for a half interest in the four homesteads which had cost them $7000.

Meanwhile, Bob Womack made a comfortable place out of his Poverty Gulch shack on the edge of the Pikes Peak Land and Cattle Company. Ida Womack had left him a real bed to use, instead of a blanket tossed on the dirt floor. He had Ida's cane rocking chair and he built a porch for it on the south side of the shack. He could sit in the rocker in the gloaming with bourbon at hand and his shotgun across his knees. He could watch down Poverty Gulch and along

Cripple Creek and if he saw a coyote chasing one of those little cottontail rabbits he could shoot him dead.

Bob didn't get along with the fellows the Thompsons hired to run the Pikes Peak Land and Cattle Company. These foremen never stayed long. They were even poorer ranchers than Bob, and the Thompson herd suffered from their bad management. The ranch had very little seasonal work for Bob and so he had to go down to the Four-Mile country to earn money to support him while he prospected in Poverty Gulch.

He found that he enjoyed his cowboy trips. Each spring and fall he and Whistler went off for weeks at a time and once they stayed all summer. The West Pikes Peak country which included Four-Mile and Cripple was part of a huge ranching environment called the South Park Round-Up District. The main idea in this vast area was to raise beef cattle to sell on the hoof. The buyers would ship the cattle by rail to Eastern markets from Canon City, or drive them to butchers at Leadville.

A big roundup involved fifty or more men and their horses. It was a complicated affair, similar to a military force on maneuvers. Men and horses had to be well fed. Arrangements had to be made for comfortable sleeping at night, since the men might be at a roundup for a week. The chuck wagon solved the supply problem, but before the chuck wagon could be used roads had to be built to accommodate it. The original road from Four-Mile Valley around Pisgah up to Cripple had been built by the Welty boys for chuck wagon use. The existence of chuck wagon roads everywhere in the West Pikes Peak country made Cripple easy to reach from several directions.

In the Eighties, at the lower elevations of these sunny

Pikes Peak uplands, ranching was of the most idyllic sort. There were none of the tribulations of plains ranching — blizzards, terrible drouths, encroachments of crop farmers and sheep men, wars between big and little operators. The weather was mild, with only a little snow before spring, and then it did not remain long on the ground.

It made Bob Womack feel good to observe how much fun the West Pikes Peak people got out of their lives. The country was so pleasant that they didn't give a hoot what went on in the rest of the world — not even in Colorado Springs, that glittering sanctuary of English tea-drinkers, European royalty, and aristocrats from Philadelphia, Boston and New York. West of the Peak there was not much money, but plenty of honey. Children grew up on horseback (if a horse wasn't handy, a steer would do). Weekly dances were held at somebody's ranch house and George Welty played the fiddle. The nearest so-called saloon was Frank Castello's store at Florissant. It was a self-service saloon at two bits a serving — by tin cup from a whiskey keg.

Small-time rustling was overlooked, which was wise because such tolerance prevented feuds over petty suspicions. But when the Watkins rustling gang ran amuck, a posse of ranchers tracked it down and hanged Watkins from the First Street bridge in Canon City. Every now and then the ranchers brought out shotguns and set up road blocks when word came that escaped convicts from Canon City might be heading up Eight-Mile or Oil Creek. Bob Womack joined a posse once to trail three Kansas stick-ups who robbed Frank Castello of $300. All three were captured.

One spring day, in 1885, an eastern dude called on Bob at his Poverty Gulch shack, just as Bob was leaving for the roundups. The dude said he was Phillip Ellsworth, half owner

of the Pikes Peak Land and Cattle Company. He wore shiny
boots, tight breeches and a hard, round hat. He had come
from New York to Cripple to see if he had doubled his
$75,000. Instead he found the cattle company going to
wrack and ruin. He asked Bob what the trouble was and
Bob said maybe Ellsworth had paid too much for his half
interest. Bob added that in '76 the Womacks had acquired
two of the four Cripple Creek homesteads at a capital out-
lay of $500 and two pigs.

Ellsworth rode off sadly. In July, 1885, he was back again.
Bob saw him riding down Poverty Gulch with two newcomers. As the three passed the shack Bob rose from his
rocker to greet them. One of the newcomers was a brisk
youngster named Horace Bennett. The older, smaller, quieter
man was Julius A. Myers.

It seemed that when Phillip Ellsworth had left Bob in
the spring he had hurried to Denver and had secured full
title to the Pikes Peak Land and Cattle Company, by threat-
ening to sue the Thompsons and Frank Anderson for fraud.
Then a friend sent him to Horace Bennett. This young Bennett had come West from Michigan, at twenty-one. He
started on his path to fame and fortune by hawking second-
hand brass beds, porcelain cats and chamber pots on Denver's
Larimer Street. In 1884 he had sold enough junk to set up
as a real estate agent on Seventeenth Street. The next year
he invited Myers in with him and the two formed the firm
of Bennett and Myers.

When Ellsworth presented himself at the offices of Bennett
and Myers he thought Bennett was the office boy. Bennett
informed him haughtily that he was the firm's *senior* partner
(Myers was fifteen years older than Bennett but Bennett
always treated him as though Myers were his son) . Ellsworth

told Bennett his tale of Cripple Creek woe and Bennett replied that Ellsworth should have known better than to sink
$75,000 in land at an altitude of 9500 feet. Ellsworth offered
Bennett the entire four-homestead outfit, plus the public
land controlled by it, plus buildings, fencing and a few hundred beef cattle, for $25,000. Bennett said, "No, thanks."
Ellsworth persisted. At last Bennett agreed to go to Cripple
with Myers at Ellsworth's expense just for the holiday.

They rode General W. J. Palmer's Denver & Rio Grande to
Colorado Springs. Ellsworth rented horses and hired a guide
at the Antlers Stables and they climbed to Cripple around
the south side of Pikes Peak, over the Cheyenne Mountain
trail. They were worn out by the time they reached Poverty
Gulch and they responded with indifference to Bob Womack's
warm welcome. Bennett was more than indifferent. He was
hostile. He sized up Bob as being a crackpot prospector who
would be assailing him for a grubstake in an hour or so.

Next day, Julius Myers asked Bob about fishing in the
district and was delighted to discover that Bob was an avid
angler like himself. Soon the two were off to see what the
rainbows looked like on West Beaver. Ellsworth took Horace
Bennett over the four homesteads of the Pikes Peak Land and
Cattle Company and said that Bennett could have them for
$5000 down. He could pay the remaining $20,000 if and
when.

Although Bennett was surprised at the richness of the grass
along Cripple's waterfront pastures he could not for the life
of him make the inventory of the property add up to more
than $10,000. The Allen Gullion homestead, on Grassy
Creek, was way the hell and gone over Bull Hill. The 160-
acre homestead up Pisgah's slope was a gravel patch unfit for
anything — except perhaps a cemetery. The Arequa Gulch

homestead was full of hummocks. The headquarters ranch
was centered around Cripple Creek spring and the spring did
not look dependable. The old Welty cabin sagged in the
middle, the springhouse was rotting, and the corrals were
falling down. Parts of the free range were potted with prospect
holes which must have been dug by that grinning nincom-
poop, Bob Womack. These holes were dangerous to grazing
cattle.

In the cool of the evening, Myers joined Ellsworth and
Bennett at the Welty cabin. Myers had left Bob Womack at
Bob's shack and he was ecstatic about his creelful of twelve-
inch rainbows. He told Bennett some of the things Bob had
told him about the wonderful hunting in the Cripple Creek
district. Ellsworth brought out some fine Scotch, and Bennett
grew mellow as he watched the colors of sunset deepen on
Pikes Peak. He began to realize that in a single day Myers
had developed a love for the place. When Bennett suggested
that Cripple Creek probably ran dry every fall, Myers looked
wistful. When Bennett commented sourly on the dilapidated
condition of the buildings, Myers assumed an expression of
dignified dissent. When Bennett asserted that the outfit
wasn't worth $10,000, Phillip Ellsworth poured Bennett an-
other Scotch.

Before Bennett went to bed that night he threw in the
sponge. The Bennett and Myers firm would buy the four
Cripple Creek homesteads from Ellsworth for $5000 down.

And before that year of 1885 had ended, Bob Womack saw
that things would be very different at the Cripple Creek ranch
under Horace Bennett's management. Through wide advertising, Bennett found in Garden City, Kansas, an experienced
cattleman named George Carr who wanted to come to the

mountains with his wife and her cowboy brother, Jack Edwards. Bennett gave Carr permission to hire Bob Womack for
odd jobs if he thought he could get any work out of him.

Bennett changed the name of the Pikes Peak Land and
Cattle Company to the Houseman Cattle and Land Company
(Alexander Houseman was a dummy director). But George
Carr called the outfit the "Broken Box Ranch" and that
name was the designation used throughout the West Pikes
Peak country. Carr demonstrated from the first that he was
the man to run the Broken Box. In two years he made the
place break even. In three years Bennett was able to cut
down on the size of the Ellsworth note.

Julius Myers was very happy that the Broken Box was a
paying proposition because he felt responsible for the purchase. Bennett may have been secretly pleased though he
never displayed anything but acidulous skepticism. Many
things about the place irritated him, and particularly the
presence in the neighborhood of Bob Womack. Each time
Bennett visited the Broken Box, Bob would come moseying
over, unshaven, often smelling of whiskey, mumbling about
gold-bearing float, and urging Bennett to grubstake him.

Invariably, Bennett invited Bob to stop pestering him. But
he softened once to the extent of accepting some of Bob's
float samples for assay. In Denver he gave them to the celebrated assayer, E. E. Burlingame, who tossed them into the
wastebasket.

And that, Horace Bennett thought, was precisely where
they belonged.

CHAPTER V

Bob Hits Pay Dirt

THE ARRIVAL of the Carrs at Cripple Creek boosted Bob's morale. Bob was a retiring man when he was sober, but he was by no means a hermit and he had suffered from loneliness after the departure of the William Womacks. George Carr's red-haired wife, Emma, was a bustling, cheerful woman who loved company. George was a happy-go-lucky Kansas cowboy who told Bob corncob jokes by the hour, accompanied by roars of laughter and sly leers at the blushing Emma. Bob blushed too. If George Carr had been a city man he would have been an ardent civic booster, a bad but brave poker player and an all-round good fellow usually described as a "card."

Because of the Carrs, Bob cut down on his solitary drinking. He began to block out the slopes of Poverty Gulch in a much more systematic way than he had done before. And finally, on October 13, 1886, he staked a gold claim, the first actually recorded by him since he began his search at Cripple in 1878. It was a spot on the north slope of Poverty Gulch, about two thousand feet above his shack. He had not struck a true vein, but assays showed that his float trail might end here. Bob called the claim the "Grand View" and it certainly had that if nothing else. Nine miles to the northeast was the blunt summit of Pikes Peak. In the south and south-west were the glorious Sangre de Cristos and the Big Divide.

All winter Bob tunneled and trenched on the Grand View. Just when he was about to give it up he had a stroke of luck. A St. Louis man, Edwin Wallace, appeared in Poverty Gulch, examined the Grand View and gave Bob $500 for a two-thirds interest.

That vast sum, which Bob received on April 23, 1887, was his first return for nine years of Cripple Creek prospecting. Wallace seemed to have great faith in the district because he stayed several months working on the Grand View and staking two other claims. Bob, meanwhile, dizzy with success, began spreading over the Pikes Peak region in search of another $500 bonanza. He wound up, of all places, down on the plains at the Womack's Sunview Ranch, where he staked a placer claim on Little Fountain Creek, near Deadman Canyon.

In order to get maximum placer acreage, Bob added to the location certificate the names of Theodore Lowe, Sam Womack, Miss Lida Womack and three neighbors. The Sunview Placer was a dud, but it served as bait for the staking, on April 5, 1889, of the Summit Placer, close to the Sunview. Among those listed as locating the Summit were Charles H. White, vice-president of the El Paso Bank in Colorado Springs, and Dr. John P. Grannis, a Springs dentist.

Bob Womack had to laugh when he learned that Charles White had come in on the Summit Placer deal. White owned a red sandstone formation at Cripple Creek which he hoped to exploit as building material. He had been as contemptuous of Bob's Poverty Gulch idea as was Major Demary, and yet here he was throwing away money on really barren diggings down on the plains. White, of course, was rich, and could afford to lose money.

Dr. Grannis, the dentist, was not rich. Bob had met him

through Irving Howbert, who went to Grannis now and then to have his teeth cleaned. Grannis was a tall, somber, self-effacing man who had come to Colorado Springs from Ohio, in 1886, to try to get the tuberculosis out of his lungs. He was thirty-seven years old. Howbert had hinted to Bob that Grannis was having trouble building up a dental practice and that it would be a kind act if the Womack family tried him out.

Even though Grannis was a newcomer he had heard a lot about the "Mount Pisgah" hoax, the foibles of Bob Womack and the Pikes Peak region's continuous record of failure as a gold field. Nevertheless, when Bob went to Grannis for a tooth filling, Grannis found himself listening to Bob's routine babble about Cripple Creek.

And then Grannis began receiving Bob at his home on North Tejon Street to hear more of Bob's theory that gold *had* to exist at Cripple. It was true, Bob told Grannis over and over, that those pastoral hills did not look like gold country. It was true that there were few outcrops, few evidences of quartz formations or of iron pyrites. Not a single assayer had been able to identify the basic mineral which composed Bob's erratic pieces of gold-bearing float. There was no reason for Bob to believe that Cripple held gold in profitable quantity.

No reason, that is, excepting the fact that dozens of people had been picking up float there at least since 1873. Where did the gold in the float come from? Well, Bob had said, it didn't fall from the skies. At Bob's urging, Grannis visited the dark basement of Palmer Hall, Colorado College, where Henry Lamb had his laboratory. Lamb showed Grannis the map of the West Pikes Peak country which was published at the same time as the Hayden Report of '73.

On this map Grannis saw that the Cripple Creek area was colored yellow. The yellow color ran from south to north on the map, representing five miles. It included the gulch which Bob called "Poverty." The color-key explained that this yellow area had been the center of volcanic activity.

Grannis bought some books on gold whose authors told him that they didn't have much information on the subject. Nobody knows, they asserted, what makes gold. Nobody even knows where gold comes from, though the theory is that quantities of it are concentrated deep in the earth. When volcanoes erupt, the gold comes to the surface and scatters all over the place. If the volcanic explosion leaves deep cracks in the earth's crust, the gold is apt to be caught in the deep crevices and cracks, instead of being washed seaward.

Well, Grannis thought, that was more or less what Bob said about Cripple Creek. It was the site of an ancient volcano. Bob's float came from a volcanic crack at the top of his float trail. When Bob found the top of this crack he would have a gold mine.

The idea was so tempting that Grannis, poor as he was, decided to go into partnership with Bob. On December 2, 1889, Grannis borrowed $500 at 7 per cent interest and gave it to Bob as a grubstake. This meant that Grannis fed, clothed, and outfitted Bob in return for a half interest in anything Bob discovered. Bob's first act under this grubstake arrangement was to buy twelve dollars' worth of boots and pants in the Springs. His second act was to get drunk in Colorado City.

The Grannis grubstake had a wonderful effect on Bob. It removed him entirely from Miss Lida's maternalism and it made him feel as if he were really in the mining business.

Through the summer he scratched around on the Grand View claim which Edwin Wallace abandoned in '88. Toward the end of September, at the east edge of the claim, he became aware that the gravel wash was dotted with tiny pieces of float. He went down ten feet and pushed short drifts eastward, northeastward and northward. On the north drift the float was thicker than ever.

And one crisp October day, with the aspens turned to deepest orange, and the first snows dusting Pikes Peak — *Eureka!*

Bob struck a submerged outcrop, a shaft of solid rock two feet wide at the top. In the middle of the shaft was a discoloration. In the middle of the discoloration was a half-inch crack. That crack, Bob knew, was his gold mine. He named it the El Paso Lode.

There was still time that day to blast once. Bob climbed from the ten-foot-deep hole and rode Whistler down Poverty Gulch to his shack for his blasting equipment. He returned with a single jack, a three-foot rock drill, a spoon with a thirty-inch handle, three eight-inch sticks of dynamite, a bottle of water and a five-foot waterproof fuse attached to a one-inch primer cap.

In the solid rock of the submerged outcrop some inches away from the half-inch vein he sank a thirty-inch hole with his rock drill, giving the drill a quarter turn with each blow of his single jack. He kept pouring in water to soften the muck made by his drilling, and at intervals he scooped the muck from the hole with his long-handled spoon. Then he crimped a primer cap on one end of a stick of dynamite and stuck the stick into the hole, primer cap at the bottom and the fuse trailing upward out of the hole.

On top of the capped dynamite stick he inserted a second

stick and he put a third stick on top of that. That made a total of twenty-four inches of dynamite in the thirty-inch hole. Bob was very careful to put the primer-capped stick in first, at the bottom of the drilled hole, to make sure that all three dynamite sticks exploded simultaneously. If he had put the primer-capped stick at the top of the drilled hole with the other two dynamite sticks beneath it, the lowest stick might have failed to explode — a dangerous business. Bob had seen many tenderfeet killed at Idaho Springs because they were careless on this point. After the blast they would go poking around with picks and hit the bottom stick of unexploded dynamite.

Bob straightened out his five-foot fuse and tamped dirt into the top six inches of his drill hole. He lit his fuse and scrambled from his shallow shaft, retiring behind a hummock a hundred yards or so away. In two minutes came the explosion. Debris flew out of the shaft and pelted down short of the hummock. It would take Bob a whole day to remove the shattered rock from the El Paso shaft before he could blast again.

For a week or so, Bob blasted along the face of his vein. On October 20, 1890, he knocked off heavy work and spent that day measuring out a mining claim with a clothesline and pocket compass, on the north side of Poverty Gulch. It was a standard Colorado lode claim 1500 feet long, 300 feet wide. What he was doing actually was relocating the old Grand View claim to make it conform more with the trend of the El Paso Lode.

After shifting the six old stakes, Bob removed the faded notice: GRAND VIEW MINING CLAIM, LOCATED OCT. 13, 1886, BY R. M. WOMACK, PIKES PEAK MINING DISTRICT, and substituted:

EL PASO LODE

LOCATED OCT. 20, 1890

BY

R. M. WOMACK AND JOHN GRANNIS

UNKNOWN MINING DISTRICT

Bob changed the name of his mining district from "Pikes Peak" to "Unknown" because many people were using the "Pikes Peak" appellation lately, to cover gold and cryolite claims on the north and southeast slopes of Pikes Peak.

He celebrated the staking by picking up a pint of whiskey at his shack and strolling a half mile southwesterly past the old Welty springhouse, to the Carr place. There he poured out drinks for George Carr, Emma Carr and the hired man, Jack Edwards. The four friends hoisted glasses to the success of the El Paso claim. And that was that.

At some point between October 20 and December 1, 1890, Bob Womack and Dr. Grannis hired Professor Henry Lamb to examine the El Paso. Lamb went up to Cripple Creek by way of Florissant and expressed guarded approval of the vein. He chipped out a dozen samples of ore, assayed them in the Palmer Hall laboratory at Colorado College, with some of the samples assaying as high as $250 a ton.

Buttressed with this very favorable assay, Bob and Dr. Grannis began a campaign in Colorado Springs to raise fifteen or twenty thousand dollars to pay for real development work on their gold mine. They showed pieces of the dull-gray ore to various mining men. None of them displayed the slightest interest.

Even with the gold-bearing vein found, even with an assay of undeniable accuracy at hand, the ghost of the "Mount Pisgah" hoax was present to deny that the truth could be true. Finally, in despair, the two promoters placed the gold ore in the South Tejon Street show window of J. F. Seldomridge and Sons, a grain store with which the ranching Womacks did business.

Each day, Bob and Dr. Grannis would call at the store to ask if anyone was showing interest in the ore. Harry Seldomridge, son of the grain-store owner, always had to tell them No. It began to get on Harry's nerves. Harry was a softhearted man and at last he stopped in at the *Gazette* and asked his friend Hiram Rogers to inspect the ore and give it a boost in the paper, if there were any justification at all.

Rogers, once a colleague of Eugene Field in Denver, and now the best reporter in the Springs, spent the rest of his life kicking himself in the pants for the scoop he missed that day. His chagrin was doubly painful because he had wanted to do something nice for the Womacks in gratitude for a couple of baskets of Sunview Ranch raspberries which Miss Lida had presented to the *Gazette* staff in August.

Many years later, Rogers wrote: "I remember seeing Bob's latest ore with indifferent curiosity, for who that has lived in the Rocky Mountains has not been shown oceans of such stuff that came from a future bonanza? As a newspaper man I looked Dr. Grannis up and asked about it. His replies were not sufficient to impress me, and I let it pass. Naturally, a discovery by Bob Womack was discounted in Colorado Springs . . ."

Rogers let it pass. And so Bob's ore just sat there in Seldomridge's show window — a tiny bit of neglected matter containing within itself a material and emotional force that was to blow Colorado Springs sky high and change its aspect forever.

CHAPTER VI

Little London and Ed De LaVergne

COLORADO SPRINGS was nicknamed Little London, not so much because it had more Englishmen than some other Colorado towns (which it probably didn't), but because the mood and tempo of the place seemed to derive from the English idea. At the time of its founding, in 1871, General William Jackson Palmer was determined to fill his sagebrush townsite with nice people — to make it a cultural oasis in a desert of American savagery. He succeeded so well that nineteen years later the *Colorado Springs Gazette* reported that "hoboes always wash up before entering our city."

The General was a warmhearted man but he had a horror of public adulation which explained his seeming coldness, baronial hauteur and untouchability. To keep people from discovering that he was painfully shy, he pretended to regard the world with the detachment of an entomologist studying an anthill.[1]

He planned Colorado Springs as a resort on the European model — a haven for rich invalids, retired capitalists, blasé Continentals bored with Switzerland, and young members of Eastern society, drawn by the climate, sports and possibilities of romance, at the foot of Pikes Peak. In December, 1890,

the Springs was a beautifully upholstered town of 10,000 people at least half of whom were there because of tuberculosis in
the family. Few American towns were as cosmopolitan or as
rigid in their class divisions. Top society was composed of
men and women who seemed to have been everywhere, and
to know everything.

Little London's leading citizen, next to General Palmer,
was James J. Hagerman, a Napoleonic little fellow with a
red beard whose large fortune was about to be augmented
by an income of $50,000 a month from his Mollie Gibson
silver mine at Aspen. Hagerman lived in a great stone house
on Cascade Avenue, which he built in '85 at a cost of
$110,000. A feature of this house was the woodwork and
cabinetry created by a sad-eyed carpenter, Winfield Scott
Stratton.

The Colorado Midland Railway was Hagerman's crowning achievement. It was built in the late Eighties to compete
with the Denver & Rio Grande. It breached the Front Range
at Colorado Springs, crossed South Park, reached Leadville,
and continued on to Grand Junction — some three hundred
miles of terrific construction. It had stretches of 4 per cent
grade and it crossed the Continental Divide at almost 12,000
feet. It was the most spectacular standard-gauge railroad ever
built and the most expensive to operate.

The Midland went up Ute Pass and through Florissant
from the Springs.[2] This Florissant station was a great boon
to the ranchers of the West Pikes Peak country, but many
Colorado Springs residents hated the Midland. Its effect
had been to double the Springs' population, raise wages and
attract rowdies who ate peas with their knives and beat
their wives on Saturday night. High society complained that
the adjacent settlement of Colorado City was suddenly full

of saloons, parlor houses, and Chinese opium dens. It couldn't be worse if gold had been found around Pikes Peak.

During the summer of 1890 astute people like Irving Howbert began to suspect that hard times lay ahead. The Sherman Silver Purchase Act, passed in July to bolster silver prices, was a weak measure that might be repealed by the gold-standard Republicans and sound-money Democrats like Grover Cleveland. Colorado's economy depended on a high silver price. Another sad situation was the failure of the great London bank, Baring Brothers. English capital was a big factor in the prosperity of Little London. Many Springs residents lived on English incomes.

So much for the Springs' general outlook at the close of 1890. The protagonist in our plot, remember, is some dirty-gray rock from Cripple Creek which Bob Womack placed in the South Tejon Street display window of Seldomridge and Sons. As we have seen, Bob and his partner, Dr. John Grannis, were getting nowhere with the El Paso Lode. Plainly, another man was needed to sell Cripple Creek to the world, a man of reputation, willing to buck the distrust created by the "Mount Pisgah" hoax and by Bob's habit of drinking so much and making such a lot of noise in the process. If Edward Morton De LaVergne had not materialized it is possible that Cripple Creek would have remained a cow pasture, conceal-ing beneath its sod the richest concentration of gold in history.

Ed De LaVergne was born of well-to-do parents, at Marietta, Ohio, in 1846. He was a descendant of General Horatio Gates, but he was hardly a chip off the General Gates block. Ed was just fairly everything — fairly smart, fairly big, fairly attractive. He was fond of saying, "I'm just an ordi-nary sort of fellow. I drink my coffee out of the saucer and if I get married I'll keep my wife for life." In the fashion of the Sixties he moved West with his family by stages, first to Tennessee, then to Clinton, Missouri. In 1878, Ed's father came to Colorado Springs to retire. Three of his children came with him, Catherine, George and Ed.

Ed was the youngest and he grew up in the shadow of his handsome brother, Colonel George, a sterling character. George had been a colonel in the Eighth Tennessee Mounted, had been hit by a shell at Chickamauga and had served as judge of court-martial at Cleveland. In Colorado Springs, George managed his father's estate, was elected a Colorado College trustee, read papers at the Phoenix Society on how to ripen tomatoes, and lent his distinguished name to the Board of Directors of mining companies. He platted a subdivision called Lihue, the name of a Sandwich Island town where his wife was born. In 1889, Colonel George set up a furniture store on South Tejon Street, across from Seldomridge's grain store.

Meanwhile, Ed De LaVergne was trying to be a mining man. He started in the Ruby silver district north of Gunnison and later ran the Old Man Mine at Camp Fleming, the Blackhawk Mine in New Mexico and the Orient silver mines at Lawson, Colorado. Ed's home base was Colonel George's fine place in the Springs, but it depressed Ed somewhat to spend time there. George had everything — money, social standing and the delightful prestige a man gains when he has had the misfortune to get hit by a shell at Chickamauga. At forty-four, Ed felt that he was a failure, a mining bum frittering away his life in search of a bonanza that would never come. He had no glamorous wife from the Sandwich Islands, and no one ever dreamed of asking him to speak before the Phoenix Society.

But Ed kept plugging, no matter how discouraged he might be. Finding himself jobless in November, 1890, he went home to Colonel George's and signed up for an assaying course under Professor Henry Lamb. While taking Lamb's course, Ed got to dropping in at the De LaVergne Furniture Company, to chat with George's manager, an upholsterer named Fred Frisbee. Ed talked a lot to Fred about gold mining and imbued him with the fever. Fred was a typical henpecked husband dominated not only by his wife, Claire, but by his precocious daughter, Kittie M. Sixteen-year-old Kittie was already notorious in Colorado Springs because of a high school lecture she had given, taking a strong affirmative stand on the subject, "Is Marriage a Failure?" Fred told Claire and Kittie all that Ed had told him about mining. The two women instructed Fred to quit the furniture trade and find a gold mine.

Early in December, 1890, Ed received his assayer's certificate from Henry Lamb, who mentioned casually that he ought to go on the other side of Pikes Peak and have a look at a volcanic area called Cripple Creek. The next day Ed noticed Bob Womack's ore samples in the Seldomridge Grain Company window, across the street from the De LaVergne Furniture Store.

Something about the appearance of the dull-gray ore posed a problem in Ed's mind. He had seen once before a stuff much like it — a gold-silver-tellurium substance called sylvanite which the smelting hero, Nathaniel P. Hill, had spotted in his Red Cloud Mine, northwest of Denver, and which F. V. Hayden and his government chemists had identified. Sylvanite was associated, often, with a telluride called calaverite, a bronze-yellow compound of gold and tellurium. The gold content of calaverite and sylvanite could be exposed in the form of bubbles, by roasting on a stove.

Although Colorado Springs residents regarded Ed De La-Vergne as nothing much compared with Colonel George, they did give him credit for having more practical knowledge of mining than anyone else in town. Young Harry Seldomridge was surprised and excited when Ed entered the Seldomridge Grain Store, in December, 1890, and asked where the gold ore in the show window had come from.

Harry told Ed what he knew about it and, during the next few days, Harry arranged a meeting attended by Ed, Fred Frisbee, Dr. Grannis, Professor Lamb and Bob Womack. The meeting had to be postponed once because Bob had made the mistake, the previous night, of wandering from alcoholic Colorado City into temperance Colorado Springs, during a binge. He was nabbed by one of Marshal Dana's bobbies before he had a chance to shoot out more than a couple of Tejon Street lamps. The Springs bobbies, like everyone else, had an affection for Bob. He was never arrested for being tight, merely carted off to the jail room in the City Hall basement to sober up.

At the meeting, Ed De LaVergne plied Bob with questions. Bob explained how, for twelve years, he had followed a trail of gold-bearing float from below the source of Cripple Creek up Poverty Gulch and how, at last, he had struck a gold-bearing vein in the hard rock. It was a thin vein of unknown composition and of unknown dimensions with a gold content assaying $250 a ton.

Ed said nothing about his suspicion that Bob's El Paso vein might contain one of the two gold tellurides, a suspicion that grew stronger as Bob's account tallied with the experience of mining men who had encountered the rich mineral. Ed made no comment when Henry Lamb discussed Hayden's theory of a Cripple Creek volcano. Lamb added his own belief that the explosion at Cripple had blown away the granite crust that overlies most of the Colorado Rockies. Then, as volcanic activity subsided, the 10,000-acre Cripple Creek hole filled up gradually with blown-out minerals which had been deep in the earth.

Silent Ed let Bob and Henry Lamb talk. He did not reveal the grandiose conception that was building up in his mind. Bob Womack assumed that his gold-bearing float came from a single gold-bearing vein — two or three veins at the most. But, Ed reasoned, prospectors had been picking up float not only along Poverty Gulch and Cripple Creek, but along the courses of many gulches all over Cripple's grassy hills. If gold-bearing float had been found everywhere, gold-bearing veins could be found everywhere, too, provided people scraped off the topsoil that hid them.

Ed realized that if his hunch were correct, he might have on his hands a gold field of incomparable richness and variety. To develop such a field, Ed figured, to remove the thin, gold-bearing veins from rock around them would require immense amounts of capital, immense man-power. Hundreds of prospectors would be needed to find the gold veins beneath their dirt covering and thousands of miners would have to be hired to drive vertical shafts and horizontal drifts. There would have to be mills to refine the gold tellurides, using processes as yet in the experimental stage. And railroads to haul the ore to the mills. And freighters to supply the rail-loading bins. And towns to house the miners and saloons to quench their thirst and stores and restaurants and stock-brokers and gamblers and schools and churches and dance halls, and doctors and women. Hail, Cripple!

So went Ed's dream. But after that first December meeting

Ed kept away from Bob Womack and Dr. Grannis. He did not want to be obligated to them. Besides, if Cripple became the American epic that Ed had in mind, why should that half-baked cowboy get all the credit? Edward Morton De LaVergne, co-discoverer of the World's Greatest Gold Camp! Every bit as good as getting hit by a shell at Chickamauga.

For some weeks, Ed mulled over Cripple and waited for good weather. On January 24, 1891, he collected Fred Frisbee, and the two men rode the Colorado Midland up Ute Pass thirty-five miles to Florissant. Here they rented a buckboard and rattled south toward Mount Pisgah and the Broken Box Ranch. It began to snow when they had reached the Weltys', at the junction of Hay Creek and Four-Mile. As they pushed up Pisgah's slopes, past the Harkers' and Riggs', it was snowing harder.

At Copper Mountain they went wrong, perhaps passing north of Mineral Hill, above the Broken Box. They wandered around all day in the high valley of West Beaver and bedded down miserably with several dozen pack rats in one of Reuben Wise's cattle shelters. Fred Frisbee, a resourceful Boy Scout, lassoed a pack rat and cooked him over a cowdung fire. Ed refused to eat any part of the pack rat and that made Fred sore.

In later years, when Ed De LaVergne was a well-known millionaire and State Senator, he spoke often of this trip, the tale getting wilder with each telling. A snake bit one of the horses. A baleful raven (Ed said) swooped down and bit him. They got sick on snow water. In the afternoon of their third day out, the two men, very weary, rode the buckboard down the slope of Mineral Hill toward the Broken Box Ranch.

As first seen by them, the Broken Box consisted of a large corral enclosed by a snake-and-rider fence of aspen poles, the old Welty cabin with second story added, a small shack for the hired hand, and the log springhouse — the construction of which had led Levi Welty to remark, "This sure is some cripple creek!" The Broken Box buildings sat on relatively flat land in the southern half of the L-shaped 160-acre William Womack homestead, a half mile south of what is now the center of Cripple Creek town.

Ed and Fred could see Bob Womack's shack, northeast of the ranch, at the foot of Poverty Gulch. As they gazed beyond the ranch they saw low, rounded hills in every direction. Cattle grazed placidly on the hills, as the snow was melting and evaporating. Emma Carr was at the kitchen door to greet the explorers and soon she was warming them with fragrant hot coffee and her own, well-padded brand of innocent sex appeal. In no time they had recovered from the effects of their frightful trip. George Carr came in at supper time and they all had fun talking about the eccentricities of Bob Womack.

Then Emma and George put up a double bed for the visitors in the kitchen. Next morning George supplied them with saddle horses and told them how to get around the Cripple Creek district. And they did get around. For a solid month, Ed and Fred roamed the 10,000-acre area, marking the volcano's rim, studying the gulches, choosing spots for mining claims. Ed's experienced eye led him to quantities of gray float, presumably gold-bearing.

One evening, as Ed and Fred relaxed in the Carr kitchen, Ed took a piece of ore from his sack — a bronze-yellow ore — and placed it on Emma's hot range. After a bit a gurgling sound came from the ore, and a rash of golden bubbles appeared on the surface.

Ed must have been pretty happy about it. He knew that the bubbling ore was the gold telluride known as calaverite. So far, Cripple Creek was living up to his expectations.

CHAPTER VII

Bob Lands in the Clink

WHILE DE LAVERGNE AND FRISBEE were poking around at Cripple, Bob Womack stayed in the Springs and tried to make capital out of their trip. The El Paso Lode must be a whale of a mine, Bob argued, if Ed De LaVergne thought enough of it to go up there in the dead of winter. And still Bob made no headway. In addition to the old prejudices against Cripple he and Dr. Grannis found themselves faced by stiff competition.

The silver camp of Creede, in southwestern Colorado, was beginning to boom. Mining people in the Springs did not want to talk of anything except the fortunes pouring out of the Holy Moses, the Solomon, the Phoenix, and other rich Creede silver mines.

You may recall that Bob went on a bender in December of 1890, and landed in the clink at the Springs City Hall. Late in January, depressed by Creede's competition, he got reboiled. Once more the bobbies nabbed him off limits and put him in City Hall to sober up. The city offices were on the second floor. The ground floor was a volunteer fire station. Directly beneath the fire station was the jail.

In those days the volunteer fire companies in Colorado Springs were similar to the service clubs of today. They threw parties and held benefits and worked at politics and made themselves generally useful. The one thing they did not do very well was to fight fire.

The reason for this was that the various companies rushed to fires in a spirit of intense rivalry. Sometimes two companies would attach their hose lines to the same fireplug, with the result that the water pressure was too low to spray the fire properly. Sometimes fist fights would start and the firemen would drop everything to settle the issue while the building burned to the ground.

The most important volunteer company was Hook and Ladder Company No. 1, with headquarters at City Hall. Its leader was a volatile Scotch-Irishman of forty-one, named James Ferguson Burns. Jimmie hailed from Portland, Maine. He had arrived in the Springs from New Orleans in '86, to look out for his three sisters, Kate, Jane, and Mary Anne, and his wild brother, Tom. Before that time he had had a romantic career in Cuba and in South America, engaged in the cane sugar business. Once while running a sugar plantation in Cuba, Jimmie fell into a pit dug to catch wild animals. This pit had caught a boa constrictor instead. While Jimmie's men rushed for ropes to pull him from the pit, the boa moved slowly on him. In those few seconds Jimmie's hair turned a dazzling white — and remained white. Or so Jimmie used to say.

Jimmie Burns started life in the Springs driving a road grader, then went to work as a plumber and steam fitter. Jimmie had no ordinary mind. He was quick and aggressive and he had great capacity for detail. He had the acquisitive face of a sparrow and an urgent, high-pitched voice. He was perpetually in a dither about something, not from frustration but from an intellectual distaste for the *status quo*. He was raised a good Catholic, but he made his pious sisters unhappy because he questioned parts of Catholic doctrine. He had a contempt for Springs high society. He felt that he had seen much more of the world than most of these aristocrats and that it took more brains to repair a toilet than to talk bad French or race a gig along Cascade Avenue.

The city fathers in 1890 turned down Jimmie's request to be named sewer inspector but he got revenge by forcing the City Council to pay him $10 damages for the loss of a $5 pair of pants which were burned while he was on fire duty. He had many enemies because of his peppery disposition, yet he was elected foreman of Hook and Ladder Company No. 1 for three years running. Among his doting admirers was a harum-scarum Irishman named Jimmie Doyle, aged twenty-three. Jimmie Doyle, like Jimmie Burns, had been born and raised in Portland, Maine. He was an orphan and as he grew up the Burns girls became fond of him and appointed themselves his protectors. When the sisters moved West to Colorado Springs, teen-aged Jimmie Doyle moved with them, and worked as their errand boy in the seamstress business.

In the 1890 fire company elections Jimmie Burns resigned as foreman of Hook and Ladder Company No. 1, and he saw to it that Jimmie Doyle got the job. One of Jimmie Doyle's unofficial duties was to let Bob Womack out of City Hall jail when Bob indicated, by pounding on the ceiling, that he had recovered sufficiently to walk straight. On an afternoon following Bob's latest spree, Burns, Doyle and other volunteer firemen were relaxing in the fire station when Bob's pounding signal was heard. Jimmie Doyle removed the jail key from its peg and descended to the basement to release the prisoner.

Bob came upstairs in a petulant mood, charging false arrest, the bobbies having stepped out of the City to get him. He went on to inform the fireman that the day would arrive when nobody would dare to throw him in the clink because of his wealth derived from the gold which he would take out of his new Cripple Creek mine. He announced that Ed De LaVergne was up at Cripple now, verifying his discovery. He added, sourly, that probably his listeners were full of bunk about Creede, but if they really wanted to become millionaires they ought to hear what De LaVergne had to say about Cripple Creek.

To Bob's surprise, the firemen, especially Burns and Doyle, seemed to be paying attention to him. And they had good reason. They were worried about the future. The building trades in the Springs had enjoyed four prosperous years. Now business was slowing down. The real estate boom was over and contractors had little construction signed up for the spring. Although Burns and Doyle did not know anything about gold mining, they realized that it might be a good idea to watch this Cripple Creek thing. They had nothing to lose. Cripple Creek was almost in their back yards.

The two Jimmies were good talkers, with the Irish gift for making things vivid. As a result, Bob Womack noticed that during the next week many people were discussing Cripple. He was asked about his mine at El Paso County Court House by Frank Howbert, who now held the county clerk position formerly occupied by his brother, Irving. He was questioned also by Commissioner Plumb, Treasurer McCreery and Judge Samuel Kinsley. The real estater, Charlie Tutt, stopped him on the street, and so did Judge Colburn, the burly lawyer who had done patent work for Miss Lida. At Colburn's request Bob looked up Old Man Stratton, the moody Springs carpenter who had been prospecting throughout the Colorado Rockies for seventeen years.

Bob told Stratton how to reach Cripple. Stratton said he might go, but it didn't sound good to him.

And then, while De LaVergne and Frisbee were still at Cripple, Bob picked up the *Gazette* to find there the first big story on a local gold discovery since the "Mount Pisgah" hoax in '84. For a moment Bob thought that Cripple was being publicized at last and his heart turned over. Then he saw this was something else. Under the date February 12, 1891, Hiram Rogers' headline was:

THE REPORTED GOLD!

A GAZETTE REPRESENTATIVE VISITS
THE FLORISSANT MINE!

How the Lead Was Discovered By
CAPTAIN HENSLEY

Complete and Accurate Statement
OF FACTS!

Specimens of the Metal Tested At
COLORADO COLLEGE

Rogers' opening paragraph read: "On last Tuesday morning a report was circulated in this city, that a very rich strike of gold had been made at Florissant, and that the whole town had gone wild."

Three columns of details followed. The "very rich strike of gold" was located by Captain J. N. Hensley on his ranch just south of Florissant near the cemetery. One hundred and fifty claims had been located, taking up all of Hensley's potato patch and the rest of the ground northward to Florissant. Over one hundred Florissant lots were sold. The Colorado Midland was running an excursion train to the spot. Charles Craig, the celebrated painter, had drawn a sketch of toiling miners on their way to the bonanza.

After reading this thrilling buildup, Bob came to Hiram Rogers' casual letdown: "I took samples of Hensley's ore to the laboratory at Colorado College. Strong nitric acid was poured on the suspected flakes of gold. They promptly dissolved. The metal was only copper." Hiram's final paragraph read:

> The talk about the find at Florissant brought to light a matter that the *Gazette* had promised to keep quiet until better developments gave it foundation. About one month ago a young ranchman well known in the city came here to report that he had found a vein of rich ore. A company has been formed with Dr. J. P. Grannis at its head. A claim has been staked and recorded. The find is eighteen miles south of Florissant and not far from Mount Pisgah.

Bob Womack, now forty-six years old, was pleased to be described by Rogers as "a young ranchman." In other respects he thought that the story was terrible. The position of the paragraph about Cripple Creek, following disclosure that Hensley's potato-patch mine was a bust, could not have been more unfortunate at this time when a number of Springs people were about to take Bob's El Paso Lode seriously. As a matter of fact, Jimmie Burns and Jimmie Doyle had decided to make a mid-winter trip to Cripple. Bob could not blame them for postponing this trip after reading about the Florissant fiasco.

And so, because of Hiram Rogers' story, the flurry of interest died a sudden death. When, Bob wondered, would his bad luck end?

Despairingly, he ceased promotion in the Springs and asked Dr. Grannis for more grubstake money so that he could develop the El Paso a little further. By this time Grannis wished he had never met Bob but he decided that he had to stay with him. He went to the Exchange National Bank, pleaded his case before the dubious officers, and finally was granted a loan of $600 at 12 per cent interest. The officers refused to accept Grannis' Cripple Creek property as security. Instead, they slapped a lien on his dental equipment.

In the last days of February, Bob bought fresh mining supplies and rode the Colorado Midland to Florissant. Here he met De LaVergne and Frisbee on their way home. Ed didn't have much to say but he did admit staking a claim, the El Dorado, adjoining the El Paso on the northwest, and a second claim called Old Mortality just west of the El Dorado. For three days Bob hung around Florissant, sleeping at night on sugar sacks in Frank Castello's store. It cheered him to find that Florissant residents, at least, weren't making cracks about Cripple. A dozen and more had gone in — fellows like Marion Lankford and grocer J. S. Lentz and the carpenter Matt Sterrett. Several of them, with George Carr, had staked the Blanche, Hobo and Blue Bell claims, even before De LaVergne and Frisbee staked the El Dorado and the Old Mortality.[1] As Bob left for Cripple, Frank Castello announced that a miners' meeting would take place at Broken Box Ranch, on April 5, to form a mining district.

March came in mild. Bob got his El Paso shaft down only six feet more. He felt lazy. He had lots of company. A dozen prospectors, of course, didn't make a gold rush but they made a big difference to Bob and to the company-loving Carrs. In mid-March De LaVergne and Frisbee returned briefly and told Bob that the Springs was still on the fence about Cripple. Ed had written a long, glowing report for the *Gazette*. Hiram Rogers cut it to four lines, buried between the Key West Cigar ad and a letter to the editor deploring promiscuous kissing in Alamo Park.

For three days before the April 5 miners' meeting, Emma Carr cleaned house and baked pies. The meeting day was a Sunday. Castello rode in early trailed by three mules loaded with bourbon and beer. De LaVergne appeared, and Fred and Claire Frisbee. Claire had spent a month boning up on gold, so she knew all about it. The Groses and Piggs came from West Four-Mile, the Weltys and Wilsons from Four-Mile. There were fifteen from Florissant. Major Demary refused to attend.

Before the meeting began, Ed De LaVergne asked if Bob Womack's El Paso Lode really qualified for the honor of being called "The Discovery Shaft." Emma Carr stood on a chair. With rolling pin raised above her head she proposed a toast to "Bob Womack, the Discoverer of Cripple Creek!" All glasses went up, Ed's included.

George Carr was elected president of the meeting. The first item on the agenda was the name to be given the mining district. "Womack" was suggested, and "Mount Pisgah" and "Golden Heaven" and "Big Bull." Ed De LaVergne said that the simplest name was usually best, the name most closely associated with the area — in this case, "Cripple Creek." In the voting, "Cripple Creek Mining District" won, though by only a few votes over "Womack Mining District."

De LaVergne reviewed the region's natural boundaries and it was decided to make the district somewhat larger than the apparent limits of the Cripple Creek volcano. The highest surrounding hills were chosen as boundaries — Rhyolite Mountain on the north, Big Bull Hill on the east, Straub Mountain on the south, Mount Pisgah on the west. The summits of these four mountains were just under 11,000 feet.

The area enclosed by them was six miles square — 23,000 acres. Its core was a mile and a half due east of the Broken Box.

It did not take long to draw up laws for the new district. They followed old custom — the liberal United States laws which had prevailed (and still prevail) from the time of the Forty-Niners. Cripple Creek prospectors could hold a lode claim indefinitely on free range by setting out six location stakes, telling County Clerk Frank Howbert about it and doing $100 worth of labor on the claim each year. To get title would be harder, requiring a survey and $500 worth of labor — a total investment of $1500 or more.

Claire Frisbee wanted to know why anybody would bother getting an expensive patent when he could hold his claim by doing $100 worth of work on it each year. Ed De LaVergne explained that assessment work can become a nuisance. None is required on a patented claim. Patented claims, Ed added, can't be jumped and it is hard to attack them in court. And patented claims bring higher prices than unpatented claims.

The Broken Box meeting designated that Cripple Creek lode claims could be staked by one man or by many men in partnership. Each lode claim, like Bob Womack's El Paso, was limited to 1500 feet long and 300 feet wide — about ten acres. A person could stake as many lode claims as he wished. His lode claim gave him a right down to China to all ore within the outside surface measurement of his claim, provided the claim antedated surrounding claims.

The ranchers set limits for placer claims. If located by one man, a placer would consist of twenty acres. It gave the locator the rights to dirt and sand as far down as bedrock. Eight people could combine in staking a single placer claim. An eight-person placer would contain 160 acres. Nobody thought that placer mining would amount to much at Cripple, but placer claims had other uses. Townsites, for instance.

During the entire meeting Bob Womack sat huddled in a corner and said nothing. He was a bit tight at the start and he got progressively tighter on Frank Castello's bourbon — like everyone else. He became almost frightened. He was overwhelmed more and more by what was going on, this creation of a concrete form for his old, old dream. Cripple Creek!

The worst time for Bob was at the end when George Carr rose and delivered a eulogy to the man whose faith and courage had brought them all this great opportunity. Loud applause. Everyone was looking at Bob. He bent his head as Claire Frisbee stepped over and patted him on the shoulder. He felt wonderful and awful. And then he passed out cold.

CHAPTER VIII

O Pioneers!

AFTER THE April 5 Miners' Meeting, some professional prospectors from South Park and Aspen drifted into Poverty Gulch. Grizzled experts like John and Tom Houghton, crazy Irishmen like Tim Hussey, eager youngsters like John Harnan. Another expert pounded at the door of Bob Womack's shack, early one May morning. It was Old Man Stratton, weary and apathetic. Bob brought out a pint. The cowboy and the carpenter polished it off for breakfast.

Stratton told Bob that Cripple showed less promise than any camp he had ever seen, far less than Kokomo or Robinson or Rosita or Red Cliff or Aspen or Tincup or even Chalk Creek. He said he was up by accident. He had started out in late April, from Manitou, to look out for cryolite beds around St. Peter's Dome. For company he had along a semi-invalid boy named Billie Fernay, and he had two burros, one with a scab on its side. The scabby burro had a bucking spell, and Stratton smacked it with a board. Blood oozed from the scab. Two Manitou housewives bustled up, complained of Stratton's mistreatment of the burro and sent word to the Humane Society to arrest Stratton. But he escaped safely with Fernay up Cheyenne Mountain trail.

In a week Stratton and Fernay were back in the Springs without any cryolite. A plasterer friend of Stratton's, Leslie

J. Popejoy, had been talking to Jimmie Burns at City Hall, and was fired up about Cripple. Popejoy offered $275 to grubstake Stratton if he would investigate. So Stratton and Fernay went again over Cheyenne Mountain to West Beaver and got lost beyond Charlie Love's ranch. While they were wondering how to proceed, a jolly, pink-cheeked Santa Claus of a man, J. R. McKinnie, came bouncing along with a wagonload of freight. McKinnie led the newcomers into camp.

When Bob Womack and Stratton finished drinking break-fast, Bob decided to change Stratton's low opinion of Cripple. He mounted Whistler, Stratton climbed on his burro, and the two prospectors toured the Gulch and part of Gold Hill south of it. Nothing aroused Stratton's interest. Bob insisted that the camp must have something, because men were arriving at the rate of four or five a day. Stratton replied that most of them were Springs tenderfeet who didn't know nuffin' from nuffin'. They were just trying to get the business slump off their minds.

Stratton wasn't the only prospector who complained of tenderfeet. Many others wondered if they had come to find gold or to keep the tenderfeet from killing themselves. It wasn't merely the problem of teaching them not to treat dynamite like stick candy. They didn't know what a claim was, or how to hunt for one, or what ore looked like. They didn't know how to build a fire or raise a tent or cook beans. As Tim Hussey said, "Folks claim they got sense enough to keep their pants buttoned in a blizzard . . . I'm mean enough to doubt that statement."

For some days Bob urged Stratton and Fernay to stay near Poverty Gulch. He aided them in staking a claim on Gold Hill, the Lone Star. He showed them how Matt Sterrett and others were mining rich float with plows on top of Globe Hill. But Stratton couldn't stand the tenderfeet. He and Fernay pushed out of the main area to Wilson Creek, at the southern edge of the Cripple Creek district. They raised their tent above the creek, on the lower slope of Battle Mountain. They had the place to themselves.

Next morning, as Stratton was enjoying a tenderfoot-free breakfast, he heard the rattle of gravel up the slope. At the top of the ridge he saw three heads. Then three grinning men and their burros marched down the hill toward him. They were all Springs tenderfeet — the lather, J. R. McKinnie; the lumber hauler, Sam Strong; the grocer, Bill Gowdy. They had observed Stratton's departure from Gold Hill, concluded that he had a hot idea, and trailed south after him.

By mid-morning Stratton could gaze at three white tents gleaming in the sun beside his own tent, on the lower slope of Battle. And soon a fifth tent appeared. It belonged to Jimmie Burns. Jimmie Doyle, Burns' protégé, couldn't come up until fall because he was superintendent of irrigation. But Doyle gave Burns his horse and borrowed a buckboard for him.

The new tenderfoot plague climaxed Stratton's displeasure with Cripple. He almost left when Billie Fernay fell ill and went home. But Fred Trautman, an old carpenter friend, took Fernay's place. Stratton called his first Battle Mountain claim the Gold King Lode. As he staked it, McKinnie and Gowdy stood by forlornly like kids outside the circus. Stratton took pity and gave them the claim. Then he and Fred Trautman slipped away up Wilson Creek. Stratton located several claims — the Legal Tender, the Lillie, the Vindicator — and abandoned them as valueless. On June 6 he staked No Name

Placer. But the next day he packed his tools, loaded his supplies on his burros, shook hands with the tenderfeet and
returned to Colorado Springs.

But he couldn't get Battle Mountain out of his head. He
kept seeing that south slope with the five tents in line near
the bottom. And he kept seeing a dreary, weathered granite
ledge that cropped out of the slope a few hundred feet above
the five tents. He had tested a piece of this ledge with his
blowpipe. It had contained no gold. And yet there was something strange about it.

He reviewed what he had noted of Cripple's volcanic structure and he tried to fit that granite ledge into the district's
geological story. And finally the answer came to him. The
ledge must mark the outer edge of the ancient volcano. If
so, a good-sized vein might exist along the face of the ledge,
under ground. Such veins were common at the perimeters
of volcanoes. A good-sized vein at a perimeter might contain
a rich deposit of gold.

Stratton hurried back to Cripple. The granite ledge was
still open. On July 4, 1891, he staked a claim enclosing the
ledge. He put his location notice on a two-by-four that happened to be lying around. He called the claim the Independence. Southward, down the slope along the trend of the
presumed Independence vein, he staked a second claim, the
Washington. He had to tack his notice for this claim to a
tree limb, because he couldn't find another two-by-four.

Three days later Stratton staked the Professor Lamb claim
(Stratton, like De LaVergne, had taken Henry Lamb's assay
course). Then he began sinking a shaft along the face of
the ledge at the Independence. He hit something several feet
down that resembled a vein, but it assayed poorly. When he
ran out of money he sent Fred Trautman to the Springs to

tackle Leslie Popejoy for more grubstake support. Trautman took with him new samples from the Independence. One of them assayed $360 a ton. And yet Popejoy refused to advance more cash.

The favorable assay pleased Stratton and he decided to hang on without Popejoy. He asked Bob Womack if anybody in the district had any money. Bob sent him to Sam Altman, who was running a sawmill at Squaw Gulch just below Poverty Gulch. Sam loaned Stratton $950. Stratton spent most of it clearing up obligations to Popejoy, Billie Fernay and Fred Trautman. In the end he had $125 capital and the sole rights to the Independence, the Washington, and the Professor Lamb.

All the while the Poverty Gulch area around Bob Womack's shack got thicker and thicker with tenderfeet — one hundred in May, two hundred in June, four hundred in August. A tent boardinghouse was set up by D. C. Williams (his full name was Denver Colorado Williams). Alonzo Welty was operating a rickety stage to Florissant. Dutch Henry ran a saloon, consisting of a plank across two beer kegs. N. B. Guyot quit his job at the Guggenheim smelter in Pueblo and opened an assay shop in Squaw Gulch. George and Emma Carr had real company, though it is a mystery how they could finance so much hospitality at the Broken Box. It was not simply a matter of feeding and housing those temporarily destitute. Every emergency — snake bite, poison ivy, broken tools, lost burros — was brought to the Carrs for solution.

In late summer a Texas tenderfoot, Chick Gatewood, was killed in the cave-in of Charles McGee's shaft. D. B. Fairley, the Springs undertaker, sent up to Cripple the first of many coffins. Unfortunately for Gatewood, his next of kin elected to have him buried at Florissant and so he failed to attain the immortality that would have been his if he had initiated the Cripple Creek cemetery.

Claire Frisbee was Cripple's first lady prospector. The second was Blanche Barton — or, anyhow, that's what Blanche called herself. She was a Colorado City madam, and when she reached Cripple to size up the situation she called on Bob Womack. Bob loved and was beloved by all God's fallen creatures. Bob advised Blanche to place her tent below his shack, at the foot of Poverty Gulch, but up the slope so she would not be washed out by a flash flood.

Blanche hadn't had much education. One evening she stopped to see Bob. Tim Hussey, she explained, had been a steady customer for weeks and had given her so many eighth interests in claims that she figured she must own most of the camp. Would Bob check Tim's IOUs? Bob did. There were twenty-seven eighth interests in all, every one assigned to the same claim.

As the pressure of people around Poverty Gulch increased, prospectors and tenderfeet pushed further afield. Ed De LaVergne found something he liked on Raven Hill, between Squaw Gulch and Stratton's Battle Mountain. William Shemwell, a Springs blacksmith, staked a claim next to Ed's Raven claim — the Elkton. C. C. Hagerty, a Springs tailor, bought an eighth of the Elkton; Smith Gee, a Negro ash-hauler, gave Shemwell his mule for another eighth. Steve Blair, a carpenter colleague of Stratton's, took a claim on Bull Hill called the Buena Vista. Near the top of Bull Hill, A. D. Jones, the drug clerk, and his boss, J. K. Miller, staked a spot which they named "The Pharmacist." Jones solved the problem of where to dig by throwing his hat in the air, digging where it fell. He hit a vein assaying $600 to the ton.

All these events made Bob Womack happier than he had

ever been. For a decade he had endured the derision of men. Now, some of these same men hung on his words. The new attitude made Bob feel good but it didn't spur him to get along with the development of the El Paso Lode. Bob had little time to work for Dr. Grannis. He was too busy advising people, finding claims for them, basking in their gratitude and enjoying their whiskey.

Perhaps the camp's busiest man was Ed De LaVergne, who had a heart as big as Bob's. Ed was working eighteen hours a day — half the time to help the tenderfeet. Many of them would bring him ore and he would explain to them the importance of proper assays. It was no use, he would tell them, to take an assay or two and try to promote their property on the results. They must take dozens of samples from all parts of their exposed vein throughout its depth and strike an average of the combined gold content. In that way they could reach an estimate of the value of the gold ore actually in sight, an estimate that would be good ammunition for the claim-owner trying to bag a capitalist.

But, on the whole, Cripple's first summer was difficult for everyone. There was one day of excitement when Leroy Case arrived to inspect the camp for General Palmer. Case decided it was another "Mount Pisgah" hoax. That was as close as the patron saint of Colorado Springs ever got to supporting Cripple. Perhaps the most discouraging thing was the fact that the place didn't remotely resemble Sutter's Mill or Fraser River or Gregory Gulch. The placer beds of the Forty-Niners and Fifty-Niners offered immediate daily profit to any man patient enough to wash gravel in a gold pan. Quick profits were not possible at Cripple. The placers in most cases were false alarms. Everyone had to believe Bob Womack and Ed De LaVergne when they insisted that

Cripple's future depended on the costly business of taking out gold ore hidden beneath the surface of the ground in veins enclosed by hard rock.

Womack and De LaVergne were true believers. But to most of the professionals the future contained an enormous if. Old Man Stratton was one of the most skeptical. After he staked the Independence and the Washington he often sneaked off to the Springs to try to unload his claims. He offered the Washington to James J. Hagerman for $500. He offered the Independence for the same price to a young invalid named Albert E. Carlton, aged twenty-five. Carlton turned down Stratton's offer on the grounds that he had no use for a gold mine. In six months, he said, he would be dead of T.B.

It was all outgo and no income. It is doubtful if as much as $25,000 of actual gold was realized from the hundreds of claims staked between January and September of '91. Alonzo Welty had teams hauling in huge amounts of beer from Florissant. The same teams hauled out no gold ore to speak of.

And so the pioneers sat on their prospect excavations and watched with anxiety the turning of the aspens. They felt that large amounts of investment capital for mine development would have to appear soon if the camp were to survive the winter. Something would have to happen.

Well, something did happen. That something was Count James Pourtales.

CHAPTER IX

Count Pourtales to the Rescue

COUNT POURTALES was a Bismarck imperialist, an advocate of selective breeding, master of the ancient Silesian estate, Glumbowitz, and lord of nine Silesian villages. He had great charm. He came to Colorado Springs in '85 to make money to support Glumbowitz and to marry his beautiful French cousin, Berthe de Pourtales.

Berthe was living on a ranch near Florissant with her brother, Louis Otto, who had been sent there by his doctor to get away from the wearing aspects of society, champagne in particular. Berthe was just a youngster but she was already a celebrity, having wed and divorced a Boston millionaire. She had caused quite a commotion on two continents as a breaker of hearts.

When she married Pourtales, Colorado Springs accepted the newlyweds joyfully and for a while the big homes of the North End were enveloped in an atmosphere of festival. Count James, however, was only a part-time playboy. He loved folderol but his main interest was sound investments paying 12 per cent. He teamed up with a Philadelphian, William J. Willcox, who was doing a bad job of running a dairy farm called Broadmoor, five miles south of Colorado Springs. With German thoroughness, Pourtales studied this dairy and decided that Willcox was doing everything wrong.

So Willcox took Pourtales' town house and Pourtales took Berthe and moved to Broadmoor where he introduced German genetics to the surprised Brown Swiss cows, improved the water facilities and experimented with new feeds. The Broadmoor dairy began to make money because of greater milk production and because it was unfashionable in Springs households not to buy the Count's Broadmoor "Gilt Edge Crown Butter."

Still, it took more than butter to support Glumbowitz and Berthe. In 1889, Pourtales set up a real estate development on the part of the Broadmoor farm closest to Cheyenne Mountain. He borrowed $250,000 from friends in New York and London, started building a casino and prepared ground for an artificial lake to enhance the beauty of the casino's Broadmoor setting. When he turned water into the lake bed it ran out again.

Pourtales figured out why. Hundreds of prairie dog mounds had been smoothed over in preparing the lake bed. The water was leaking through the prairie dog holes beneath the mounds. Pourtales hired an army of diggers, who uncovered four hundred holes and filled them with potter's clay. Then the lake held water. And still people hesitated to buy lots in the platted area below the Broadmoor dam for fear they might wake some morning and find their homes floating into the plains. Pourtales had the answer to that, too. Instead of placing the Broadmoor Casino on solid rock beside the lake he placed it right on top of the earth dam. This act created faith in the dam's stability and the Broadmoor lots began to sell.

The glittering Casino opened in June, 1891, just in time to get caught in the gathering financial storm set off a few months before by the Baring Brothers failure in London.

The Count had expected to make a killing out of roulette and had imported a crew of French croupiers to run the Casino wheel. General Palmer disapproved. He spoke a word or two. A flood of county officials swept over Pourtales and foundered his roulette plans. Then he almost unloaded the Casino on George Pullman, the palace-car man. Pullman withdrew at the last moment.

With a mortgage coming due on Glumbowitz, Pourtales was in a tough spot in August of '91. One afternoon he got to chatting with Ed De LaVergne over a glass of beer at the El Paso Club. Ed unburdened himself of his hopes and fears about Cripple Creek. He said that a couple of hundred men were up there discovering gold lodes by the dozens. He stressed his belief that these lodes contained unlimited amounts of gold in tellurides. Only capital was lacking to create a great gold industry and a lot of millionaires. He explained that hard-rock gold mining had fallen into disrepute during the Seventies because of refining problems. But many of the headaches had been cured by metallurgical discoveries in the South African Rand which had reduced the cost of removing gold from difficult ores.

Smelting charges which had been $65 a ton in 1870 were down to less than $20 a ton in 1891. The cost of lumber for mine shaft timbering had fallen from $60 to $18 a thousand, dynamite from a dollar to fourteen cents a pound, fuses from $30 to a dollar each. All in all, hard-rock gold mining cost only 30 per cent of what it had cost twenty years earlier. The cost might become even lower at Cripple Creek if the government decided to stop buying silver for currency at an artificially high price. Such action would force most of Colorado's silver mines to close. Thousands of men would be thrown out of work, and the average wage of hard-rock miners would fall below the level of $2.50 to $3 a day.

Pourtales wrote down Ed's figures and discussed them next day with his best friend, Thomas C. Parrish, an amateur prospector and an artist of sorts.[1] Parrish was impressed by De LaVergne's argument and recommended an inspection trip to Cripple. In mid-August, Pourtales and Parrish rode the now-worn Cheyenne Mountain trail to Love's ranch, past Big Bull Mountain to Wilson Creek and south around the curve of Battle Mountain. They saw the five white tents of Stratton and Company, and headed for the path above them leading over the ridge. A head popped out of a prospect hole a dozen yards below them. A stocky figure emerged from it in one hell of a hurry. It was Sam Strong, the Springs lumber hauler who had joined Stratton on Battle in the Spring. Sam was red as a beet from sun and booze. He was working on a claim named after himself. Sam yelled, "Git out of here, you crazy fools! Can't you see I'm blasting?"

Pourtales and Parrish did git before debris from the blast could pelt down on them. The path took them over the ridge past De LaVergne's Raven and Shemwell's Elkton claims, and across Squaw Gulch where Frank Castello and the Houghtons were digging a hole called the Mary McKinney. Another mile brought them to the Broken Box ranch house.

Cheerful Emma Carr took a fancy to the big, laughing German. Pourtales told her in heavy Teutonic accents that she reminded him of the Lorelei, and Emma returned the compliment by permitting him to sleep late if he wanted to. She assigned to him the bed in her kitchen. It was her custom to make biscuits on a dough board at the foot of this bed, which she managed by propping apart the large feet of the snoring master of Glumbowitz, so that she could set the dough board between them. Pourtales could sing with gusto, if not with accuracy. One night he astounded the Carr household and Bob Womack by presenting the score of *Fidelio,* singing all the parts himself.

For many days Pourtales and Parrish roamed the Cripple Creek district, staking placers and taking hundreds of samples for assay. Bob Womack accompanied them to Battle Mountain to discuss the situation with Stratton. It was at Stratton's suggestion that they went to the north side of Bull Hill to look at Steve Blair's hole in the ground called the Buena Vista.

All the while Cripple's tenderfeet were growing more and more gloomy. By October fellows like Jimmie Burns and Fred Frisbee and Sam Strong were on their last legs financially. They knew that if capital didn't arrive soon they could not continue the assessment work required to hold their claims, and their sacrifices of the spring and summer would come to nothing. The outlook was especially wearing on Bob Womack. In June and July he had been happy, not because he was making money but because his faith in Cripple seemed justified. Now, as the snow deepened on Pikes Peak, that justification seemed as far away as it had thirteen years before, when he had outlined his hopes to Theodore Lowe.

Ed De LaVergne was as disturbed as Bob, but Ed's emotion was closer to angry frustration than to anything else. Ed knew by this time, without any possibility of error, that the gold was there for the taking. His assays of exposed veins in a dozen prospect holes had disclosed high-grade ore worth ten times the asking price of the claims. But would any of these wealthy invalids and millionaire playboys in the Springs advance money to triple their fortunes? No, not even his own brother. Capital for Creede? Certainly! For Aspen or Leadville or Lemhi, Idaho, or Joplin, Missouri? Sure thing! But

Cripple? "Hard times, Ed," they would tell him. "And, besides, Cripple will never pay."

Pourtales was a feudal overlord in Germany, but he was a real democrat at Cripple Creek. He and Tom Parrish made many friends. The attitude of the camp toward them was one of good-natured amusement and it seldom occurred to anyone that these two might be up there for a serious purpose. Pourtales in his flat Silesian hat, string tie and green velvet frock coat talked a great deal about alpine flowers. He said that he meant to establish a Colorado rock garden at Glumbowitz. Parrish spent much time sketching windlasses, burros and slouch-hatted miners.

During the last week of October, Pourtales and Parrish packed up and left Cripple. And, on November 10, 1891, the sensational news broke, the totally unexpected news about what they had been up to. On that day, the Colorado newspapers announced that Pourtales and Parrish were going to buy, for $80,000, Steve Blair's Buena Vista claim on Bull Hill, two miles east of Poverty Gulch. In the announcement Pourtales stated dramatically that the Buena Vista contained a million dollars' worth of gold ore in sight. He added that the Cripple Creek district had at least a hundred other claims as valuable as the Buena Vista.

The Count's sense of timing, his social prestige and the glamour of his name made the announcement immensely effective. It changed the entire attitude toward Cripple Creek, removed the memory of the "Mount Pisgah" hoax, and broke the dreary stalemate. Capitalists from the Springs, from Canon City, from Denver, from Pueblo and Aspen, sent engineers by the dozens to the camp, and soon claims were being snapped up right and left.

Nothing succeeds like success. The excited pioneers, who

would have sold their holdings for a song in October, raised their prices ten and twenty times. Winfield Scott Stratton removed the $500 label from his Washington claim and sold it to Pourtales' dairy partner, W. J. Willcox, for $80,000. Bob Womack threw away his half interest in the El Paso Lode to Dr. Grannis for $300, and Grannis sold four fifths of this claim to Claire Frisbee for $8000.

Claire's purchase terrified Fred Frisbee, but, even while he berated himself for failing to control his spouse, Claire collected $8000 from William Lennox, the Springs coal dealer, for a *three-fifths* interest in the El Paso, thus retaining one fifth as clear profit. Soon after, Judge Colburn paid $10,000 for a tenth interest in the claim. Then William Lennox and Colburn teamed up with Ed Giddings, the Springs department store owner, to take a $60,000 option on Sam Strong's Battle Mountain prospect hole, the Strong Mine.

The snowballing of confidence helped everyone except the two fellows who had created it. Pourtales and Parrish had their Buena Vista Mine, but they had trouble raising funds for its development. One day the Springs druggists, A. D. Jones and J. K. Miller, hit a streak of $510-a-ton ore in their Bull Hill mine, the Pharmacist. The claim was four hundred yards west of the Buena Vista. Pourtales took a piece of Pharmacist ore to James J. Hagerman, the richest man he knew. He told Hagerman that the same kind of high-grade ore existed in the Buena Vista. Hagerman ordered Wolcott E. Newberry, boss of his famous Mollie Gibson silver mine at Aspen, to inspect the gold camp.

Newberry, one of the most respected mining engineers in the United States, approved of the Buena Vista. That solved the development problem of Pourtales and Parrish. In the

months that followed, Hagerman put up $225,000 for work-
ing the Buena Vista and for buying twenty-one other Bull
Hill claims. These claims were consolidated under the title,
Isabella Gold Mining Company. The name "Isabella" was
popular for babies and bonanzas in '92, because of the four
hundredth anniversary of the discovery of America by an
old-time prospector called Columbus, grubstaked by Queen
Isabella of Spain.

"Hagerman" was a magic word in Colorado investment
circles, and Pourtales lost no time exploiting it for the benefit
of Buena Vista stock sales. When Hagerman's participation
in the Buena Vista became known, the stock rose from
twenty-five cents to $7.50 a share. Other mining stocks like
the Gold King (originally the El Paso) and the Pharmacist
shared in the boom and an informal mining exchange was
set up on the sunny north side of Pikes Peak Avenue, in
Colorado Springs.

And so Bob Womack and Ed De LaVergne had their gold
rush at last, a rush reaching such proportions in '92 that
Marshal Dana of Colorado Springs declared, "Crime in our
fair city is at an all-time low. All the criminals have moved
to Cripple Creek." But, for the second time, members of
Springs society were critical of James J. Hagerman. In
the late Eighties his Colorado Midland had disturbed them.
Now Hagerman's support of the Buena Vista was causing a
cataclysm again. Their cooks, butlers, nursemaids, gardeners
and ash-haulers were so engrossed in Cripple Creek stocks
that they couldn't work properly.

And yet, in actual fact, the throngs who poured into
Cripple during '92 had little more to encourage them than
had the pioneers of '91. Only the Buena Vista and the
Pharmacist were producing gold in quantity. But nobody

worried any more. Big production was around the corner. In the meantime, there were other ways to make money.

The population of the gold camp was increasing at the rate of a thousand a month. This stream of arrivals had to be fed, clothed, housed and entertained. A town had to be founded, laid out, sold off and built. And so we resume the curious saga of Bennett and Myers.

CHAPTER X

A Town Is Born

YOUNG HORACE BENNETT thought it was plain foolishness when he bought the Broken Box in '85 for the Denver real estate firm of Bennett and Myers. The terms for the four 160-acre homesteads, you may recall, were liberal: $5000 down, and $20,000 owing, if and when. Still Bennett thought he was paying far too much just to give his midde-aged partner, Julius Myers, a place to catch trout.

Bennett's pessimism increased with the years, even though George Carr was making a profit for the Broken Box. Bennett detested Cripple's high altitude, its frightful lightning, Bob Womack and his perilous prospect holes. Bennett believed in the judgment of the Denver assayer, E. E. Burlingame, who had declared that Womack must be crazy to keep hunting for gold at Cripple. Thereafter, Bennett always referred to Poverty Gulch's sole resident as "Crazy Bob."

Carr never wrote Bennett about ranch affairs during the winter, and so Bennett heard nothing of Womack's El Paso Lode or of the Cripple Creek explorations of De LaVergne and Frisbee. Bennett could not have been more incredulous when, two weeks after the April 5 miners' meeting at the Broken Box, George Carr wired him from Florissant: GOLD PROSPECTORS DIGGING UP THE RANCH EVERYWHERE. SHALL I MAKE THEM JUMP?

Bennett hurried to Cripple Creek. He saw a handful of old-time prospectors and a bunch of bewildered tenderfeet scratching on the hills. He saw Bob Womack rushing hither and yon flashing a pocketful of greenbacks. But he didn't see anything that resembled gold and he concluded that another "Mount Pisgah" hoax was in progress. He told George Carr to get out his shotgun and keep these gold-seeking maniacs off the 160-acre headquarters ranch around Cripple Creek spring, and off the Arequa Gulch homestead, two miles south. This was not difficult since the favored gold grounds were the free range gulches and low hills east and southeast of the Broken Box ranch house.

There was one slight puzzlement to mar Bennett's conviction that Womack and his pals were staging a hoax. Some Colorado Springs fellows had staked a 140-acre claim called the Hayden Placer around the north and east borders of Broken Box headquarters. The stakers made no pretense that they were working the placer claim for gold. On the contrary they seemed to encourage prospectors to put up tents on their placer ground and build shacks here and there.

On his way back to Denver, Bennett looked up the names of the Hayden Placer locators at El Paso County Court House. He found that the placer had been staked on April 4, '91. The first three names listed as locators — Ed De LaVergne, Fred Frisbee and Harry Seldomridge — were unknown to him. But the next four made Bennett suspicious. The names were County Clerk Frank Howbert, County Commissioner J. C. Plumb, County Treasurer H. C. McCreery and Judge Sam Kinsley. These four men were not prospectors. They were El Paso County's four top Republican politicians.

It didn't take Bennett long to figure out what those four

names meant. Hayden Placer was a blind, a slick way of getting control of government land for a townsite. The four Republicans included as locators were the same men who had engineered the election of Hosea Townsend to Congress in Washington. They could depend on Townsend to rush a quick patent through the government land office so that Hayden Placer could be platted into lots.

Of course Bennett didn't believe for a minute that a real town would ever be needed at Bob Womack's gold camp. But it might be possible to unload in "town" lots a few acres of the Broken Box at prices a hundred times higher than the acres were worth — provided the Springs politicians didn't beat Bennett to it. It happened that Bennett had on his neck a young half brother, Melvin Sowle, whom Bennett was supposed to teach the real estate business. Bennett had nothing special for Sowle to do in the Denver office of Bennett and Myers.

And so Bennett explained the Hayden Placer threat to Sowle and sent him up to Cripple with instructions to keep his eyes open for several weeks until the camp folded. Sowle packed his fishing rod, an extra pair of pants and one blanket in case it got cold in August. But Bennett's assignment was destined to last a bit longer than either Bennett or Sowle expected. Sowle would not get away from Cripple again until the start of the Spanish-American War.

Upon arriving at Cripple, Melvin Sowle saw at once that action was necessary. Sam Altman's sawmill at Squaw Gulch was turning out quantities of lumber for shacks, and new prospectors were arriving at the rate of a dozen a day. The Hayden Placer people, Sowle discovered, were planning to plat into lots their 140 acres adjoining the Broken Box. They expected to sell these lots even before they received a government patent to the placer land by giving bond that the patent would materialize.

Melvin Sowle wrote Bennett advising an immediate survey of the Broken Box Ranch and the filing of a townsite plat. Bennett mulled the matter over for a week and wrote Sowle to have a survey and plat made if they could be made cheaply. Bennett stipulated that only the northern, hilly half of the Broken Box's 160 acres was to be platted. Bennett didn't want this inconvenient, ridiculous, temporary gold flurry to interfere with the ranch buildings and the corral in the southern, flatter half of the ranch.

The hilly half, Bennett decided, was too cruel a habitation for cattle, but it would do probably for these cock-eyed tenderfeet from the Springs if they were determined to have a town. Bennett stipulated that if people bought lots in the Bennett and Myers townsite they must agree to leave their shacks behind when they abandoned Cripple Creek as a gold field. The ranch company could use the wood in these abandoned shacks to repair fences and cattle shelters after the gold nonsense was over.

Melvin Sowle wanted to call the proposed townsite "Cripple Creek" but Bennett vetoed it. Bennett had a stubborn streak. For some weeks an official United States post office called "Fremont" had been operating on Hayden Placer ground.[1] So Bennett announced that his townsite would be named "Fremont." If Fremont post office didn't like it, the United States government could move it down the hill of Hayden Placer and on to Bennett and Myers land. Bennett would show these Springs politicians that they couldn't put anything over on him!

The Bennett and Myers townsite, Fremont, was duly platted and the plat filed on November 6, 1891. It consisted of eighty acres, oblong in shape. From east to west, starting almost at Bob Womack's old shack near the entrance to Poverty Gulch, it ran for 2620 feet toward the lower slopes of Mount Pisgah, with the blocks marked by five north-south streets. The distance from south to north, an unholy climb, was 1350 feet, divided into five east-west streets.

The total of thirty blocks contained 766 lots priced at $25 for inside lots, $50 for corner lots. The cheap platting job was done in a hurry and no serious effort was made to have the streets conform to topography. Even if the effort had been made it probably wouldn't have improved things much. As you look at Cripple Creek town today you can see the point of the old joke: "A man broke his neck last night, falling off Bennett Avenue." There is a spot on the main street where the south side is fifteen feet lower than the north side.

Just before filing the Fremont townsite plat, Horace Bennett and Julius Myers stretched the map out on Bennett's desk in Denver, and Myers suggested that maybe the streets ought to have names. Bennett noticed that most of the north-south streets were narrower than the east-west streets, and presumably less important to the coming metropolis. So he merely numbered them, First to Fifth Streets, moving from west to east. Then Bennett wrote BENNETT AVENUE on the widest and most central of the east-west streets, and passed his pen along to Myers, who wrote the fateful words, MYERS AVENUE, on the east-west street just south of Bennett Avenue. Throughout his life, Julius Myers, a singularly pure and childlike spirit, never ceased shaking his head in wonder and amusement that one of the country's best-known red-light districts should be named after him.

Three more east-west streets remained. The one north

of Bennett Avenue was easy. Bennett wrote CARR AVENUE on the plat in honor of the amiable foreman of the Broken Box, George W. Carr. But then both Bennett and Myers were stumped. Time was a-wasting as they had a date in a few minutes at the Arapahoe County Court House. Bennett thought of his half brother, Melvin Sowle, but discarded Sowle as being too unusual for a street name. Glancing around, his eyes fell on Seymour Warren, an insurance man who rented desk space in the Bennett and Myers office. WARREN AVENUE went down on the street south of Myers Avenue. The door opened and in walked William Eaton, Julius Myers' brother-in-law. Myers picked up the pen and inscribed EATON AVENUE on the plat north of Carr Avenue.

There was no immediate boom in the sale of Fremont townsite lots, despite the November influx of capital initiated by Count Pourtales. But Melvin Sowle sold enough lots on Bennett Avenue to saloon men, dance hall men, parlor house madams, gamblers and mining brokers, to give that street a head start as the center of the business district. Ed De La-Vergne and the rest of the Hayden Placer townsite group could not get their adjoining land platted until February 15, 1892. It comprised 140 acres laid out in 1320 lots, the slopes of which were even better adapted to mountain goats than the slopes of Fremont. The popular name for Hayden Placer townsite was "Cripple Creek."

Horace Bennett worried incessantly about the Hayden Placer "Cripple Creek" and he spent considerable time concocting small skulduggeries for Melvin Sowle to execute. Stage drivers, for instance, were bribed not to deliver passengers up the hill.[2] But Bennett really had nothing to worry about. The force of gravity alone was a sufficient guarantee that business would be concentrated down on Bennett Avenue.

Furthermore, Bennett was helped because Ed De LaVergne was somewhat of a Puritan. His moral scruples impelled him to bar from Hayden Placer the normal enterprises of a new mining camp — saloons, dance halls, habitations for frail sisters. This attitude forced Ed to rely on snob and scenic appeal if he and his politicians expected to sell lots in competition with Bennett's wide-open Fremont. A Hayden Placer announcement read: "All the best people are building homes out of the saloon and gambling area. From Hayden Placer, residents can gaze southward on the glories of the Sangre de Cristo Range, instead of on the degradation of the Four Hundred."

The infant townsites, Bennett's Fremont and Hayden Placer's Cripple Creek, developed side by side with only one police officer, good-natured Peter Eales, who wandered around, brandishing his six-shooter as El Paso County sheriff. There were no municipal services of any kind, and the general disorder was increased by the fact that Fremont residents and Cripple Creek residents took up the cudgels for the proprietors of their respective townsites and insisted on separate town administrations.

Fremont held the first city election with Peter Hettig running for mayor against Rancher George Carr. Carr won easily, but the opposition got to playing catch with several shoeboxes full of Carr's ballots and an accurate count of the votes was impossible. Consequently, for almost four months, Fremont's municipal life, such as it was, was managed by two full sets of officers until a second election could be arranged.

At this second Fremont election, George Carr ran against Dr. John A. Whiting. The pre-election odds were six to one for Carr, which was natural since half the town had imposed on George and Emma Carr's generosity in one way or another. However, on the night before election George and his election manager, Bob Womack, loaded up on campaign enthusiasm and whiskey and got to lassoing opposition leaders and dragging them down Bennett Avenue behind their cow ponies on the grounds that they were low-down mavericks who rightfully ought to carry Carr's brand. Everybody enjoyed the fun. But Cripple's pioneers contained a high proportion of law-abiding tenderfeet from Colorado Springs and they felt that being mayor of Fremont was a serious matter, after all. On election day most of Carr's supporters switched sides, and Dr. Whiting was elected mayor of Fremont, in a landslide.

John Simington was elected first mayor of Cripple Creek (Hayden Placer). He didn't serve a full year, because in February of '93 residents of Fremont and Cripple Creek decided that they had had enough of municipal uproar with mayors all over the place issuing conflicting orders, and they voted to consolidate the two townsites under one name, Cripple Creek, with a single set of officers. In the ensuing election, Dr. Whiting became mayor of the consolidated towns.

While these events were transpiring, Bennett and Myers had another look at that part of Broken Box Ranch which lay up the east slope of Mount Pisgah. It was a mile above Fremont, and Myers felt it was useless even as a town dump. Bennett, a cosmic thinker, agreed that this gravel patch could not attract living people, but many living people in Cripple would soon be dead, what with tenderfeet misusing dynamite, and miners engaging in saloon brawls. And so Bennett set aside one end of the gravel patch and labeled it "Mount Pisgah Cemetery." In a matter of weeks, the Bennett and Myers firm was doing a brisk cemetery business. One

of the first people buried there was A. A. McGovney's faithful
Negro coachman, Solley Bufford, who curried McGovney's
mare one last time, left Colorado Springs for Cripple Creek
and died of pneumonia three days later.

Next, Horace Bennett platted the southern portion of
Broken Box Ranch into the First Fremont Addition, tore
down the precious corrals and ranch buildings that he had
tried so hard to protect the year before against this townsite
absurdity, sold the cattle and turned George Carr out to
pasture. This was fine with George, because he was making
much more money now buying and selling mining claims
than the $50 a month Bennett had paid him to run the
Broken Box.

Within two years after reluctantly platting Fremont, Bennett and Myers saw their town transformed into a comfortable settlement with a population of 5000, a water system,
electric arc lights and twenty restaurants on Bennett Avenue.
The white tents had mostly disappeared from the low hills
and so had the groves of spruce and aspen. Thousands of
acres of government timber were cut down without permission, and eight lumber yards sold boards which were made
into hundreds of unpainted shacks and privies. The shacks
were one- and two-room affairs, often with attic rooms for
children, heated by wood and coal stoves. They were built
with the outside boards running vertically, the cracks covered
with wood strips. The inside boards ran horizontally and
were lined with newspaper. The gable and hip roofs were
not pitched steeply because rains and snows were rare. Ceil-
ings were lined with canvas. These kerosene-lighted homes
could be built for $500 or less. They brought high rents —
$15 a month.

Bennett Avenue, between Second and Third Streets, filled

solidly with business establishments, and so did Third Street south to Myers and along Myers back toward Second Street. Melvin Sowle raised prices of lots almost weekly. Business lots that went for $25 and $50 in November of '91 were bringing $3000 and $5000 in '93. By that time Cripple Creek town had twenty-six saloons and gambling houses, four dance halls, twenty-four grocery stores, ten meat markets, nine hotels, nine laundries, three large bathhouses, eleven clothing stores, ten barber shops, nine assay offices, seven bakeries, six bookstores, forty-four lawyers' offices, eight stenography offices, thirty-six mining stock and real estate offices, eleven parlor houses and twenty-six one-girl cribs. There were also five fraternal lodges and a dozen or more literary and social clubs.

Horace Bennett and Julius Myers had very little to do with the gold camp of Cripple Creek beyond paper work accomplished in their Denver office. And yet they made at least a million dollars at Cripple. Their profits from the sale of Fremont lots came to $500,000. Gold ore in quantity was discovered on the Arequa Gulch homestead of the Broken Box Ranch — Bob Womack's original 160 acres; Bennett and Myers plotted this Arequa homestead as a townsite and sold it off for a total of $320,000. They sold the Allen Gullion homestead at Grassy to Frank and Harry Woods for $180,000. All in all, a tidy return for an investment of $5000 down, $20,000 owing! [3]

CHAPTER XI

Happy Days!

Miss lida womack, still living at Sunview Ranch down on the plains with her frail father, Sam, saw little of Bob during the gold camp's childhood. It was a nice time for Bob. He was much too busy to do any work, and he never needed money. Always, somebody was around pleased to pay for anything he wanted. His tall, stooped frame composed one of the first sights pointed out to visitors. He loved to hide behind the door of his shack and listen to tenderfeet telling each other, "There's Womack's place — the feller 't discovered Cripple Creek."

Until the start of '93, the saloons, gambling places, restaurants and dance halls of Cripple Creek town were concentrated along Bennett Avenue. Upstairs over the Anaconda, Buckhorn and some other saloons were the parlor houses operated by Minnie Smith, Mollie King, Lollie Lee, Blanche Barton and the like — old hands from Leadville, Aspen and Colorado City. Alcohol and sex got so mixed into everything that a man could hardly enter a store to buy groceries without being propositioned. So Marshal Hi Wilson moved the girls and the dance halls a block south to Myers Avenue, between Fifth and Third Streets. Wilson promised that nobody would bother the girls on Myers, as long as they paid their head tax, gave to church funds, and behaved demurely when out shopping.

Bob Womack tried his hand at faro, roulette, twenty-one and craps in the Bennett Avenue gambling houses, but he liked poker best. More than once he sat in games at Johnnie Nolon's, with Melvin Sowle and Jimmie Burns and Tim Hussey, that went on for three days. Johnnie Nolon, an ex-pony express rider from St. Joe, ran the straightest gambling house in town. He was a small, impeccably dressed, soft-spoken Irish Catholic with great tact and a very soft heart. He was a sucker for a touch and any hungry hobo could always get a meal at Nolon's. At night Johnnie covered the pool tables with blankets and let the bums bed down.

Although Bob Womack danced badly he worked at it hard in the Myers Avenue joints — the Bon Ton, Red Light, Great View, Topic and Casino. Taxi dances were the rule: quadrille, waltz, schottisch. For one short dance Bob paid twenty-five cents, which included a shot of rotgut whiskey and maybe a kiss or two. The girl received half of the two bits. It always took Bob quite a while to gather a lady into his arms and some more seconds to get started on the beat. Consequently, by the time he took his first steps the dance was over and the caller was shouting, "Promenade to the bar!"

Sometimes the dance-hall floor would be cleared for a boxing match. The contestants were miners brought in off the street and tagged with names like "Dynamite Dick" or "Giant Powder George." But the most exciting dance-hall nights took place when Old Man Stratton and Jimmie Burns got their checks for ore from the Pueblo smelter and tried to outdo each other in buying drinks for the house. The bartenders would turn out beer in such quantities that soon the sawdust around the bar would be soaked with it.

Many things went on as a matter of course in early Cripple

that were banned by Colorado law, but the gold camp had its own unwritten rules. Chinese and South Europeans, for instance, were taboo. As one lawyer put it, "Beyond the fact that these rules seem to repeal most of the ordinary laws of the United States, they are a damn' good set of laws for Cripple."

As we have said, Cripple's predominant population was made up of law-abiding Springs tenderfeet and so the camp had a certain orderliness. It took a long time even to acquire a murder. Bob Womack thought one had happened in November of '91 when Pegleg Ricketts attacked a hotel manager, F. S. Appleton, with a buggy whip in front of Bob's porch. The two men had been arguing about which of them had the meanest wife. Tom Houghton and Bob pulled Ricketts off Appleton and for some days Appleton "hovered between life and death," according to the *Colorado Springs Gazette*. In the end it appeared that what the *Gazette* meant by "hovering" was that Appleton refused to sober up. Forty-rod, not buggy-whipping, was his main trouble.

The first actual murder occurred when a colored ex-convict named Charles A. Hudspeth went berserk in the Ironclad Dance Hall, in April of '92, and tried to shoot Bartender McMicken. Hudspeth missed McMicken, but the bullet killed Reuben Miller, the piano player. At the Ironclad one month later Bob Womack stopped to see the first touring troupe to visit Cripple. The stars included a team of German comedians, Oscar and Sallie Kerns, and a handsome gymnast and clogger of eighteen years called Fred Stone.[1]

Cripple had no professional badmen in the early days. The police chief, Hi Wilson, was a tough hombre who had served many years as a fast-shooting cop in Denver. When Bob Ford, the killer of Jesse James, and Soapy Smith, the

Denver bunco artist, arrived from Creede to take charge of the underworld, Wilson met them at the city limits and sent them flying down the mountains again. Occasionally, some of the tenderfeet would deck themselves out with six-shooters and would swagger down the street trying to look like the Dalton Gang. Then Hi Wilson or Deputy Sheriff Pete Eales would walk up and remove the weapons. "Listen, Bub," Pete Eales would say, "no gun-totin' here. I'll just take that for the school fund." After confiscating the gun, Pete would sell it to a gun-hawker who would sell it to another tenderfoot. Before '92 ended, the school fund from Pete's gun sales was large enough to start the school system.

Almost every afternoon Bob Womack parked himself on the horse trough in front of Joe Wolfe's Continental Hotel to await the arrival of the Florissant stage. Alonzo Welty's rickety wagons, hauled by cow ponies, were replaced by tourist carts from John Hundley's Antlers Livery in the Springs. It was an eighteen-mile run from the Florissant railway station to the gold camp with a stop midway at the Welty ranch house on Four-Mile. The Midland Railway saw to it that the stage was always full. The Midland people were advertising Cripple Creek as far away as Chicago and San Francisco. One ad in '92 ran:

> CRIPPLE CREEK is not only a HEALTH but a WEALTH resort.
> Location near Pike's Peak.
> GOLD! Bright yellow gold is found at grass roots in the rock formation.
> Reliable experts claim this is today the richest camp in Colorado.
> Assays average over $100 per ton, and have run as high as FIVE THOUSAND DOLLARS.
> 100 people a day are now rushing into this DISTRICT.

A chance of a life-time is worth looking after.

The ONLY WAY to reach CRIPPLE CREEK is via Florissant and the COLORADO MIDLAND RAILWAY.

Inquire of local agents for particulars, or *Chas. S. Lee, genl. passenger agent, Denver, Colo.*

John Hundley's stage horses were big, strong animals, but John did not believe in punishing them. They were given all the time in the world to pull up the long hill above Cripple. At the top, with the town spread below, the horses paused to get their breath and the driver would warn the passengers to hold tight. This was the moment which Bob and fifty other people hung around at the Continental to see. The six horses would plunge downgrade at a wild gallop, past the cemetery, the stage careening and the passengers hanging onto the roof for dear life. At the city limits, dogs, chickens and burros would scatter. And then the stage's squealing brake shoes would squeal louder as the big horses slid to a stop in front of the hotel.

Bob was fascinated by the variety of people descending from that stage. Charlie Tutt, the Springs real estater, arrived in November of '91, and Bob helped him locate the C.O.D. Mine in Poverty Gulch. A little later came Irving Howbert in his wing collar, convinced at last that Major Demary was wrong about Cripple. Count Pourtales brought William Lidderdale, ex-governor of the Bank of England, and the French milling expert, G. de la Bouglise. Some of the stage passengers were young fellows of high social standing and fancy education. Spencer Penrose, Harvard '86, arrived in December of '92, to team up with Charlie Tutt. Harry Leonard, a Columbia grad, reached the camp a month later. Frequent visitors were the Massachusetts blue-blood, Henry M. Blackmer, and Verner Z. Reed, novelist and promoter.

Charlie MacNeill, son of a Denver doctor, arrived on the stage to stay in '93, and so did Albert E. Carlton and his brother, Leslie. Each of the Carlton boys was backed by a $10,000 grubstake given to him by his well-to-do father. Another father, Warren Woods of Denver, sent up his two sons, Frank and Harry, under a similar financial arrangement.

Cripple Creek's first hotel was Wesley Gourley's place opened in the summer of '91.[2] Soon after, Jim Cassady built the Anheuser-Busch, famed for the luxury of its appointments (it had eight separate bedrooms instead of just one room divided by canvas into cubicles as was the case with Gourley's establishment). But the Anheuser-Busch, splendid as it was, was overshadowed by Joe Wolfe's Continental, a two-story board structure with elegant false front which opened in January of '92.

The Continental had accommodations for two hundred, counting those sleeping in the halls, on the stairs, in the closets and on the dining room tables. During most of '92 silverware was never washed between customers. "Ain't enough to go 'round," the tired waitresses would say. Bob Womack thought the Continental had real class. One of its features was a gilt-framed replica of Falero's "The Twin Stars," the original painting of which had been given to the Metropolitan Museum of Art by the heiress, Catherine Lorillard Wolfe — "My Cousin Katey," Joe Wolfe would tell Bob, glancing down his long nose.

In May of '92, some of the Hayden Placer group opened the Hotel Clarendon on Carr Avenue. Furniture for the Clarendon cost $16,000, and flowers for the opening cost $300. The Clarendon became at once the social and business center. Joe Wolfe and his Continental should have taken a beating as a result, but Joe was never behind any eight ball

1876. This cabin on the future site of Cripple Creek town cost the Womack family $500 and two pigs. The springhouse at left was built under damaging circumstances which caused Levi Welty to remark, "This sure is some cripple creek!"

1891. At forty-four, Ed De LaVergne felt that he was just a mining bum, frittering away his life in search of a bonanza that would never come. Ten years later he would be a State Senator and one of Cripple's best-known sons.

1891. Count James Pourtales, a Bismarck imperialist, advocate of selective breeding, lord of nine Silesian villages and great judge of wine and women, was the first to bring big money to Cripple.

1892. Cripple was a plush place in which to be a pioneer. Tent restaurants like these even served oysters. The wood structure at left was the Hotel Clarendon on Carr Avenue, run by the shell-game artist, Joseph H. Wolfe.

1892. Placer mining never amounted to much at Cripple even though for a while men found some placer gold above Cripple Creek town. The sluice boxes and long toms were of the same types used by the Forty-Niners.

for long. Soon he leased the Continental and signed on as manager of the Clarendon.

Nobody knew much about Joe Wolfe's past excepting that he had been chased out of several mining camps before being chased out of Ouray due to his penchant for get-rich-quick schemes which multiplied in his mind like fleas on a goat. After Ouray, Joe settled in Manitou near the Springs, as hotel manager and tourist-gypper. He was a small, wiry, black-eyed man, merry as a terrier and fond of coal-black suits and purple brocade vests which sagged under the weight of his heavy gold watch chain. His hat was a two-foot-wide sombrero, giving him the appearance of an Indian looking out of a tepee.

Wolfe was a pal of the slickest sharks of the promoting fraternity. One of them, Clint Roudebush, had learned his trade in Wall Street and at Leadville. Clint decided that he could clean up among these Cripple Creek tenderfeet. After a few successes, he tried to jump a rich claim, the Deer Horn, belonging to Matt Sterrett, the Florissant carpenter. Everyone liked Sterrett. W. S. Stratton, Jimmie Burns and Bob Womack called a mass meeting and the first thing Clint knew his effigy was hanging from the flagpole in the center of Bennett Avenue. Then Clint found himself being dumped on the out-going stage.

Joe Wolfe pretended that he had had no connection with Roudebush but he had been throwing large money around the gambling tables and he certainly wasn't earning it as manager of the Clarendon. After Roudebush left, E. C. Gard, owner of the gold camp's first newspaper, the *Cripple Creek Crusher,* went after Joe Wolfe and the Clarendon. "This curious hostelry," Gard wrote in the *Crusher,* "is run by a red-faced, cock-eyed boob who ought to be back in the

Missouri flats pulling cockle-burrs out of a cornfield." Gard's attack forced Joe's removal as manager of the Clarendon. Some months later his gambling debts became so heavy that he had to leave town for a while. He headed for Oklahoma to attend the September '93 opening of the Cherokee Strip.

During these happy days Bob Womack spent his time with old Springs friends and with prospectors like Lafe Fyffe and Joe Whalen and Horace Barry — men who located dozens of Cripple's best claims and let them go for a drink or a poker ante. Horace Barry founded the village which bore his name in Squaw Gulch and he boasted that it was the cultural center of the mining district. Among its residents were such splendid intellects as Judge M. B. Gerry, whose immortal preamble in 1883 to the sentencing of Alfred Packer for cannibalism was said to have been:

"They was seven Democrats in Hinsdale County and you ate five of them. Stand up, you man-eatin' son-of-a-bitch and take yo' sentence."

The cultural nucleus of Barry Village was the Squaw Gulch Amusement Club, "with a membership of 400, of which 399 are from the high-toned aristocratic circles of Squaw Gulch." The president of the club was George Carr, chosen because he could call square dances with a voice like the six bulls of Bashan. The nonresident member and sergeant-at-arms was Robert Miller Womack. It was up to Bob to maintain the club's high tone by excluding prostitutes. Since Bob thought all women were wonderful it never did any good to inform him that a chippy was present. He was apt to take a poke at the plaintiff for defaming womanhood.

Since about one third of the gold camp was composed of Irish Catholics, it had a strongly religious element from the start. The first regular church, however, was the Congregational. It was conducted by the stern Bostonian, Rev. Horace Sanderson, up on Carr Avenue in a large tent labeled "WHO-SOEVER WILL." This tent served also for the civic and social affairs of the respectable residents of Hayden Placer. It inspired one of the worst of many terrible puns created by Burt Pottinger of the *Cripple Creek Crusher.* "Frozen lumber," Burt wrote, "was used to make the seats in WHOSOEVER WILL. Soon the seats were all 'kiln' dried, and didn't kiln any miners, either."

Bob Womack was not a church-going man, but he did attend Cripple Creek's first Sunday school. It was held in the rear of the Buckhorn saloon operated by the celebrated faro dealer, Mother Duffy, a large, rosy, muscular woman with the poetic vocabulary of a mule-skinner. Mother Duffy had a batch of girls above the Buckhorn and on the Sunday morning of this first Sunday school they brought out their long traveling dressses and sat in a prim row along the top of the bar. Mother Duffy covered the bar and gambling layouts with canvas on which cavorting cherubs had been painted by the Springs artist, Walter Paris. Count Pourtales paid for the painting of these cherubs and instructed Paris to make them look as much as possible like Emma Carr.

Bishop Matz of Denver had sent down young Father Volpe to organize the Catholic Church, and Volpe delivered the Sunday school prayer. In the middle of it Bob Womack and the rest of the congregation heard a commotion at the saloon's street door. A drunken freighter stood there demanding breakfast from Mother Duffy.

Quietly and politely Mother Duffy asked the freighter to wait, but he was not the waiting kind. "What the hell do I care for this Sunday school business?" he said. "I want a drink and some grub and I want 'em quick!"

Mother Duffy rose, turned purple and flexed her biceps. Then she exploded. "I'll show you, you low-down drunken bum, not to bust up the first Sunday school ever held in this camp! Now get out of here, damn your soul!" And she grabbed him by the collar, pushed him through the door and heaved him all the way across the boardwalk and into the line of saddle horses hitched to posts in front of the Buckhorn.

Happy, happy days! Each month Bob Womack watched Cripple's gold production increase — from $50,000 to $100,000, and then to $200,000 and more a month during 1893. The district's population climbed from 2000 in February of '92 to 12,500 on January 1, 1894. Around the clock the grassy hills swarmed with men and teams, echoed with yells of "Fire!" followed by blasts of powder. In the evening when the sun sank behind Mount Pisgah, Cripple's electric arc lights came on. To the east and southeast were innumerable spots of soft color on the hills — the glow of kerosene lamps in a thousand shacks.

It was all wonderful fun. Bob loved the pretty Chinese lanterns swinging in the breeze on Bennett Avenue during Fourth of July. He would never forget Tim Hussey shinnying up the Bennett Avenue flagpole on St. Patrick's Day. He could chuckle any time thinking of abstemious Charlie Howbert (Irving's brother) going into Johnnie Nolon's on business, to be greeted by Johnnie's command, "Bartender! A lemon squash for Mr. Howbert!" Bob did not care much for water, but if he had to drink it he liked its taste coming from the big iron tanks on wagons, sold at five cents a bucket, thirty-five cents a barrel.

And Bob would remember Terence Coyle proudly posting his claim with the notice, "including all dips, spurs and

angels of minneral barren rock." And Wizard "Professor"
L. J. Campbell, a distinguished magician who trod the hills
with a triangle held in one hand. From the triangle hung
three magnetized pieces of metal, signifying, in turn, gold,
silver, and copper. If one of them swung in a circle, that metal
was sure to exist underground. Wizard Campbell had stiff
competition from Madame Vida De Vere of the Cabinet
Saloon. Vida could locate mines in her crystal ball.

The kind of life Bob was leading could not last. As he
approached fifty his drinking began to wear him down. He
lost weight. Just before Christmas of '93, he caught a bad
cold which could develop into pneumonia. Milda James, a
Negro madam who ran a place near Bob's shack in Poverty
Gulch, put her girls to nursing him in shifts. Milda's medica-
tion was kerosene taken by the tablespoon every two hours.
The kerosene cured Bob but he felt rocky as the holiday
season started. He realized that he was approaching the end
of something. Cripple's pioneering days were almost over, and
Bob's celebrity as the pioneer of pioneers was waning too.
The newcomers who poured in from the closed silver mines
of Idaho and Nevada and Montana had never heard of Bob,
and didn't want to hear. Tenderfeet who used to treat him
with reverence ignored him now.

The day before Christmas Bob sold his Womack Placer
and changed most of his sale money into five hundred one-
dollar bills at Johnnie Nolon's. Early Christmas morning, he
had four or five drinks and posted himself on the busy corner
of Third and Bennett. To every passing child Bob gave a
dollar bill. Soon the line of children extended down Bennett
almost to the Palace Hotel. By degrees the children got
taller, and Bob saw that grown men were accepting his bills
and were rejoining the line for more. Bob threw his fist at the

very next face. Someone struck back and Bob fell to the sidewalk. Johnnie Nolon picked him up and Deputy Sheriff Pete Eales carted him home. Pete wired Marshal Dana in the Springs and Dana sent a message to Miss Lida at Sunview.

Miss Lida reached Bob's shack the following afternoon. She had not seen Bob in a year and his thinness distressed her. To make her feel worse Bob wept copiously and said he ought to jump down the nearest mine shaft. Miss Lida prepared a huge bowl of soup and made Bob drink it all. She asserted, gently, that Bob's work at the gold camp was done, but that he would never be forgotten as the discoverer of Cripple Creek. She added that she was selling the last portions of Sunview Ranch and planned to start a boardinghouse in the Springs on Cascade Avenue. She badly needed Bob to be her partner in this enterprise.

Between the soup and Miss Lida's placid talk, Bob began to feel better. Then he felt much better. Before bedtime he felt almost normal — the same amiable, grinning Bob who had enjoyed himself before gold came into his life and who would enjoy himself again now that he was leaving gold behind. Next morning Bob turned his shack over to Melvin Sowle to rent. As he and Miss Lida rode the stage out of Cripple Bob didn't look back once.

They arrived in the Springs as newboys were howling the *Gazette's* headline for the day: CRIPPLE CREEK'S FIRST MILLIONAIRE! Bob thought it must be Ed De LaVergne or Fred Frisbee or Count Pourtales or the druggist, A. D. Jones. But the *Gazette* informed him it was none of these. "Winfield Scott Stratton," the story ran, "can write a check in six figures. His Independence Mine is valued in the millions."

It must have been a worrisome moment for Miss Lida

when Bob read her the story of Stratton's success. Long afterward she recalled that Bob's face was sad as he laid down the paper. And then he smiled — a big, wide smile. "Poor Old Man Stratton!" he said. "All that money to worry about . . . I don't envy him one bit!"

PART TWO

Stratton & Company

CHAPTER XII

First He Was a Carpenter

OLD MAN STRATTON was a heavy-handed, heavy-footed, overly serious sort of fellow whom one could not imagine as ever having been young. His father had named him Winfield Scott because that was what fathers named their boys in 1848 when Old Fuss and Feathers was riding the crest of his Mexican War wave. The place of Stratton's birth was Jeffersonville, Indiana, a few miles over the river from the Kentucky "plantation" where Bob Womack was born.

Stratton's father, Myron, was an Ohio River boatbuilder. The two didn't get along well. Myron often told his son how to behave and it made the boy so angry that he got out his rifle one day and fired at him. But he missed. Winfield Scott's mother was a smothering female who spent all her time having babies. She had twelve all told, eight of them girls. Of the four boys only Winfield Scott survived. By the time he was ten he was so sick of being surrounded by women that he decided never to have anything more to do with them.

Those were great days. If you didn't like home you packed up and went West. At twenty, Stratton visited a married sister in Eddyville, Iowa, where a phrenologist examined his head and told him he ought to be an undertaker or a lawyer. He moved on to Sioux City and Council Bluffs and Omaha and Lincoln and, in 1872, to Colorado Springs. Stratton's father had taught him carpentry and so he set up a carpentry shop on Pikes Peak Avenue. The Springs was growing very rapidly. Stratton had more work than he could handle. He designed the gingerbread for the Episcopal Church, and built the house which would be famous as the residence of Helen Hunt, author of *Ramona*.

He was a fine carpenter. He had a good grasp of mathematics and he could make estimates quickly. The estimates always turned out to be close to actual costs. But he was nervous, high-tempered, impulsive and neurotic. He could not enjoy life. He did not like people very much. By May of '74 three of his business partnerships had ended in fights, and he was sick to death of carpentry. So he sank $2800 of his profits into a mining claim called the Yretaba Silver Lode and set out for the San Juan Mountains in southwestern Colorado to look it over.

He spent two months on this Yretaba claim, learning the facts of mining life. The facts in this case were easy to learn. He had thrown away $2800. And yet he was not unhappy about it. Hunting for mines suited his temperament. Here was the sort of career he wanted. It gave him excitement without the headaches which line the path of ordinary ambition. He enjoyed the aloofness of mountain scenery, the tinkling sound water made up there, the simple way everything was put together. He liked traveling around with a burro for a companion. Burros did not talk back, quibble, complain, belittle, overcharge, boast or make unreasonable demands. They just did what they were told.

For the next seventeen years hunting for a mine would be Stratton's absorbing passion. During the winters he worked at carpentry in Colorado Springs to finance his summer prospecting. Only once did he break his routine. In June of '76 he married a little seventeen-year-old named Zeurah Stewart after courting her four months. It is reported that they had been married only a few days when Zeurah told him she thought she was pregnant. Right away Stratton remembered that he still hated women. He threw a tantrum. He told Zeurah that he had had nothing to do with her pregnancy. He renounced their marriage, and Zeurah left the Springs for her old home in Illinois. Her baby, a son, was born near Danville, Illinois, six months later. Stratton did not see Zeurah again. In '79 he divorced her. He did not see Zeurah's son until he was a young man.

Stratton got around in those years. He plodded across South Park and prospected the lovely Chalk Creek area at the southeast shoulder of Mount Princeton. He combed the gulches near Granite north of Mount Princeton. He covered Baker's Park in the San Juans and hurried to Leadville during the early days of the world's greatest silver camp. He found nothing at Leadville though H. A. W. Tabor, Leadville's silver king, paid him well to place on top of the Bank of Leadville a huge metal disc carved to represent a silver dollar.

At the time of the "Mount Pisgah" hoax, Stratton was in the Blue River country northeast of Leadville — at Kokomo and Robinson. Then he swung south, to Rosita in the Wet Mountain Valley, below Canon City. Next he prospected the Elk Mountains and had a try at Red Cliff and Aspen.

In the Seventies and Eighties thousands of prospectors like Stratton examined every inch of the Continental Divide and the other beautiful mountains of Colorado. They shaved rarely, wore ancient felt hats, chewed tobacco, drank quantities of whiskey and lived mainly on beans and hope. They were an uneducated, hermitlike breed guided more by super-

stition than by science. That is why everything worth finding was found by them, instead of by the mining engineers
who held them in such scorn. Gold is where you find it, not
where it ought to be.

But Stratton wasn't an ordinary prospector. He was a man
of intelligence even though he had had little formal school-
ing. He was acquisitive, canny, curious and ambitious. To
improve his knowledge of the nature of ores he worked for
a summer in the Nashold Reduction Mill at Breckenridge.
And you may remember that he took a course in blowpipe
analysis from Professor Lamb at Colorado College. He
studied metallurgy at the Colorado School of Mines at
Golden. Each day at Golden on his way to class he crossed a
spot to be occupied many years later by a three-story granite
and red sandstone building named Stratton Hall.

The time usually comes when an absorbing passion begins
to pall, particularly if it leads nowhere. In 1890 Stratton estimated that he had spent $20,000 of his own hard-earned
money on futile prospecting since 1874. He had not found
a single paying mine. The knowledge and experience which
he had gained seemed of no earthly use to him. He had become so disgusted with the search for gold and silver that he
turned to hunting humdrum minerals — potash for paint,
cryolite for making aluminum, and such.

And it was this disgust for gold and silver that remained
uppermost in Stratton's mind after his arrival at Cripple
Creek in May of '91. He was forty-two years old, a thin, pale
fellow with silky white hair who looked as though he never
got enough to eat. He had a way of holding his head a little
to one side as though he were trying to make up his mind.
Probably he was trying to make up his mind, and the evidence
suggests that he never did.

Stratton had a lot of sympathy for Bob Womack, but he did not believe in Bob's Poverty Gulch and the Gold Hill area south of it. Bull Hill, a mile east of Gold Hill, didn't look a bit better to him in spite of the hullabaloo over the Buena Vista and the Pharmacist. In choosing Battle Mountain, a mile south of Bull Hill, for his operations, Stratton thought merely that he was picking ground somewhat less unpromising, and freer of tenderfeet, than the remaining 10,000 acres of the Cripple Creek district. Stratton was certain that the south base of Battle was at the edge of the ancient Cripple Creek volcano.

Battle Mountain was an irregularly shaped hill of about five hundred acres. It was 10,300 feet above sea level, some five hundred feet lower than the top of Bull Hill. Wilson Creek skirted Battle to the south and Squaw Mountain adjoined it on the southwest. Over its ridge to the northwest was Ed De LaVergne's Raven Hill. A mile northwest of Raven Hill was Gold Hill, at the bottom of which was Cripple Creek town. These low hills, rising five hundred feet or so above their bases, were connected by broad saddles. They drained on the west into Cripple Creek by way of four main gulches, Poverty, Squaw, Arequa, and Eclipse.

Of course it tickled Stratton to collect from William J. Willcox, in February of '92, $10,000 as part payment for his Washington claim. But it didn't lessen his pessimism about Cripple Creek in general, Battle Mountain in particular. He knew that Willcox planned a wildcat stock promotion to exploit the flurry of confidence created by Count Pourtales. Willcox wouldn't find much ore in the Washington. He would never pay off the remaining $70,000 to take up his option. And, sure enough, in August of '92 Willcox gave the Washington back to Stratton.

Meanwhile, Stratton was aware that curious things were happening on Battle Mountain. He couldn't get excited about them and yet he couldn't ignore them. Not four hundred feet west of his Independence, J. R. McKinnie was pulling good ore from a claim called the Black Diamond. Just below the Black Diamond that hard-drinking roustabout, Sam Strong, was finding pay dirt in his Strong Mine. Sam was broke in the spring of '92. Six months later he had sold enough ore to buy a winter home in Houston, Texas.

And what, Stratton wondered, was the exact situation on Battle Mountain, seven hundred feet above his Independence? What were those temperamental Irishmen, Jimmie Burns and Jimmie Doyle, going to find in their hole up there? In recent months Stratton had come to regard Jimmie Burns with admiration, even with affection. During the pioneering summer of '91, Stratton had had Burns at his heels for days on end, the most irritating sort of trailing tenderfoot. But Burns had something. He had eagerness, a sure grasp of what he wanted, a zest for life. He had what Stratton wanted most himself to have, and didn't have because he was too disillusioned, too suspicious, too tired.

Jimmie Burns gave Stratton vicarious pleasure. Stratton would always remember the time he asked Jimmie what he was going to do with his life. "Well," Jimmie said, in his high, raspy voice, "I'm going to make a million and get a beautiful wife and send my brats East to school and build a house as big as General Palmer's. And then I'm going to tell those god-damn millionaires in Colorado Springs to go to hell!"

The Burns-Doyle claim above the Independence was hardly a hot prospect for a would-be millionaire. And yet Stratton got a kick out of the way the Irishmen buzzed around it. He had to smile at the crazy events that brought them to it. Jimmie Burns, you remember, had come to Cripple Creek alone, because his protégé, Jimmie Doyle, had to wind up his summer job in the Springs as Superintendent of Irrigation. Burns, strictly a city man, did not take to gold-camp life, and it irked him that he did not strike a bonanza right away. All he could find were two ratty locations called the St. Patrick and the Professor Grubbs.

Burns had expected to get financial aid from Jimmie Doyle. But when Doyle reached Cripple in the fall of '91 he had to tell Burns that he had lost nearly all his summer savings in a crap game at the fire station. A day or so later, Jimmie Burns began to wonder how he could survive living with Doyle. At twenty-three, Doyle was an irresponsible puppy who never hung up his clothes, never washed the dishes, left lighted cigars in inflammable places, and kept Burns awake at night with his loud snoring. Burns, of course, was old enough to be Doyle's father, and he felt more and more like a bewildered parent as he observed Doyle's scatter-brained prospecting methods. Jimmie Burns' ignorance of gold mining was almost as profound as Doyle's, but Burns at least tried to learn. Doyle seemed to believe that gold was found near the claims of those prospectors who were most generous with their whiskey.

Burns had been impressed by Stratton's monotone comments about gold occurrence on the south slope of Battle Mountain. But the south slope seemed to be fully staked. Burns and Doyle couldn't find a location. Now it happened that an important 160-acre stretch of Battle's south slope was the Mount Rosa Placer which J. R. McKinnie had staked in September of '91.[1] On January 4, 1892, M. S. Raynolds platted the Victor C. Adams homestead into a town called

Lawrence. McKinnie, watching this platting from the slope above, decided that the lower part of his Mount Rosa Placer was better suited for a townsite than Lawrence, especially if he shifted the Mount Rosa Placer southward a hundred feet or so until its south limit coincided with the north limit of Lawrence townsite. Accordingly, McKinnie relocated the Mount Rosa Placer. His action led two or three other men who held lode claims just north of his placer to relocate *their* claims some dozens of feet southward down Battle's slopes. Their idea was to get closer to Stratton's claims, as Stratton was the fellow on whom the Battle Mountain gang pinned their faith.

Jimmie Doyle and Jimmie Burns had no notion what this general shifting of stakes was about. But, on January 22, 1892, while Doyle was plodding up Battle northwest of the Independence, he realized that he stood on a fragment of land which had been vacated by one of the stake-shifters. Doyle staked it in a hurry, named it the Portland after his and Jimmie Burns' home town in Maine, and placed his name and Jimmie Burns' name on the location notice. Later surveys showed that this fragment consisted of 69/1000 of an acre, about the size of a fifty-by-sixty-foot house lot.

Shortly afterward, Burns and Doyle brought Stratton up the hill and proudly showed him their Portland claim. Stratton was in one of his black moods. He told Doyle, heartlessly, that he had a nerve making him climb that far to look at such a bust. Doyle, sore as a boil, invited Stratton off the claim.

Then the two small Irishmen started to dig. In some weeks they got their hole down thirty feet. But their blasting seemed to uncover nothing. Their windlass kept breaking down. They bickered constantly as to whose turn it was to descend the hole and load the bucket. They became very unhappy. Doyle was sorry now that he had kicked Stratton off the Portland. Stratton's advice was badly needed.

One afternoon, as Burns was emerging from the Portland shaft, he saw John Harnan strolling across the tiny claim. Harnan, also Irish, had been sorting ore at Stratton's Independence for some weeks. He was a Pennsylvanian, thirty-one years old, and a brother of the Harnan who had located the great Hilltop bonanza near Fairplay. John had been handling ore since his teens, and he had a good working knowledge of geology. Burns called Harnan over to the shaft, and Doyle joined them. Burns told Harnan that they couldn't find a vein and that they weren't even sure what a vein looked like. Harnan glanced once at the Portland dump and right on top he spotted a chunk of sylvanite — telluride of gold! He asked Burns and Doyle what they would give him if he found a vein. They offered him a third interest in the Portland.

Harnan accepted. He descended the shaft, studying the sides carefully. At the bottom he called up to Burns and Doyle to help him shift the ladder to the opposite side. Then he examined the side of the hole where the ladder had been. Halfway down he found the sylvanite vein.

Within a week, Burns, Doyle and Harnan had their drift running along the Portland vein, and began sacking ore. Assays were excellent. Harnan saw that their position was precarious, due to the tiny size of the Portland claim. When the owners of the surrounding claims learned of the Portland's rich vein they would fill the courts with lawsuits, contending that the Portland vein originated on their earlier claims.

Burns suggested that they remove their sacked ore by night and cart it secretly to Pueblo for refining. In this way they might be able to accumulate money with which to defend themselves when the secret of their bonanza was out. The ore sacks were heavy and Burns invented a complicated kind of harness to ease the carrying. These harnesses were sewn together in Colorado Springs by Burns' seamstress sisters, Kate and Jane. One night Burns came down the hill with an ore sack and stumbled right near Stratton's shack. He fell and couldn't work free from his sisters' harness. He began to cuss. Stratton came from his shack to learn what was the matter. Stratton cut Burns loose and the two went in Stratton's shack to have a nip or two.

Before the evening had ended, Burns had described to Stratton everything that had happened at the Portland claim since the day when Doyle had ordered Stratton off the ground. Burns disclosed that the three of them, Burns, Doyle and Harnan, had amassed $70,000 to date, from ore sales at Pueblo. He added that the ore they had removed wasn't a tenth of the ore in sight. But they couldn't possibly keep the secret much longer. Burns was afraid that, under the circumstances, $70,000 might not be enough money to win lawsuits. What ought they to do now?

Stratton considered. Then he replied that he, too, had a secret. And he had a proposition to make to Burns. Quite a proposition.

CHAPTER XIII

The Luck of the Irish

Sᴛʀᴀᴛᴛᴏɴ's sᴛᴀᴛᴇ ᴏғ ᴍɪɴᴅ in mid-August of '93 when Burns told him the truth about the Portland was far different from what it had been three months earlier. In May, Stratton despaired of finding pay dirt in the Washington and Independence. Almost two years had passed since he had staked them. His boots were worn thin from hiking over the ridge to Squaw Gulch where N. B. Guyot had his assay furnace. Nine times out of ten, Guyot would tell him his samples contained no gold. "Of course," Guyot had said in mid-May, "when you want to sell I'll give you a seller's assay that'll knock 'em dead." Every good assayer could produce a seller's or a buyer's assay to fit the case.

Next day, Stratton hit a streak of telluride in the Washington. Guyot said it assayed $150 a ton, buyer's assay. But, Guyot added, it was not oxidized telluride. It wouldn't separate easily. Stratton sent it to Tomlinson's stamp mill at Beaver Park. Tomlinson pounded it, ran it over the amalgamation table and recovered only $25 worth of gold per ton. The rest remained in combination with the telluride and was washed on to the dump. Stratton tried the new French stamp mill, the Rosebud, at the foot of Squaw Gulch. It didn't do any better. Mining and hauling costs absorbed his gross profit and he ended up broke.

And so he said to hell with Cripple. He told Guyot to rig up a seller's assay and to spread the word that his claims were available. He laid off his small development crew, closed his shack and went down to the Springs. He decided to resume carpentry. For some weeks he visited with Joe Dozier and other contractor friends. Dozier, the biggest builder in town, didn't have a single job in progress or in prospect. He told Stratton that the Springs had never known a slump like this. Poor people along Shook's Run were eating prairie dogs and jack rabbits. Silver prices had collapsed. That put a great strain on Springs banks and ended the incomes of some of the town's richest men. Dozier urged Stratton to return to Cripple and to try once more to find gold.

Stratton went back to his shack above Wilson Creek. It was late in June now. A fellow named L. M. Pearlman was waiting for him. Pearlman represented a San Francisco mining syndicate. He wanted to buy the Washington claim because it was near the rich Strong Mine. Pearlman kept asserting that the Washington was an unpromising property. Stratton got peeved and decided not to sell the Washington. He told Pearlman that he could have the Independence instead, on a thirty-day option. Terms? Merely $5000 down; $150,000 owing.

Stratton knew that this asking price of $155,000 for an unproved mine was ridiculous. It was almost twice as high as the highest price to date. But he didn't like Pearlman. So he flipped out the price and prepared to bid Pearlman farewell. Pearlman didn't bat an eye. He sat down at Stratton's pine utility table and wrote a check for $5000, closing the thirty-day option deal.

After Pearlman left, Stratton sat for a bit recovering. In 1893 $155,000 was a fortune. Then Stratton pulled himself together. Pearlman's crew would take over the Independence in the morning. Stratton would have to get his tools and lamps out of there.

The Independence shaft was eighty-five feet deep. It had four crosscuts at the fifty-foot level. Stratton removed his equipment from three of them. He had abandoned the fourth crosscut a year ago and it occurred to him to check that one, too. It was choked with debris, but he wormed his way in. He found a rusty drill and he poked with it at a loose rock in the wall. The rock fell and behind it was the discoloration which marks the outer edge of a thick vein. Stratton kept poking. In a few hours he had established roughly the scope and trend of the vein. Then he backed out of the musty crosscut. He replaced the debris as it had been when he entered.

He took his bag of samples from the new vein to Guyot. The results were what he had expected. The vein assayed $380 a ton pretty regularly along the crosscut for twenty-seven feet. It could not be less than nine feet wide. The vein must extend a hundred feet downward at the very least. That meant $3,000,000 worth of ore in sight!

The month of July, '93, was the most nerve-wracking of Stratton's life. Pearlman's option would expire on July 28. His crew was working steadily in the Independence. Stratton had continuous dreams in which the crew entered the abandoned crosscut and discovered the mine's value. Stratton could betray no interest in the Independence and he had to keep away from Pearlman. On the night before the option would expire, he took Pearlman to dinner. The best hotel in Cripple Creek was the Palace, at the northwest corner of Bennett Avenue and Second Street. Joe Wolfe had built it and had named it the Joseph H. Wolfe. After Joe skipped town the new owners changed the name to the Palace. It became the meeting place of everybody who was anybody in the gold camp.

The Palace lobby had a huge fireplace. Pine logs always burned there on summer evenings. When Pearlman and Stratton finished dinner they took easy chairs near the fireplace and talked about how Cripple wasn't developing into anything much. Pearlman began discussing Stratton's Independence and the trouble he was having with it. His crew had found hardly enough ore to cover the $5000 down payment to Stratton. The men had explored thoroughly the ground along three of Stratton's crosscuts. Pearlman had intended to put them to work next morning cleaning out the abandoned fourth crosscut. But he hated to spend a day's wages on it.

Then he said, "Look here, Stratton, I want to leave town early in the morning. How about taking back my option tonight?"

Stratton managed to murmur that he wouldn't object. When Pearlman took the option from his pocket and thrust it toward him, Stratton trembled so that he was afraid to reach for it. "Just toss it in the fire, will you?" Stratton said.

The two men watched the option burn in the big fireplace. The Independence belonged to Stratton again! Two days later he had a crew of eight working in that abandoned crosscut. In two weeks he doubled his crew. He designed his surface buildings and signed a contract for their erection. He completed freighting arrangements to ship his ore to the Pueblo smelter. He estimated that he could be in full production by September — thirty tons a day. He decided to limit his net to $2000 a day. If smelter returns exceeded this average income, he would curtail production. Gold in

1893. The Fourth of July was a gloomy day in most American towns during the Panic of '93. But not in Cripple Creek. Bennett Avenue was just about the busiest and most prosperous street in the whole United States.

1893. You never knew who might step from the Hundley stage which arrived daily from Florissant or Divide. An afternoon load might include a Baptist minister, Lord Lidderdale of the Bank of England, Fred Stone the variety artist, young Bernard Baruch, and three frail sisters up from Denver.

1893. The world's finest swindlers congregated nightly in the Palace Hotel lobby to see who could squeeze the most money out of the tenderfeet.

1893. Winfield Scott Stratton began to hit pay dirt in his Independence Mine in July. Six months later he became Cripple's first millionaire — which figures out to a daily wage of $5500. Before he went to Cripple, Stratton earned three dollars on good days as a carpenter.

the ground, he believed, was worth more than gold in circulation.

Stratton could fret like a peevish old woman over small affairs. He showed now that big affairs never fazed him. The longer he thought about his bonanza the cooler he became. His long experience told him that he had on his hands maybe the richest mining property on earth. The princes of India, the kings of Europe, the railroad barons of America — he might become wealthier and more powerful than any of them. He, Winfield Scott Stratton, a weary, defeated carpenter who had spent most of his forty-four years working for three dollars a day! And still he refused to be impressed. His first extravagance as a potential multimillionaire was to write Bert Robbins in the Springs to send him two new pairs of boots and a light-gray hat.

He had a colossal job ahead. Yet he made plans as calmly as though he were laying out the design for a kitchen cabinet. He knew exactly what he wanted. The Cripple Creek District must be kept a true gold camp as long as possible. It must be developed to benefit a large number of people instead of being exploited to enrich a few. Promoters and speculators and absentee owners must be controlled.

Some of these slick promoters with their lawyers and engineers were getting to be a nuisance. One of them had swindled Tim Hussey out of the Prince Albert, and poor old Tim had gone bats. Dave Moffat, the Denver banking and railroad tycoon, had consolidated most of Gold Hill under the name Anaconda.[1] Dave's agent, Clint Roudebush, had manipulated Anaconda stock so violently that Irving Howbert had to intervene to save the mine. Moffat had bought the rich Victor Mine on Bull Hill. He had opened the Bi-metallic Bank in Cripple Creek and he was building a narrow-gauge railroad into the district from the south. Plainly mighty Dave planned to gobble up the place in a few years.

Stratton would try to keep Moffat in check. He would watch James J. Hagerman of the Isabella, too, though he knew the ailing Hagerman did not have Moffat's drive. Of course Stratton could not hold the line alone, even with an income of $2000 a day. He would need help from Ed De LaVergne on Raven Hill, and from the Bernard boys nearby. Sam and George Bernard were the Springs grocers who owned most of the Elkton.[2] Stratton could count on the support of Frank Castello of the Mary McKinney. And Giddings, Lennox and Colburn, the new owners of the Strong Mine, would ride with Stratton because he owned Battle Mountain ground east of them. Sam Strong would string along. Sam was about to buy Sam Altman's Free Coinage on Bull Hill.

But Stratton wanted a firmer grip on Battle Mountain. That is why Jimmie Burns' revelation in mid-August of '93 about the Portland bonanza was such a gift from heaven. The Portland — a Battle Mountain claim so rich that three small Irishmen carrying off a sack of ore each night for seven months had earned $70,000! Here was the missing link in the chain Stratton hoped to forge. That big Portland vein must be a continuation of Stratton's Independence vein. All Battle Mountain ground between and around the Portland and the Independence was certain to be bonanza ground.

So, when Burns finished unburdening himself to Stratton about the Portland, Stratton disclosed to Burns the secret wealth of his Independence. He got out paper and pencil and explained with drawings why the Portland and the Independence were twin keys to the inexhaustible treasure of Battle Mountain. He emphasized that the $70,000 which

Burns, Doyle and Harnan had accumulated would not begin to protect the tiny Portland from lawsuits when the surrounding claim-owners found how rich the Portland was. Even if the Irishmen put the Portland into full production they could not make money fast enough to stave off injunctions.

Then Stratton made his proposition to Burns. "You boys come in with me," he said. "Between the Portland and the Independence, we'll lick every jawbone lawyer in Colorado. And we'll buy Battle Mountain."

Next morning Burns put it up to Doyle and Harnan. Harnan took a look at Stratton's vein and emerged from the Independence, his eyes sparkling. The three Irishmen shook hands with Stratton and the deal was on. No papers, no precise commitments. It was just a mutual assistance pact between friends.

And it worked. Stratton began producing around the clock at the Independence. Burns hired a dozen miners and started hauling ore from the Portland in wagons. The hauling was still done at night to keep the secret as long as possible. And it wasn't until October of '93 that the richness of the Portland was fully known. No lawsuits reached the courts until mid-November. By then Burns had $125,000 in reserve. Stratton had piled up almost as much and he had unlimited credit at Irving Howbert's First National Bank in Colorado Springs.

Twenty-seven people filed suit against Burns, Doyle and Harnan, claiming prior rights to the Portland bonanza vein by virtue of the law of apex. This law of apex stated that a vein belonged to the claim on which it surfaced, even though that vein might run far beyond the boundaries of the claim. The Portland vein did not apex on Portland ground. One of the suers might be able to prove that it apexed on his nearby claim. The twenty-seven suits involved a total of $3,000,000. Stratton had to decide whom to hire to fight the suits. He didn't want any big-shot Springs or Denver lawyers for fear they would double-cross him and grab the property. For years he had watched the brilliant real estate operations of a Springs youngster named Verner Z. Reed. Stratton believed that Reed had the imagination, the gall, the energy and the knowledge of high finance to beat the Portland's enemies. He hired Reed on behalf of the Portland, and Reed moved into the Palace Hotel.

Reed was a Scott Fitzgerald character twenty-five years before the Jazz Age. He had a Fitzgeraldian beauty and Fitzgerald's love of gilded living and his ability to earn money with great ease. Reed had started out as a Chicago *Tribune* reporter and had moved to the Springs in the Eighties to help his father run a livery stable. In no time he was famous locally as a writer of gaudy tourist folders and as a seller of more Springs real estate than had ever been sold before.

He went to work on the Portland mess with such speed that the twenty-seven suers never caught up with him. First off he optioned the Portland to Walter Crosby for $250,000. Crosby was a Springs broker whose chief assets were his gorgeous daughters, Gladys and Nina, who would later become Mrs. Mark Hopkins and the Marquise de Polignac. While the suers tried to figure out whom to sue now, Reed bored from within, buying the lesser claims of lesser enemies. Then he approached bigger enemies and threatened suit on the grounds that his claims held prior rights to their prospect holes.

The suers went on the defensive and began to get scared.

As their suits against Walter Crosby opened in court, Crosby suddenly surrendered his Portland option to the Burns-Doyle-Harnan partnership. Reed dissolved the partnership and formed the Portland Gold Mining Company. Then Reed arranged the declaration of a $90,000 dividend and Portland stock rose in price like a rocket. Almost overnight the Portland Gold Mining Company became one of the richest enterprises in Colorado. In a panic, the enemies called Reed into conference. Before it ended, all claims in the lawsuits were sold to the Portland Company, thereby expanding its holdings from 69/1000 of an acre to 183 acres.

Purchase of the claims cost the Portland Company $1,025,-000, much of the money being borrowed from the bank by Stratton. Reed issued 3,000,000 shares of Portland stock. Stratton took 731,000 shares. Burns, Doyle and Harnan took 600,000 shares each. Most of the remaining 469,000 shares went to J. R. McKinnie and to Frank Peck, a Springs cigar store owner. Peck was courting Jimmie Burns' sister, Mary Anne. Peck and McKinnie owned the Black Diamond claim. They gave it to the Portland Company in exchange for stock. Stratton didn't attend the first stockholders' meeting and he was elected president of the Portland Company. He resigned, stating that Burns, Doyle and Harnan had developed the Portland and it was their job to run it. So Jimmie Burns became president.

During these Portland goings-on, Stratton had a man at work on his own behalf. Jonah Maurice Finn, a Cripple Creek lawyer, soft-shoed around and bought for Stratton eleven claims adjoining his Independence, Washington, and Professor Lamb claims. That gave him altogether 112 acres. Thus, by the spring of 1894, Stratton and the three Irishmen virtually owned Battle Mountain, just as Stratton had predicted in mid-August of '93, when he made his proposition to Jimmie Burns.

Even as semisecret operations, Stratton's Independence and the Portland Mine had a tremendously stimulating effect on the gold camp. As Stratton and Burns hired more and more miners, other owners followed suit — Dave Moffat at the Victor, Hagerman at the Isabella, Irving Howbert at the Anchoria-Leland. The gold camp's population reached and passed 10,000. Lots of people were making money hand over fist.

And yet, in spite of the splendid isolation on the high slope of a great mountain, nobody could ignore the catastrophe that had come to the rest of the world. The international economic crisis had its beginnings in 1890. It was a bewildering thing to Americans, and, little by little, it became the bitterest public issue since the Civil War. Americans everywhere convinced themselves that the depression was caused by United States monetary policy. Americans in the East, who owned most of the gold, told Americans in the West that bimetallism was the trouble. The United States must adopt the gold standard and cease buying silver as required by the Sherman Silver Purchase Act of 1890. Americans in the West, who owed huge sums to Eastern bankers, demanded a much larger proportion of silver in United States currency so that they could pay their debts in money as cheap as money had been when they contracted the debts. The people of Colorado were particularly distressed because the production of silver was their chief means of livelihood.

The East won the argument. President Grover Cleveland took the advice of Wall Street instead of that of Colorado's Senator Henry Teller. Cleveland secured repeal of the Sherman Silver Purchase Act. But, to the surprise of the gold bugs, going on the gold standard did not end the depression. The national crisis became more acute as banks crashed, factories closed, bankruptcies glutted the courts and millions of people began the heart-rending business of trying to stave off starvation. In Colorado — outside of Cripple Creek — the situation was worse than anywhere else. With the government out of the silver market, the price of silver fell from $1.25 to less than sixty cents an ounce. Almost every silver mine in the State ceased production and laid off the miners.

In July of '93 these unemployed men started to trickle into Cripple Creek. They came from Leadville and Aspen, from the San Juans and from the Gunnison country, from Boulder County and from Idaho Springs. By August the trickle had reached the proportions of a flood. In the wake of the miners came their hungry wives and children, the busted saloon-keepers, gamblers, prostitutes, lawyers, storekeepers, labor union leaders. During the year ahead, the population of the Cripple Creek district would rise to 20,000. The saloons in Cripple Creek town alone would increase from thirty to seventy. The slopes of Mount Pisgah west of First Street would become populous new additions. A rival town at the foot of Battle Mountain, Victor, would be born and would grow rapidly. District villages such as Altman, Independence and Elkton would pop out like the hives.

And so Cripple's happy pioneer days had to end, the neighborly, cozy, generous days when everybody knew everybody else and there were plenty of gold mines to go around and plenty of work for all.

To Winfield Scott Stratton the situation was a paradox. He was Cripple's first gold millionaire. He might become soon the most powerful mining figure in the United States. He desired to protect working people from exploitation by the rich. He was heart and soul behind Senator Teller. He wanted free coinage of silver.

And yet here he was harming the cause of silver, the cause of working people, by producing gold. More gold was precisely what Wall Street bankers needed. If gold production increased, deflation would be checked. Bankers could claim credit for it and could keep the gold bugs in power.

Stratton was worried and perplexed as he watched storm clouds gathering over Cripple Creek.

Preface to a Nightmare

LIKE ALL GOOD STORM CLOUDS, the ones over Cripple had a storm center. His name was Davis H. Waite, a sixty-seven-year-old Moses with a flowing white beard and a voice like Rocky Mountain thunder. Waite, a nonentity unable to rise higher heretofore than justice of the peace at Aspen, was Populist candidate for Governor of Colorado in '92.

Populism was more than a third party. It was a widespread protest against the uncurbed power of money — forerunner of Bryanism, Progressivism, Wilsonian Democracy and the New Deal. The Populist plank called for an income tax, eight-hour day, secret ballot and direct election of senators, but these crazy notions meant nothing to the Republicans and Democrats of Colorado. They voted Waite into the governorship because their own parties had let them down. The Populist plank alone favored the free coinage of silver.

And they were at once sorry. Waite was a good and a brave man, but he was not smart. He put some awful lemons in State offices. He horrified conservatives by such flaming remarks as: "And if the money power shall attempt to sustain its usurpations by the strong hand, we shall meet the issue when it is forced upon us, for it is better, infinitely better, that blood should flow to the horses' bridles rather than our national liberties should be destroyed."

This "Bloody Bridles" speech had a mixed reception in El Paso County. Irving Howbert and James J. Hagerman regarded it as the opening gun to overthrow the United States government. Stratton and Jimmie Burns thought it was fair warning to mine owners who had made silver fortunes and then had deserted their employees. The silver miners who had rushed to Cripple applauded it because it showed that Waite would side with the miners if conflict arose between them and the mine owners.

And conflict did arise. Miners at Hagerman's Buena Vista worked eight hours a day for three dollars, but some mines worked their men nine hours for three dollars. In August of '93, Bradford Locke, super at the Buena Vista, posted a notice stating that the work shift there would be nine hours instead of eight. The pay would remain three dollars. Next morning Locke arrived at the Buena Vista and was surrounded by one hundred Bull Hill miners. Locke began an oration on his constitutional rights. Somebody said, "Well, boys, bring on that can of tar." Locke abruptly stopped talking, tore down the offending notice and reinstated the eight-hour three-dollar day.

But the damage was done. The classical cleavage of haves and have-nots came into sharp relief. There were lots of things to cleave over — Governor Waite; Populism; Cripple's Irish Catholics (a third of the gold camp population was composed of these "red necks") versus the predominantly Episcopalian mine owners of Colorado Springs. Some mine owners bellowed that Cripple Creek miners should be happy to accept the depressed wage scales prevailing in the country at large. The miners wouldn't swallow that one. They had as much right as the mine owners to benefit from Cripple's unique prosperity.

The mine owners did most of their bellowing at the El Paso Club in Colorado Springs. The miners did theirs in the little town of Altman which Sam Altman had platted on a short saddle between the top of Bull Hill and the top of Bull Cliff. Sam's "highest city in the world" was close to three of Cripple's largest mines, the Buena Vista, the Victor and the Pharmacist. By November of '93 it consisted of a schoolhouse, six saloons, six groceries, four restaurants, several boardinghouses, a telephone and two hundred unpainted shacks housing 1200 men, women and children.

It was 10,620 feet high and it must have been one of the most thrilling spots on earth to live.[1] The overwhelming scenery, the gorgeous sunsets, the stupendous storms and the thin air made hearts beat fast up there all the time. Day and night the shacks trembled from underground blasting. When blasts occurred near the surface, whistles shrieked and housewives took down their washing so that it would not be torn by flying gravel.

Altman overlooked the six square miles of Bull Hill and Battle Mountain like a medieval fortress overlooking its feudal domain. From the porch of Smith and Peters' Saloon a man could observe what was happening anywhere in the area. The population was completely homogeneous — miners, miners, miners.

One of the miners was a Scotsman named John Calderwood, an old Aspen friend of Governor Waite's. Calderwood had worked in Scotland's coal mines at the age of nine, came to the Pennsylvania coal fields at seventeen, graduated from the McKeesport School of Mines in '76 and was blacklisted from the State for joining the Mollie Maguires — a sort of early I.W.W. He was a grave, courteous, sandy-haired Catholic who loved to expound the teachings of Pope Leo XIII.[2]

The Pope was making some wealthy Catholics nervous by urging workers to demand the eight-hour day, old-age pensions and child-labor laws.

Calderwood was an organizer for the Western Federation of Miners. This historic union, forefather of both the I.W.W. and the C.I.O., was formed at Butte, Montana, on May 15, 1893, after a bloody battle between miners and mine owners in the Coeur d'Alene. The mine owners won the battle, with help from several regiments of the United States Army.

Some Western Federation men were Mollie Maguires, who longed to barbecue all capitalists. Their militancy was too much for Calderwood, but the W.F.M. was young and full of beans, and Calderwood decided to work for it at Cripple. He worked fast. In two months every Altman miner joined his Free Coinage Union No. 19, Western Federation of Miners. He formed smaller unions at Cripple Creek town, Victor and Anaconda. He organized eight hundred men in all — two thirds of the miners in the district. He promised them a standard three-dollar eight-hour day.

The mine owners in the Springs opposed Calderwood and the Western Federation as bitterly as they opposed Governor Waite and Populism. They couldn't understand what ailed Stratton and Jimmie Burns, who insisted on treating Calderwood as though he were almost human. But the mine owners' biggest worry was the fact that they couldn't agree among themselves on uniform wages and hours. At last, twelve of them came to an agreement. After February 1, 1894, their mines would run on a three-dollar nine-hour day. Jimmie Burns was one of the signers of this agreement though he soon withdrew his signature and never did put the Portland on a nine-hour day. Other signers included Hagerman, Dave

Moffat, Sam Altman, Irving Howbert, Ed De LaVergne and William Lennox.

Calderwood met the challenge of the nine-hour agreement by calling his men — five hundred of them — out of every nine-hour mine during the first week of February. Some seven hundred men, union and nonunion, kept working in the eight-hour mines. Bull Hill and Battle Mountain comprised the main area affected, because most of the nine-hour mines were within its limits.

At first the nine-hour owners pooh-poohed the strike. Some of them had won strikes from the inept Knights of Labor at Leadville and at Aspen. The miners would get hungry shortly and go back to work.

However, as the weeks passed, it began to dawn on the mine owners that they faced something new. The power of the State as represented by Governor Waite was behind the miners. And John Calderwood wasn't like the fumbling leaders of the Knights of Labor. Calderwood didn't bluster around looking tough — and accomplishing nothing. He behaved more like a professor, quartermaster and banker. He lectured daily to his men on the aims of the Western Federation of Miners. He maintained friendly social relations with the biggest mine owners in camp, Stratton and Burns. He organized a central kitchen for strikers at Altman. He instructed pickets in legal intimidation. He collected funds. In February he took in $1400 from Cripple Creek businessmen, $800 from Butte headquarters, $700 from Federation members in the San Juan and $4500 from working miners at Cripple. The assessment for each working miner was $15 a month.

By the middle of March the nine-hour mine owners had

to accept the dismaying fact that the Bull Hill strikers didn't seem to be starving to death. People generally criticized the nine-hour mine owners for trying to establish a nine-hour day when so many owners were running profitably on an eight-hour day. Everybody was tickled when Jimmie Burns praised his men for joining the Western Federation of Miners. "Every worker," Jimmie said, "has a right to improve his status by bargaining collectively." In its report the *Cripple Creek Crusher* added: "Upon receipt of Mr. Burns' statement at the El Paso Club, three members collapsed on the pool table and died of apoplexy."

Then the crowning blow — a veritable stab in the back. Old Man Stratton asked John Calderwood to confer at his Wilson Creek shack. There Stratton proposed a day wage scale of $3.25 for nine hours' work, thus offering a compromise on the nine-hour issue by higher wages. Night shift miners would work eight hours for $3.25.

Calderwood accepted Stratton's compromise and a *contract* was signed. A contract with a labor organizer! To the nine-hour mine owners, Jimmie Burns' statement about the miners' right to bargain collectively was ill-mannered heresy. But Stratton's act in signing a contract with the common enemy was incredible folly. It was blasphemous for Stratton to admit that Calderwood existed. It was obscene of him to recognize by contract such an anarchistic gang of extortioners as the Western Federation of Miners.

Up to now Irving Howbert had kept the nine-hour mine owners from foolhardy action by reminding them that it would be bad politically. Howbert was chairman of the Republican Central Committee charged with booting "Bloody Bridles" Waite out of the governorship in the '94 elections. If the owners lost their tempers and tried to use force to

get Bull Hill back from the strikers, Calderwood would ask
the Governor to protect them. Waite would come flying up
to Cripple in a cloud of Biblical oratory, would side with the
workers and would use the militia to help the Federation
win the strike.

That might win back for Waite many votes that he had
lost lately because of his lack of political skill. Howbert
explained this again to the nine-hour mine owners but they
wouldn't listen any longer. They wanted open war with the
W.F.M. in defense of Americanism — and their bank accounts. If Stratton and Burns wished to behave like damn
fools, that was their business.

The nine-hour mine owners went to Judge John Campbell and secured an injunction restraining the Western
Federation from interference with the operation of their
mines. They announced that they would run their mines
with scab workers. On March 15, Frank Bowers, the sheriff
of El Paso County, climbed to Altman and served papers on
Calderwood and one hundred other members of Free Coinage Union No. 19. Well-meaning Frank was just like the
harried cops in the old Keystone comedies, handlebar mustache and all. He had a big heart and he yearned to be loved
by everybody, which was why it almost killed him to have
to be a key figure in the strike conflict. He had been elected
sheriff in '92 with the financial aid of the mine owners. His
past experience as a distinguished criminologist derived from
experience as marshal of Manitou where he had tried to keep
Joe Wolfe from scalping tourists. He had served also as
bouncer in Johnnie Nolon's Manitou saloon.

The loyal subjects of the kingdom of Bull Hill did not
know what Sheriff Bowers and the injunction meant but
they suspected the worst. They buzzed around Bowers like

angry bees. Frank had never endured such an unhappy half hour. When he finished reading the names of those whom the court ordered to cease interfering with the mines he hurried back to Cripple Creek town, his mustache drooping in discouragement.

A phone call awaited him. The superintendent of the Victor Mine, Charles Keith, was at the other end of the wire. Keith said that a gang of Altman miners was about to destroy the Victor. Frank put six deputy sheriffs in a wagon, and sent it lumbering up the long, steep road toward Altman and the Victor Mine. Soon after midnight, Keith phoned the sheriff that the six deputies had been seized by Altman town officers and a posse of miners claiming to be the Altman police force.

Poor Bowers appeared wearily on Bennett Avenue and called the citizenry to arms out of the bars and gambling houses. But just as Bowers ordered the advance on Altman the six missing deputies came into view. They reported their release by Altman authorities. They said that they had not been harmed physically or spiritually. So Bowers' expeditionary force returned to the bars. The Sheriff of El Paso County went gratefully to bed.

Things were hung-over and jittery next morning. Leaflets issued by the nine-hour mine owners stated that Dave Moffat's Victor and Anaconda mines, Ed De LaVergne's Raven and the Summit were going to open. Bowers received frightening reports of carnage among scabs seeking jobs. Only people with passports signed by King Calderwood himself could enter the kingdom of Bull Hill. Bowers considered regrouping his barfly cavalry but decided that capturing Altman was no task for a hung-over army. He phoned James J. Hagerman for guidance. Hagerman dove into his store

of wisdom and came up with instructions to sit tight, bring
nothing to a boil, keep everything under control and not
cause a rumpus that would glorify Waite and lose Republican votes.

Sit tight! Not cause a rumpus! With the top of Bull Hill
about to blow off! At midnight, nearly crazy with anxiety,
Bowers phoned Governor Waite for military aid.

Colorado's bedeviled chief of state was seeking composure
after the political farce called "the City Hall War" which
had followed his dismissal of two of Denver's fire and police
board. The dismissed men had refused to be fired. They
locked themselves in Denver City Hall and dared Waite to
come and get them. They were defended by the entire Denver
police and fire departments plus Soapy Smith, the bunco king,
and his friends. Waite sent the State militia to go and get
them with Adjutant General Thomas J. Tarsney (prophetic
name!) in command. The militia drew up in Fourteenth
Street facing City Hall. Cannon were loaded and aimed. Rifles
were at ready, and sabers were drawn. To match this belliger-
ent show, the defenders of City Hall had guns poking from
every window.

Ten thousand Denverites took ringside seats along Fourteenth Street and waited for the battle to begin. They waited
seven hours while Waite struggled with the problem of
whether to order the attack. At 9 P.M., March 15, he recalled
the militia to its barracks and handed the dismissal issue
over to the courts.

Sheriff Bowers' plea to Waite next day gave the Governor
a heaven-sent chance to draw attention from the Denver farce
and perk up the humiliated militia. He ordered most of the
militia to entrain to Cripple Creek. Adjutant General Tarsney and General E. J. Brooks were in command. The militia

reached Cripple early Sunday morning, March 18. The men encamped on the site of George Carr's ranch house and fell asleep.

General Tarsney was a queer one. At forty-four he was a sort of middle-aged Peck's Bad Boy who enjoyed peppering those he disliked with his figurative beanshooter. He disliked practically everybody, and vice versa. He had been an obscure Durango lawyer in '92 when Governor Waite chose him for Adjutant General. He was perhaps the worst of Waite's many bad choices. He was a Populist not by conviction but merely because he hated Republicans and Democrats. He was far from loyal to Governor Waite, whom he habitually referred to as "that old fool."

Upon his arrival at Cripple, Tarsney conferred with Sheriff Bowers, who explained that King Calderwood had seized Bull Hill, that a reign of terror existed and that he needed the militia to arrest people for him. Tarsney told Bowers that the militia was not supposed to be called unless Bowers had evidence of resistance to arrest. Bowers replied that he would get evidence in a hurry. But first he would have to rush to the Springs for warrants.

When Bowers departed, Tarsney called Calderwood to the Palace Hotel. He told Calderwood that he would have to send the militia against the strikers if any of them resisted arrest by Bowers upon his return to Cripple. Then the mine owners could move in their scabs, the strike would be lost and the old fool Governor Waite would bite nails in wrath because he was a Populist pledged to prevent usurpations by the money power.

King Calderwood promised that no Federation members would resist arrest. Thereupon, Tarsney woke his militia and set it to marching up Tenderfoot Hill and away from Cripple. Sheriff Bowers came back with his warrants. When he found the militia gone, he complained that Tarsney and Governor Waite were handing the gold camp over to the murderous strikers. It would be suicide, Bowers declared, to try to arrest strike leaders on Bull Hill without the militia's Gatling guns to back him up.

Tarsney — ah, Iago! — suggested to Bowers that maybe he was imagining things. Why didn't he go to Altman to see if the strikers *would* resist arrest? Bowers strapped on his six-shooters, set his jaw in a martyr mask, left a farewell note to his wife and set out grimly for Altman.

Instead of running a gantlet of hot lead, he was greeted pleasantly along the five-mile road by unarmed miners. At Altman he was received by Calderwood as an honored guest and plied with the best bourbon in Smith and Peters' saloon. When he read the eighteen names on his warrants, Calderwood and his privy council submitted to arrest like college seniors stepping up for diplomas.

The bewildered Sheriff of El Paso County couldn't understand what had happened until his return to Cripple Creek town. He realized then that Tarsney and Waite had conspired with Calderwood to fake peace on Bull Hill so that Waite could recall the militia and demoralize Judge Campbell's injunction. Bowers' men reported that armed strikers had resumed guard of all roads to Altman. Passports were required again at the border, and it was difficult to get visas. The kingdom of Bull Hill had resumed its proud status as an independent principality completely surrounded by the United States.

In a few days, the eighteen officers of the Western Federation of Miners whom Bowers had arrested and jailed in Colorado Springs won acquittals or release on low bail.

And what brilliant attorney achieved this miracle? None other than Thomas J. Tarsney, the impartial Adjutant General of Colorado!

The Battle of Bull Hill

EARLY IN APRIL, John Calderwood decided to tour the State's mining camps on behalf of the Western Federation of Miners and of Governor Waite. Stratton and others hated to see him go. They were afraid that the strike would get out of hand during his absence.

It did. Before he left, King Calderwood named an Aspen friend, Junius J. Johnson, as regent of the kingdom of Bull Hill. Johnson had been a West Pointer a few years before and had been expelled for hazing during his senior year. He had taken his dismissal hard and had left his Kentucky home for remote places where he would not meet classmates, which was how he got to Aspen and to Cripple.

Cripple's March troubles had drawn all kinds of men to Bull Hill, criminals especially. "General" Johnson began to feel that he was the employment office for every ex-convict fresh out of the Canon City pen. These fellows were truly rugged individualists. They had a gang leader, "General" Jack Smith, whom "General" Johnson had to accept as his right-hand man. "General" Smith favored forthright action. When two spies for the mine owners, Bill Rabideau and W. S. Ferguson, defended the nine-hour day at a miners' meeting, Smith and his gang grabbed them, carted them to Altman, made them drink from cuspidors, threatened to cut off useful parts of their bodies and drove Rabideau out of camp. Ferguson was thrown down an eighteen-foot prospect hole, suffering a broken leg.

Rabideau and Ferguson were gorillas who were asking for what they got, but the mine owners claimed that they were saintly men. They demanded punishment for the "General" Smith gang. "General" Johnson hastened to improve Bull Hill defenses. He built a log fort atop Bull Cliff, its fake cannon pointed at the Victor Mine below. He designed a bow-gun which could hurl beer bottles filled with dynamite to the bottom of Bull Hill. He collected rifles from the hardware stores and homes of the district. Bull Hill and Battle Mountain roads were mined. Strikers were supplied with pencil-sized dynamite cartridges to blow up attackers at close range.

Johnson tried to maintain discipline on the Hill, but he couldn't control Jack Smith and Company. This bunch roamed around soothing the complexes of its members by wrecking saloons, robbing stores, beating nonunion men and disturbing the peace of parlor houses. Their lawlessness was given full publicity by newsmen in the pay of the mine owners. The general public began to get tired of the strike. That gave the mine owners a chance to enlist support for raising an army of El Paso County deputy sheriffs to capture Bull Hill from the Western Federation. No more appeals to "Bloody Bridles" Waite. No more truck with Adjutant General Tarsney. From here on El Paso County would handle its own affairs.

There was one hitch. Very few residents of Colorado Springs knew how to hold a gun, let alone aim one at a mob of mountaineers led by a West Pointer. The solution, supplied by Irving Howbert, seemed too good to be true.

What large body of tough and expert marksmen despised Governor Waite, Tarsney and all their Populist rabble, including the Western Federation? Why, the ex-police and ex-firemen of Denver, whom Waite had just kicked out of their jobs for resisting his militia in the Denver City Hall war!

And so it happened that 125 "El Paso County deputy sheriffs" — all from Denver — passed through the Springs, changed trains at Florence and approached the gold camp from the south on the new narrow-gauge Florence & Cripple Creek Railway. "General" Johnson got the news at Altman and decided on drastic action. These phony deputies hired by the mine owners must not be allowed to take Bull Hill. They must be given a scare they would never forget.

At 9 A.M. on May 25, two F. & C. C. flatcars loaded with the Denver ex-police and ex-firemen moved along the last curving mile toward Victor town. The ex-police looked forward to showing the Bull Hill strikers how professional toughs operated. From the flatcars they saw nothing unusual on the south slope of Battle Mountain — just a work gang and a two-horse wagon pulling toward Stratton's Independence from the Strong Mine.

As the flatcars moved near the Strong, the whole sky over and around Victor town seemed to explode. The Strong Mine shaft house flew three hundred feet into the air and disintegrated under the force of a great blast. While the Denver force stared in terror, a second blast shook the district and re-echoed along the Rampart Range. The Strong's steam boiler shot skyward like a cork from a popgun. The ex-police dropped their rifles and covered their heads as hunks of gallows-frame, cable, and iron wheels pelted around the flatcars. They weren't tough hombres now. They were scared senseless, as "General" Johnson hoped they would be. The locomotive engineer lunged at his lever and set his wheels spinning in reverse. The dinky train backed off toward the southern hills, slowly at first, then in urgent flight.

Half an hour later, the whole gold camp went into an emotional tailspin. A boil of resentment spilled over the district — resentment at Springs mine owners, Springs millionaires, Springs Episcopalians, Springs Republicans. It was a real mass orgy. Yelling mobs smashed the doors and windows of liquor warehouses, and drenched themselves in whiskey. "General" Johnson's crew who had blown up the Strong Mine seized a flatcar, loaded it with TNT and rolled it downgrade to try to smash into the Denver force. Instead it left the track on a curve and exploded, killing a cow and three goats. The same crew drove twenty-one guards from Stratton's Independence and took over the mine. In Victor town Stratton heard of the seizure. From then on he opposed the strikers.

"General" Jack Smith collected his drunken battalion, loaded two wagons with dynamite and set out to blow up every mine shaft, every super's home, every ore bin in the district. "General" Johnson intercepted Smith and ordered him to sober up and chase the retreating Denver force. Smith and Company stole a work train at Victor and met the enemy around midnight some miles south of Victor. In a brief, confused battle two men were killed. The hired Denver deputies captured five strikers.

Early next morning John Calderwood arrived back at Cripple from his speaking tour. It was a sad homecoming. His fine work was ruined. The strike's original purpose was forgotten. It had degenerated into a futile class war. Calderwood had to move quickly to stop a renewal of the orgy. He got the saloonkeepers to close their doors. He locked up "General" Smith in Altman. He persuaded "General" Junius Johnson to leave the district. He asked Father Volpe and other church leaders to restore order in their settlements. He asked wives to get their men home. By nightfall the hysteria was over.

It was Colorado Springs' turn next. Stratton and Sam Strong got down the mountain a dozen hours after the Strong Mine explosion. Their reports started a reaction that swelled and roared until it equaled the reaction in Cripple Creek. The Springs people had great grievances too. They hated the gold campers because they were Populists; because they admired Governor Waite; because so many were Irish red-neck Catholics. They hated the miners for capturing Bull Hill. Their fury hit a peak when they learned that Superintendent Sam McDonald and two miners were in the Strong Mine at the time of the explosion. The strikers took them from the mine afterward and jailed them at Altman. McDonald was all right, but one of the others lost his mind from shock.

The eight-hour issue was forgotten in the Springs as completely as it had been forgotten in Cripple Creek. It was replaced by a conviction that the Bull Hill strikers would pour down the mountain to capture the Springs — for the greater glory, some said, of Pope Leo XIII. A town meeting was held in North Park. Cries went up to phone President Cleveland and the United States Army, to lynch Calderwood, to impeach Governor Waite, to hang Adjutant General Tarsney. In a stirring speech Judge Colburn said: "I call on every able-bodied man and boy to wrest Bull Hill from the insurrectionists before the insurrectionists despoil the Springs'

fair womanhood and slit the throats of its little children!"
Miss Susan Dunbar announced that her Ladies' Auxiliary
was ready to make bandages and fill canteens for the city's
defenders, to bind wounds and to comfort the dying.

With the grapeshot seeming to fly already, the residents
flocked around Sheriff Bowers demanding to be sworn in as
deputy sheriffs. Irving Howbert sent coded telegrams hiring
one hundred more professional gunmen from Denver and
one hundred from Leadville. Stratton, still in high dudgeon
over the seizure of his Independence by the strikers, told
Howbert to buy him a full brigade to recapture his property.

Sheriff Bowers swore in altogether an army of 1200 deputies to oppose the 700-man miners' army on Bull Hill. The
enlarged deputy army went into campaign headquarters at
Hayden Divide, on the Colorado Midland eighteen miles
north of Cripple. At Hagerman's request, William S. Slocum,
president of Colorado College, went to Altman to try to
settle the conflict. He didn't settle anything. But he did
arrange an exchange of prisoners. It occurred on May 28,
1894, near Hoosier Pass, north of Bull Hill. The five strikers
who had been captured by the Denver ex-cops were exchanged
for Superintendent McDonald and his two comrades. The
exchange was a unique event in United States history. Neither
army had any legality, yet both behaved like international
belligerents bound by the laws of war.

The exchange convinced Governor Waite that he'd better
come up and end the explosive situation. That made it more
explosive than ever. Waite was the last person the mine
owners wanted to see in El Paso County. He journeyed to
Altman and received full power to arbitrate for the strikers,
provided they wouldn't be prosecuted for criminal acts. Then
Waite and John Calderwood came to Colorado Springs to

confer with Hagerman and other mine owners in a room at Palmer Hall, Colorado College. The mine owners stared through Calderwood as though he were so much air. It made Calderwood nervous so he remained in the hall.

The Governor tried hard. For four hours he pleaded, threatened, pounded the table. The mine owners agreed to a three-dollar eight-hour day. But they wouldn't agree not to prosecute the strike leaders for criminal acts. So the conference broke up. An angry crowd milled around Palmer Hall waiting to nab Waite and Calderwood. While Judge Horace Lunt made a speech to hold the crowd, Waite and Calderwood slipped out a back door and walked to the Denver & Rio Grande Railroad station.

Sheriff Bowers met Waite at his special train and handed him a written request for the State militia to return to Cripple. This request was, of course, against the mine owners' wishes. But Bowers was at the end of his rope once more. The army of 1200 El Paso County deputies at Hayden Divide refused to acknowledge his authority. They had selected County Commissioner Winfield Scott Boynton as their boss.

Boynton, a hotel man and former Manitou shoe clerk, had risen from sleep one morning filled with a certainty that he was a military genius. He was the man who ought to be sheriff of El Paso County. He could save Colorado Springs from destruction by leading the deputy army from Hayden Divide in a frontal attack on Bull Hill. He could and would. He made stirring orations and lectured the deputies on tactics and held drills and song-fests. He created drama by locking up the newspaper reporters at Hayden Divide and cutting phone and telegraph wires. He published a front-page announcement in the *Gazette:*

UPHOLD LAW!

CITIZENS! IF YOU HAVE THE BLOOD OF 1776 IN YOUR VEINS, IN
THE NAME OF GOD, IN THE NAME OF YOUR COUNTRY, IN THE
NAME OF YOUR HOMES, YOUR WIVES AND YOUR CHILDREN, STAND
BY LAW AND ORDER THAT THIS GOVERNMENT OF THE PEOPLE, BY
THE PEOPLE AND FOR THE PEOPLE MAY NOT PERISH FROM THE
EARTH. I AM, MY FELLOW CITIZENS, MOST TRULY YOURS,

                                          W. S. BOYNTON

All this chest-beating by Boynton had got the deputies into
such a prematurely triumphant state that Sheriff Bowers decided to protect them against themselves. That is why he
asked Waite for the militia. He knew that the strikers would
make mincemeat of the deputies if they walked up Bull Hill,
armed only with brashness, one busted Gatling gun and a
Parrott cannon [1] nobody knew how to fire.

Early Wednesday morning, June 6, General Tarsney and
the State militia left Denver for Cripple. Boynton heard of
it, broke camp at Hayden Divide and rushed his deputy army
southward. His plan was to take Bull Hill, disarm the strikers
and open the mines before the militia could interfere.

The deputies reached Beaver Park in the afternoon and
set up their tents. Boynton could see no signs of life around
Altman, three miles to the south, and he concluded that the
strikers had withdrawn from their Bull Hill fortress. He
moved jubilantly to the head of the deputy column and
ordered the final victory march. The 1200 men walked forward a mile or so. Suddenly Boynton felt his hat fly off.
Then the air was full of small noises, like popcorn warming
in a skillet. Tiny plumes of dust danced around the feet
of the deputies, who flopped on their bellies and wondered
what the hell. Boynton flopped too. The noise was rifle fire
from every rock and tree and kinnikinnick bush ahead.

The strikers were dead shots. Boynton had to pull the deputies back in a hurry. He tried a night attack and it failed. Many deputies got lost and ended up shooting at one another. By Thursday morning the deputies had retreated to their Beaver Park camp. That is where the State militiamen found them when they reached the mining district at night-fall. Adjutant General Tarsney placed the militiamen in Grassy Gulch exactly between the deputies in Beaver Park and the strikers on Bull Hill. Then he commanded Boynton to disband his army because it was an illegal force. Boynton flatly refused.

But the situation of the deputies and of Boynton was intolerable. Down in the Springs, 10,000 loyal souls awaited word of the deputies' glorious victory. The deputies had to do something, or at least seem to do something. Boynton split them into three units and sent them padding mysteriously about the fringes of Bull Hill. On Friday, the Stratton brigade marched part way up Globe Hill to within a mile of Altman. The strikers hurried forward to stop the brigade, and the militia drew between them. General Tarsney got hold of Sheriff Bowers and instructed him to assert his authority over the deputies. Bowers ordered Boynton to order the Stratton brigade off Globe Hill and back to Beaver Park. The brigade obeyed, with its Gatling gun in reverse, as at funerals. As the deputies withdrew they sang:

> The Sheriff of El Paso County
> With all the Sheriff's men,
> He marched them up the hill, and then
> He marched them down again.

With the Stratton brigade out of the way, Tarsney sent the State militia up Bull Hill. The strikers welcomed it and allowed Altman to be occupied. Most of the strikers handed their arms over to the militia.

The Battle of Bull Hill was over. But Commissioner Boynton clung still to his particular dream of glory. To jack up his morale and that of his men, he staged a grand parade of all deputies from Beaver Park through Cripple Creek town and on south toward Victor. As the deputies approached the south slope of Battle Mountain, General Tarsney appeared and asked Boynton what he had in mind. Boynton declared that the deputies were going into camp around Stratton's Independence, to protect it from the strikers. Tarsney approved this project but he warned Boynton not to move his men closer to Bull Hill. If they did move closer, the militia would be obliged to blast them right off the mountain into Wilson Creek.

A treaty of peace was signed next morning at Altman, Sunday, June 10, 1894. Sheriff Bowers and Commissioner Boynton agreed to disband the army of El Paso County deputy sheriffs. The miners agreed to surrender their arms. The militia would stick around until the mines were operating on normal schedules. John Calderwood and three hundred strikers agreed to stand trial for criminal acts. The nine-hour mine owners put their properties on a three-dollar, eight-hour day.

The strike had lasted 130 days, the longest and bitterest of all American labor disputes up to that time. It had cost $3,000,000 in lost production, lost wages, and upkeep of the three armies involved. It introduced dozens of weapons that have become standard in labor battles — spies, blacklists, propaganda, injunctions, assessments. Though rarely mentioned by labor historians among the great strikes of history, the Cripple Creek strike was tremendously important. It brought enormous prestige to the Western Federation of Miners. By winning Calderwood's demand for a three-dollar, eight-hour day at Cripple this pioneer industrial union was started well on its way to becoming the most powerful labor organization in the United States.

But nobody in El Paso County thought of historical matters on Sunday, June 10. Cripple Creekers began a victory celebration that would last for many days. And Colorado Springs celebrated, too. An ovation was prepared for Winfield Scott Boynton and the deputies whose heroism had prevented the strikers from descending the mountain to pillage the city. A band led the parade up Tejon Street in Colorado Springs, followed by Boynton, the police, the 1200 deputies, the 500-man home guard, the firemen, the county jail guards, and Susan Dunbar's Ladies' Auxiliary.

At the Court House, "three hearty groans were given for Governor Waite and his man Friday, Thomas J. Tarsney." Susan Dunbar tendered thanks "to all those women for their willing devotion in sending their dear ones to the defense of our homes. The City feels the high honor due not only to the courageous men at the front, but the quiet heroines at the fireside."

The strike left in the minds of many people wounds that never would heal, but it did not take long for the gold camp to resume a normal appearance. John Calderwood holed up in Denver for a while, submitted to arrest, stood trial and was acquitted. Thereafter, he quit the organizing game and became an assayer in Victor. "General" Junius Johnson died a colonel in the Spanish-American War. "General" Jack Smith went to Missouri briefly, returned to Cripple and was shot to death at Altman, in May, '95. Of three hundred strikers jailed by Sheriff Bowers, only two served time in

Canon City penitentiary, on charges of blowing up the Strong Mine.

Winfield Scott Stratton got over his pique at the strikers for seizing the Independence and resumed his efforts to keep the camp free of corporate domination. But he had had more than enough of Governor Waite's liberalism, and he did not support him in the November, '94, gubernatorial race. Waite was defeated by Irving Howbert's Republican candidate, Albert W. McIntire. Howbert's reward was a huge banquet at the Antlers Hotel, complete with bluepoints, roast quail and Mumm's extra dry.

"Bloody Bridles" left office with these ominous words: "I will not say 'hail and farewell.' That would be too formal. We go, but we return. We will meet you, gentlemen, in two years 'at Philippi.' " But Davis Waite never had another chance to meet his enemies at Philippi. And yet, as we have said, he was a good and a brave man. Many people thought he was an extreme radical; today we would probably regard him as a conservative on the order of the late Harold Ickes. The manner of Waite's death somehow fitted him. It came of paralysis, in 1901, while he was peeling apples in the kitchen of his Aspen home.

CHAPTER XVI

The "Tar" in Tarsney

AFTER THE PEACE TREATY WAS SIGNED, Thomas J. Tarsney came to the Springs as protecting angel for the arrested strikers, seeking their release on technicalities. In this work he was motivated less by love of miners than by hatred of everybody in Little London.

In the hour before supper, Tarsney liked to park in the lobby of his headquarters at the Alamo Hotel and narrate to admiring drummers how he had outgeneraled those damned deputies. Most of his talk was repeated everywhere. Marshal Dana twice warned him to get out of town before something happened to him.

It happened. On June 22, late in the evening, an ex-deputy, Joe Wilson, bade a fond farewell to his girl on a boarding-house porch at the edge of the Springs business district. Wilson carried a large satchel containing a down pillow, a brush and a can of tar. He had filched the tar earlier from a roofing job at Matt Conway's shoe store. He walked down Tejon Street to Pikes Peak Avenue and westward to the Antlers Hotel Park, where he joined fifteen men. Most of them were thugs who had been imported by the mine owners as deputies to help capture Bull Hill.

Shortly before midnight the group separated in twos and threes and converged on the Alamo. Simultaneously a man approached the hack stand at the corner of Pikes Peak Avenue and Tejon Street in front of the First National Bank. He asked the two hackmen there to douse their lights and drive to the Cucharras Street side of the Alamo Hotel. One of the hackmen was Sherman Crumley, reputedly a former member of the Dalton gang of Kansas outlaws.

At midnight the Alamo phone rang and night clerk George Dayton answered it. Phone Number 53 at Cripple Creek had urgent need to speak to Mr. Thomas J. Tarsney. This phone was in the Branch Saloon where Tarsney used to meet Western Federation members. Clerk Dayton wrote the message on a card and sent it up to Tarsney's room with the night porter. Tarsney woke up, read the message, dressed, descended to the lobby and went back of the room clerk's counter where the phone was located.

At that instant, Joe Wilson and his friends filed into the lobby. Three of them moved behind the counter. Tarsney looked up from the phone and started yelling for help. A masked man with two revolvers struck him on the head with a revolver butt. Tarsney was hoisted over the counter and dragged through the lobby into the street and dumped into Sherman Crumley's hack.

Policeman Sam Agard, who had been slumbering on an Alamo Park bench, woke to see Crumley and the other hack-driver leap to their boxes. As the hacks swept past him eastward on Cucharras, Sam heard a smothered yell coming from the first hack. He began running north up the middle of Tejon Street, blowing his whistle for all he was worth. At Pikes Peak Avenue he met Police Captain J. W. Gathright. Sam reported that a kidnapping may have occurred at the Alamo. Gathright ordered him sharply to stop making so much noise and return to his beat.

The two hackdrivers turned their galloping horses off Cucharras northward on Weber Street, past Irving Howbert's fine place, to Cache la Poudre Street, ducked under the railroad underpass and left town on the Austin Bluffs Road. At the country home of William A. Otis, a Cripple Creek mine owner, the hacks turned in and pulled behind the Otis barn. The conspirators unloaded Tarsney and heated the can of tar over a coal-oil fire. They stripped the Adjutant General, coated his stout body with the warm tar, and added feathers from Joe Wilson's down pillow.

Wilson told Tarsney to put his clothes on over the tar. Then the kidnappers dumped him into Crumley's hack once more. Near the Santa Fé tracks at the east edge of town they left him with orders to walk toward Denver and keep walking. As the two hacks rattled back into town, Captain Gathright appeared and told the passengers that he was hunting a gang in two hacks rumored to have kidnapped Adjutant General Tarsney from the Alamo. Gathright asked the passengers if they had seen any such hacks or kidnappers. The passengers said No, and Gathright went away.

Meanwhile, Tarsney plodded north along the Santa Fé tracks. At dawn he reached Andrew Malloy's ranch, ten miles from the Springs. Mrs. Malloy gave him breakfast and scraped off some of the tar. Malloy drove him to Palmer Lake, and Governor Waite sent an engine and caboose up there to bring him home.

Waite was thoughtful enough to put a gallon of benzine and a change of clothes on the train. The brakeman used the benzine to get the tar off Tarsney, who went to bed in his own Denver house that Saturday night, still smarting from the benzine but otherwise not much the worse for wear.

He began planning at once how to get even with the ex-deputies in the tar party.

His problem was difficult. He knew his kidnappers, and so did many residents and all the police in the Springs. But he couldn't find anyone in El Paso County who would testify that he had been tarred and feathered. And so he had to bide his time and try to upset his enemies with sarcastic remarks about Little London. When he was ordered to appear before a Colorado Springs grand jury to testify against Bull Hill strikers he enjoyed refusing, on the grounds that no man in his right mind would risk visiting such a barbarous community.

In mid-July Tarsney learned that most of his kidnappers had left their sanctuary in the Springs, and had returned to their own communities. He put the whole State administration to work tracking them down. He himself turned detective and traced Joe Wilson to a farm in Vernon County, Missouri. In a few days he managed to capture eleven of the fifteen who had kidnapped him. He corralled them just for his own satisfaction, for he realized no El Paso County jury would punish them. He passed them on to Sheriff Bowers, and all were acquitted at once.

To this day, Little London has refused to divulge the inside story of the tarring of Tarsney. We know that Irving Howbert tried to prevent it, because he feared it would reflect on the Republican Party. Stratton tried to prevent it because he wanted to improve relations between the Springs and Cripple Creek. Marshal Dana, Captain Gathright, and William A. Otis co-operated in the plot. Mine owner Ed Giddings publicly expressed approval after the event. But we don't know who made the phone call from the Branch Saloon in Cripple Creek which lured Tarsney from his hotel room. We don't know who did the planning or how the ex-deputies were chosen or how much pay they received.

Tarsney hated to see his attackers go free, but the worst blow to his self-esteem came on August 6 when he went to the Springs to answer a charge of contempt of court arising from his refusal to testify against the Bull Hill strikers before the grand jury. He took no chances of being tarred again. Accompanied by a militia bodyguard in full dress he marched in solemn grandeur from the railroad station to Pikes Peak Avenue and Tejon Street where the assemblage boarded a streetcar for Colorado City to put up at the Hoffman Hotel.

Next day, Judge Campbell found Tarsney guilty of contempt and fined him fifty dollars and costs. This was the sole punishment ever meted out to anybody in connection with the tarring and feathering of Tarsney.[1]

CHAPTER XVII

Boom, Cripple!

WHEN THE STRIKE ENDED, Cripple's great era began — eight years of outpouring wealth that would spread the camp's fame to the ends of the earth.

Gambling in Cripple Creek stocks grew to the status of a national sport. The mining exchange in Colorado Springs became the largest in the world. Cripple's gold production quadrupled. The world's best geologists and milling men rushed to Pikes Peak. School children in Texas and Oregon and Maine sang the jingle:

> Goin' up to Cripple Creek,
> Goin' on the run,
> Goin' up to Cripple Creek
> To have a little fun!

At the center of the excitement and a big reason for it was the carpenter, Winfield Scott Stratton, still thin, tired, pale, diffident and moody. He was earning a million dollars a year from the Independence now, and yet the mine was only 250 feet deep and his small crew was removing only part of the ore in sight. And Stratton got still more income from his Portland Mine stocks. The Portland wasn't nearly as rich as the Independence, but Jimmie Burns managed it well and made it pay by using a huge crew and all the latest equipment. Plumber Burns was moving into the world of his dreams. He planned to buy a big house on Tejon Street in the Springs, and he had an eye out for that beautiful wife. The best tailor in Denver made his clothes. He loved any kind of theater and he frequently attended the Butte Opera House in Cripple. He hadn't been invited as yet to dine at the El Paso Club in the Springs, but when he walked into the First National Bank there the tellers sprang to attention.

Of course, everyone sprang to attention when Stratton walked in, but Stratton didn't care two pins about that. Colorado's greatest mining king remained unimpressed with himself. His Independence Mine was being written up sensationally everywhere but to Stratton it was like an ordinary carpentry job to be worked according to the estimate and with allowance for future strains. There were no high-falutin engineers on Stratton's payroll. Old friends like Charlie Steele and Fred Trautman ran the mine. His general manager was his former shoemaker, a Swiss named Bob Schwarz. Through '94 and most of '95 Stratton lived alone in a cabin above Wilson Creek close to the Independence. Burns and Jimmie Doyle and John Harnan lived nearby and so did J. R. McKinnie and burly Sam Strong. McKinnie was married and fervently moral. The rest were hard drinkers and heavy gamblers.

For a while Stratton and Company were sturdy patrons of the Myers Avenue parlor houses, but as they grew rich this became undignified and the girls came around instead to their Battle Mountain shacks more or less on schedule like the morning milk. Nobody thought this dangerous until '95 when one of Stratton's girls, Candace Root, sued him for $200,000, alleging breach of promise to marry. Candace claimed that Stratton had lured her into his bed unfairly and got her pregnant. Stratton denied luring her, unfairly or otherwise. He told the court that Candace had been losing her virtue profitably since '92, and why should she blame her pregnancy on him particularly? The case was dismissed.

Stratton came close to being a happy man during his first three years of great wealth. He enjoyed helping the Irishmen to straighten out the Portland. He gave $85,000 to the Salvation Army, $20,000 to Colorado College, and $25,000 to the Colorado School of Mines at Golden. He gave thousands to Father Volpe to help build Cripple's St. Peter's Church and other thousands to Presbyterian and Baptist ministers and to "Parson" Tom Uzzell for his Methodist Tabernacle in Denver. When Horace Tabor of Leadville fame hit the skids and asked Stratton to loan him $15,000, Stratton gave him a check and tore up Tabor's note. Stratton learned that many poor people had lost savings by investing in W. J. Willcox's early promotion of Stratton's Washington claim. Stratton found Willcox's records and reimbursed every purchaser of the defunct Washington stock.

Any old miner down on his luck could drop in at Stratton's cabin and get a hundred dollars. For several winters Stratton supplied the poor families of the Battle Mountain area with coal. When Zeurah Stewart's son turned up, Stratton enrolled him at the University of Illinois and gave him an allowance of a hundred dollars a month. He grubstaked his old friend Jim Casey to the extent of $75,000 to go prospecting in the Klondike. He donated a bicycle to every laundry girl in Colorado Springs. During a Springs blizzard he hired men to feed the horned larks.

But his greatest pleasure was watching Cripple Creek grow, and watching the men who were helping him to make it grow. Below his shack was the town of Victor, founded by the Woods boys. Genial Frank and dour Harry Woods were in their thirties. They were quiet, mousy fellows, ardent Baptists and pillars of the Y.M.C.A.[1] In '93 they paid $1000 for McKinnie's 136-acre Mount Rosa Placer and they laid out a townsite on it. They called it Victor after Victor C. Adams, original homesteader of the adjacent Lawrence townsite.

The Woods boys told the world that every Victor lot was a gold mine. The lots moved so well that they decided to build the Victor Hotel. While Frank Woods was grading for this hotel, he struck a twenty-inch vein. It had a little gold in it, so Frank traced it to a claim called the Gold Coin which he bought for a few thousand dollars. Some months later the Gold Coin was earning $50,000 monthly for the Woods boys. As a token of their gratitude they gave the Gold Coin, later, a beautiful brick shaft house with colored-glass windows like Chartres Cathedral — the largest and fanciest shaft house in mining history.

Stratton saw at the start that Cripple must have a railroad and he pestered Harry Collbran, general manager of the Colorado Midland, to build an eighteen-mile spur up to camp from the Midland's whistle-stop at Hayden Divide. The Midland was owned by the Santa Fé, the directors of which were not interested in a spur to Cripple Creek. So Collbran went ahead on his own, getting $100,000 from a Springs millionaire, Harlan P. Lillibridge, and moral support from W. K. Gillett, passenger auditor of the Santa Fé. Collbran called his road the Midland Terminal. By September of '93 he had spent all of Lillibridge's $100,000 in building nine miles of narrow-gauge grade from Hayden Divide south toward Cripple.

And it looked as though he had thrown Lillibridge's $100,-000 away. While Collbran was building his narrow-gauge grade, Dave Moffat was building a rival narrow-gauge line, the Florence & Cripple Creek, northward from Florence toward Cripple up a steep ravine, Eight-Mile Canyon. Collbran's narrow-gauge Midland Terminal would connect at Hayden Divide with the standard-gauge Colorado Midland, requiring a transfer of freight. Moffat's narrow-gauge Florence & Cripple Creek connected with the narrow-gauge Denver & Rio Grande — no freight transfer needed.

Collbran and W. K. Gillett went to Lillibridge, informed him that they had made a $100,000 mistake and asked for another $100,000 to change the nine miles of completed narrow-gauge grade into standard-gauge grade.[2] Lillibridge refused to help them further. Thereupon, Collbran and Gillett announced that they would rebuild the Midland Terminal as a standard gauge anyway, and push it through to Cripple.

But what would they use for money? Jay Gould himself would have admired the shoestring on which they operated. Collbran was still general manager of the Colorado Midland. Gillett was still passenger auditor of the Santa Fé. Because of the depression, traffic on the Colorado Midland was light. Its employees had little to do. Collbran and Gillett used their authority as executives to put idle Colorado Midland men to work on their private project, the Midland Terminal. In a tour of the 350-mile Colorado Midland system, Collbran found quantities of "defective" material — ties, trestle lumber, tanks, spikes, switches, rails, tools. This material was hauled to Hayden Divide for use in rebuilding the M–T. The Santa Fé-Colorado Midland people knew of course what Collbran was doing, but they didn't care. If the Midland

Terminal turned out to be a success it would bring traffic to the Colorado Midland.

By January 1, 1894, Collbran had completed the standard-gauge Midland Terminal six miles from Hayden Divide toward Cripple to Midland Station. A dozen Midland Terminal trains, borrowed from the Colorado Midland, made the run each day. Then Collbran began building the difficult twelve-mile ascent from Midland Station up to the gold camp, an ascent that would cost $70,000 a mile. Hard cash was needed now. To get his hands on it, Auditor Gillett put into practice all the dodges he knew about railroad accounting.

Huge freight shipments for Cripple, sent collect from all over the United States, arrived at Midland Station. Gillett collected the total freight charges, 95 per cent of which belonged to transcontinental railroads. When passengers and freight left Midland Station for Colorado Springs, Denver, and points east or west, Gillett collected the total revenues in advance. He used all these revenues to pay Midland Terminal construction bills. Interroad accounts are supposed to be settled within ninety days. Gillett didn't get around to settling many M–T accounts until five years later.

And so the M–T was getting built after all. But Moffat's Florence & Cripple Creek entered Cripple Creek town on July 2, 1894, far ahead of the M–T.[3] The F. & C. C. got an immediate stranglehold on the ore-hauling business from the best mines of Poverty Gulch and Gold Hill. It seemed as though the M–T would find lean pickings when it finally struggled into camp. But one day a very rich gold strike was made in a neglected section of the mining district — on Bull Hill's east slope south of Altman. Prospectors stampeded to the new area from the west slopes of Gold and Globe Hills.

Many rich veins were uncovered — the Pikes Peak, Golden Cycle, Hull City, Last Dollar.

Perhaps it pays to make mistakes. Collbran's $100,000 mistake when he started the M–T as a narrow-gauge line allowed the Florence & Cripple Creek to reach camp first and snag most of the ore business. The F. & C. C. engineers ran their road along the west side of the mining district where the richest mines seemed to be located. But the new finds on the east slopes of Bull Hill showed that the west side was not the richest side. Therefore, Collbran and Gillett ran the Midland Terminal straight for those rich east slopes of Bull Hill past the Buena Vista, Victor and Vindicator and on around Battle Mountain near the Independence, Strong and Portland.

They didn't complete this long loop around the mining district and into Cripple Creek town until December, 1895, eighteen months after the arrival of the F. & C. C. During these months the F. & C. C. earned its entire $800,000 construction cost, which was lucky for Dave Moffat. After the M–T got into camp, the F. & C. C. never earned another cent. It was not only that the M–T traversed all the best territory for ore shipments. The F. & C. C. was very costly to operate, because of its steep grades and constant washouts.[4] In '99, Dave Moffat called it quits and turned over the stock of the Florence & Cripple Creek to the victorious Midland Terminal crowd.

Collbran and Gillett do not deserve all the credit for creating the Midland Terminal. They were helped by a brilliant youngster, Albert E. Carlton, who would become in time not only King Bert of Cripple Creek, but one of the greatest promoters in the Rockies. Bert Carlton was born in Warren, Illinois, in 1866. He developed serious T.B. and moved to the Springs in '89 with his family. He took the usual rest cure, lost the use of most of one lung, and recovered. He tried to get an outdoor job driving a streetcar and spent some months clerking in Ed Giddings' department store.

As we have seen, Bert heard of Cripple Creek when Stratton tried to sell him a half interest in the Independence for $500. When Collbran started rebuilding the M–T toward Cripple in the fall of '93, Bert and his younger brother, Leslie, got out their bikes and rode up Ute Pass to look at the gold camp. The frenzy of the place fascinated them and they opened a small firewood and coal business. Bert would talk people into buying fuel and Leslie would deliver it on the back of the burro. This relation between the brothers continued all their lives. Bert would get the business and Leslie would deliver the goods.

Bert believed that transport was the key to power in Cripple, and that the Midland Terminal would defeat the Florence & Cripple Creek in the long run. He called on Collbran at the Palace Hotel and explained that he and Brother Leslie had received $10,000 each as grubstakes from their father, H. M. Carlton. Bert proposed to organize a wagon company to haul ore from the mines to the rails of the Midland Terminal.

If Bert's wagons brought a lot of ore business to Collbran's M–T, would Collbran give Bert a monopoly on the local delivery of freight arriving on the M–T? Collbran promised that he would, and the Colorado Trading and Transfer Company was born, in a shack of rough lumber at the southeast corner of Bennett Avenue and Fifth Street.[5] Bert Carlton began using his genius as a salesman at once. In a short time he induced many mine owners to let the Colorado Trading and Transfer Company haul their ore to the Midland Terminal railhead at Midland.

The Carlton boys were just two of an extraordinary group of well-educated, energetic young men from prominent families in the East, who began their careers at Cripple. There was Henry M. Blackmer, a Massachusetts blue-blood, smoother than oil and sharper than a razor. And Horace K. Devereux, the Princeton football star and polo player — a pleasant fellow when sober but a terror in his cups. And pink-cheeked Harry Leonard, a product of St. Mark's School and Columbia University. Harry drove the Cheyenne Mountain stage for some weeks before going to work in '92 as an ordinary miner at Cripple. And a sharp-faced youngster named Charlie MacNeill. At the age of twenty-two, Charlie knew more about milling metal than most of the experts from the Transvaal.

They were a lively bunch — all under thirty, all ambitious, all ready for a party at the drop of a hat. And it was this gang — generally described by other gold campers as the Socialites — who kept Cripple's bars and dance halls roaring during those early days when everything was wide open and policemen existed only to see that the fighting was fair.

The gang had a sort of leader, a tall, elegant young man of twenty-seven named Spencer Penrose, startlingly handsome and solid as a Hereford bull. His nickname, a childhood corruption, was Spec and it was Spec's fists that maintained order if the Socialites tended to get unruly. Spec was one of seven sons of Dr. R. A. F. Penrose, a prominent Philadelphia physician whose great-great-great-grandfather was a partner of William Penn. Spec graduated from Harvard in '86 and spent a period in New Mexico looking for silver mines and raising fruit. The Colorado Springs real estater, Charlie

Tutt, had been a boyhood friend of his in Philadelphia. When Charlie located the C.O.D. Mine at Cripple in '91 he wrote Spec about it. Spec did not reply but one day early in December of '92 he turned up at Charlie's real estate office in the Springs.

In his quiet, offhand, tumbling speech, Spec told Charlie that he had made $2000 in a big grape deal at Las Cruces, New Mexico, but had spent most of it in a grand tour of the Far West. Charlie suggested that he take a shot at Cripple Creek and offered him a half interest in the Tutt real estate business for $500. Penrose accepted but Charlie never received his $500. As Charlie said later, "Since my business in '92 wasn't worth a plug nickel, I didn't have the nerve to collect anything for it."

During the week following, Charlie introduced Spec to Colorado Springs society. Spec tried to stay on good behavior for Charlie's sake. He got into trouble only once — a brisk brawl with Harry McKean in the main lounge of the Cheyenne Mountain Country Club, because McKean was teasing a little man named Shiner Casement.

In January of '93, Spec went to Cripple Creek to handle the affairs of Tutt & Penrose up there. He moved into bachelor quarters with Harry Leonard in a cabin high on Prospect Street near the reservoir. In March the firm of Tutt & Penrose was named agent for the Hayden Placer Company, and then a couple of leasers struck rich ore at Charlie Tutt's C.O.D. Mine. In a fever of enthusiasm, Spec wired his older brother, Boies, for $10,000 to buy a sixteenth interest in the C.O.D. Boies wired back $150 for rail fare home to Philadelphia. Spec refused to return. Instead, he put the $150 into the C.O.D., and later gave Boies $10,000 as a return on his "investment."

Spec wrote a glowing prospectus about the C.O.D. which he distributed copiously in Colorado Springs and Denver. One day the C.O.D. filled up with water. This event inspired some of Spec's friends at the El Paso Club to issue a rival prospectus entitled, "The Tenderfoot's Delight Mining, Milling and Transportation Company." Part of the text read: "The C.O.D. Mine is elevated two miles above sea-level and consequently the grade of the ore expected to be found will be very high." And then: "A large flow of water exists in this great mine, which when pumped to the surface to a canal which is projected from Cripple Creek down the mountain to Colorado Springs, will form an important artery of commerce."

Penrose was a hustler as a real estate salesman and he did not suffer from modesty in writing ads for the *Cripple Creek Crusher* about the firm of Tutt & Penrose. A typical ad in March of '93 read:

BUY A BLOC OF LOTS IN CRIPPLE CREEK FROM TUTT AND PEN-ROSE AND NET ENOUGH TO GO TO THE WORLD'S FAIR!

Another Penrose ad some weeks later read:

TUTT AND PENROSE ARE RECORD BREAKERS IN SELLING REAL ESTATE. LIST YOUR PROPERTY WITH THEM AND THEY WILL SELL IT BEFORE YOU LEAVE THEIR OFFICE!

Profits rolled in on the firm from the sale of Hayden Placer lots and from expert promotion at the new town of Gillett. Charlie and Spec spent part of them putting up a large building at Bennett Avenue and Third Street. They bought and leased the Myers Avenue building known as the Topic Dance Hall. They were agents for many absentee owners and Spec had to hire more and more office help, especially in the matter of collecting rents. One of their clients owned the parlor house which was rented to the Denver madam, Lola Livingston. One day a Harvard classmate of Spec's asked him for a job. Spec put him on collections and started out with him at 7:30 A.M. the next morning, to show him the ropes.

Spec's classmate looked spick-and-span as the two left the Tutt & Penrose office at 335 Bennett in a buckboard. He wore a black pin-stripe suit, wing collar and bowler hat. The first stop was Lola Livingston's place. The new man entered the parlor house to collect the forty-five dollars due. Spec waited outside in the buckboard.

He waited and waited and waited. Then he dropped in the Topic Dance Hall for a cup of coffee. He emerged just as his collector was stepping blithely down the steps of the parlor-house porch.

"What in the hell have you been doing?" Spec yelled at him. "It's almost 8:30. You've been in there forty minutes! Did you get the money?"

Spec's Harvard classmate grinned — a coy kind of grin. "Not exactly, Spec."

"What do you mean, not exactly? How about that forty-five dollars?"

"Now, Spec, don't be mad. I had a long talk with Miss Livingston. We decided I ought to take it out in trade."

Spec didn't fire his collector — not right away. Any man who could enter Lola Livingston's at 7:30 A.M. and stay forty minutes deserved a certain consideration.

The Socialites were by far the most attractive group of males in Cripple Creek. The camp's prettiest girls — professional and amateur — gravitated toward them naturally. The most striking among the amateurs was a husky, horse-crazy creature from Colorado Springs, named Sally Halthusen, daughter of the prominent sheep raiser and grain man, Herman Halthusen. Sally came to Cripple in search of a husband wealthy enough to supply her with the finest horse-flesh that money could buy. She was a big, beautiful blonde, and she had an additional attraction in her reputation as a *femme fatale*. People said that a Denver father had paid her $10,000 in '92 to break an engagement with his son.

For many months Sally had a fine time playing with all the Socialites, waiting for one or another to make a million dollars so that she could marry him and get started on the horse farm. One of the prettiest sights of early Cripple was Sally astride her magnificent white horse as he pranced gracefully past Johnnie Nolon's on the way to Charlie Mac-Neill's or Harry Leonard's. Sally had only contempt for lady-like sidesaddles.

But she lacked patience. None of the Socialites wanted to marry right away. And none of them seemed to be acquiring an immediate million. So she went off and married Tom Gough, a Springs confectioner who had a mine or two at Cripple.

If she had waited and had managed to marry almost any one of Spec's crowd she would have had the wherewithal to buy the best horses in the world. Before their careers ended, Penrose, Charles MacNeill, Verner Reed, Harry Blackmer and Harry Leonard would accumulate worldly goods almost beyond computation — well over $100,000,000 worth. Glamorous Sally missed her chance all right, but there is a monument of sorts at Cripple to her memory. Up near Mount Pisgah Cemetery her white horse lies buried. The tour guide will show you the place.

Old Man Stratton paid little attention to the extracurricular activities of the Socialites, though he was amused when Charlie MacNeill stole Jimmie Burns' current girl for no better reason than to win a bet from Spec. To Stratton the Socialites were just a bunch of wild Indians and yet he was impressed and interested when Spec came to him for support in a scheme to start a sampling works. A sampler is an outfit that buys ore from small mine owners, the price paid per ton being determined by assay samples. Stratton knew that many owners of undeveloped mines could not afford to ship their ore to a smelter or a mill. A sampler in the district would be a great help to them. Stratton went along with Spec's plan, Springs bankers advanced money, and the Tutt-Penrose outfit — the Cripple Creek Sampling and Ore Company — was set up along the F. & C. C. tracks south of town.

For a time, Stratton advised Spec and Charlie Tutt to ship their sampler ores to Pueblo for refining. But all the while he watched events at the experimental chlorination plant at Lawrence below Battle Mountain built by Joseph R. Lamar, the Utah mining king. Chlorination was a new process imported from the Transvaal. Stratton did not think it would work at Cripple. And it didn't work — at least not at first. In February of '94, Lamar sold the Lawrence plant to Ed Holden, the mill expert who had lured the Guggenheims into the smelting business at Leadville. Holden put a protégé of his in charge of the plant. The protégé was this fellow Charlie MacNeill.

To Stratton's astonishment, MacNeill began to get good results. He had come to Colorado in '85 at the age of fourteen when his father, Dr. J. E. MacNeill, moved to Denver from Chicago. Ed Holden took the teen-ager under his wing and kept him hopping from smelter to smelter — at Aspen, Leadville, and Denver. When silver prices fell, Holden sent MacNeill to Cripple to study gold milling. Charlie saw that stamp mills were useless there, which was why Holden bought the Lamar chlorination plant at Lawrence.

When Stratton was sure of MacNeill's milling ability he sent many Independence ores to Lawrence and induced Penrose to do the same with his sampler purchases. For nearly two years, Charlie MacNeill did a large milling business.[6] Then, in December of '95, the chlorination plant burned to the ground. By that time, MacNeill and Penrose and Tutt had become close friends. They had talked a lot about their futures. Gold mining, they had decided, was the bunk. There was much more money in gold milling. The burning of the Lawrence mill crystallized their plans. They decided to set up a series of mills that would eventually dominate the refining of low-grade ores from Cripple. As a starter, backed by Stratton, Irving Howbert, and some Philadelphians, they formed the Colorado-Philadelphia Reduction Company, with a big chlorination plant in Colorado City. During the next few years they would build or buy other mills in Florence and Canon City and would come to be referred to generally as "the mill trust."

The departure of Penrose and MacNeill from Cripple Creek early in '96 to live in the Springs left a big void in the gaiety of the place. And yet it shouldn't be imagined that the Socialites were the only ones with ideas to make life brighter. After all, it was not a Socialite but the hotel pioneer, Joseph H. Wolfe, who conceived and executed the only Grand National Spanish Bull Fight ever to be held in the United States.

CHAPTER XVIII

A Lot of Bull

THE LAST TIME we saw Joe Wolfe was in June of '93 when he left Cripple to duck his creditors. He went to Oklahoma's Cherokee Strip, made a pile of money out of assorted skin games and returned to the gold camp a year later as manager of the Palace Hotel.[1] Everyone was glad to have Joe back. His bunco proclivities caused pain at times, but even so Cripple had missed his merry black eyes, flashy vests and vast sombrero, to say nothing of the fun of wondering what he would do next.

Early in July of '95 Joe read in the newspapers that Secretary of Agriculture Morton was trying to force down the high price of meat in the United States by permitting free entry of Mexican cattle into Texas. At about the same time Joe struck up an acquaintance with an out-of-work Wild West performer named Arizona Charlie Meadows, a thirty-one-year-old cowboy who had spent several seasons with the Harmston and the Wirth Brothers circuses.

Charlie Meadows was seven feet tall, built like Hercules, and he wore long flowing hair and an early-day scout's costume with leggings. He told Joe Wolfe that he was tired of doing tame pony tricks and wanted to stage a real Wild West show with steer-busting, bulldogging and other acts using wild animals.

Right away Joe thought of Secretary Morton's edict on the free entry of Mexican cattle. That meant that you could bring in bulls — even fighting bulls. If you imported fighting bulls and Spanish bullfighters you could put on a bullfight. Joe told Charlie Meadows that no real bullfight had ever been held in the United States and that the Cripple Creek district was the perfect place for it. Charlie liked the idea and the two men formed a bullfight company with Joe as president and Charlie as producer. Two Cripple Creek merchants advanced $5000 and Bert Carlton agreed to supply hay to the bulls on their arrival.

Cripple Creek town had nothing like an arena but Tutt & Penrose had laid out a race track at Gillett along the Midland Terminal in West Beaver Park. Gillett was four miles northeast of Cripple Creek, and still closer to the Bull Hill communities. Joe hurried to Gillett, rented the race track and appointed all Gillett officials to the board of directors of the Joe Wolfe Grand National Spanish Bull Fight Company. Meanwhile, Charlie Meadows went to Colorado Springs and to Denver and held press conferences during which he announced that the bullfights would occur at Gillett on August 24, 25, and 26. Then Wolfe and Meadows departed for Chihuahua, Mexico.

The bullfight announcement set off explosions of protest in Colorado Springs. The chief exploder was Francis B. Hill, local secretary of the Colorado Humane Society. Hill had concluded a successful campaign to prevent the docking of horses' tails, and he was full of confidence and righteous energy. In addition to stirring up anti-bullfight sentiment in the Springs, Hill sent angry telegrams to National Humane Association officials. He inspired the following editorial in the *Colorado Springs Gazette,* dated August 8, 1895:

The recent announcement that a man from Cripple Creek is in Old Mexico securing an unparalleled aggregation of unforeseen attractions or words to that effect for the coming spectacular carnival at Gillett lends additional interest to a letter which we find in the *New York Tribune* to Secretary of the Treasury Carlisle by Mr. William Hosea Ballou, vice-president of the American Humane Association: "Sir: It is announced that ten bulls have been shipped from the City of Mexico to the Atlanta Exposition for the purpose of giving exhibitions of bull fights. I am informed by counsel that my appeal to President Cleveland from your department's decision admitting these bulls acts as a stay. You should, therefore, hold the bulls at the frontier port of entry, pending the decision of the President. Inasmuch as your decision has had the effect of encouraging the importation of bulls and as bull fights are being announced in various quarters of the country in consequence, I have no reason to believe that the President will uphold your decision, which was a misconstruction of the tariff law which, in effect, excludes the importation of all things of immoral use. Certainly, if you admit bulls pending the decision of the President, I am of the opinion that you will be liable to impeachment at the next session of Congress."

Then came the *Gazette's* summation:

If it be illegal to import bulls for fighting at the Atlanta Exposition, surely it must be illegal to import them across the border for fighting at the Gillett Exposition. Here is a chance for Francis Hill of the Humane Society to write to the Secretary of the Treasury, informing him that it is proposed to import bulls for the same purpose of fighting and invoking the aid of his department to keep them out of El Paso County.

Francis Hill did write the Secretary of the Treasury and he received a reply that no bullfight would take place at the Atlanta Exposition or anywhere else in the United States.

Joe Wolfe read this letter from the Secretary upon his return from Chihuahua, but it didn't dampen his enthusiasm about his own bullfight. Joe had completely rebuilt his appearance, transforming himself from Missouri Joe into Spanish José. He wore a black Spanish cape so loose that he had to adopt an oratorical stance to keep it from falling off. Speaking with a strong Spanish accent, he stated that Charlie Meadows had bulls. He scorned a suggestion that Francis Hill, or even hired four of Mexico's finest bullfighters and ten Cazaderia Hill's superior in Denver, Secretary Thompson of the Colorado Humane Society, could stop the fight.

On Monday, August 19, Joe and Charlie Meadows led an army of fifty carpenters to the Gillett race track and started building a 5000-seat amphitheater. Joe's design called for a bull pit 250 feet square enclosed by a log stockade. Above it the spider web of seats rose in twenty tiers. Joe put another army of men to work papering the saloons and shaft houses of the district with posters, offering bullfight tickets at $2, $3, and $5. All the while, Joe was getting hourly warnings from Francis Hill and other members of the Humane Society to call off the fight if he wanted to keep out of jail. Joe ignored the threats because he had inside information that Governor McIntire was not inclined to interfere, and neither was Sheriff Bowers.

Joe knew, too, that he had the tacit support of a lot of Cheyenne Mountain Country Club fellows like Charlie Tutt and Count Pourtales who couldn't stand the sight of Francis Hill because Hill had clamped down on pigeon shooting at their Country Club range. With the secret encouragement of these country clubbers, Joe asked the city fathers of Colorado Springs for permission to participate with his whole troupe of bullfighters in the Third Annual Flower Carnival

1894. Spencer Penrose (second from left), Philadelphia aristocrat, did more than just enjoy Cripple's gay life. Among other things, he and his partner, Charlie Tutt (right), built the Cripple Creek sampler. At left is Bela Kadish. Edward Newhouse stands between Penrose and Tutt.

1894. These were the sort of striking miners, mostly residents of Altman, who seized a dozen square miles of the United States and held them against all comers for four months.

Photo by T. H. Routh

1894. Altman, at 10,620 feet, must have been one of the most thrilling spots on earth in which to live. When blasting occurred there, Pikes Peak itself (extreme left) seemed to tremble and housewives took down their washing so that it would not be torn by flying gravel. Sometimes they took it down to avoid flying bullets from saloon brawls.

Denver Public Library Western Collection

1895. Matador Marrero got plenty of action out of this West Four-Mile bull during Señor Wolfe's epic bullfight at Gillett. Charlie Meadows rides at right, his brother at left. Standing by is Banderillero Carlos Garcia.

to take place on August 22. This colorful affair, conceived by
Tom Parrish, consisted of a parade led by Marshal Dana, Captain Gathright, the Fort Logan army band, a Fort Logan
regiment in full dress and a mile or so of flower-decked carriages bearing beauties like Nina and Gladys Crosby and
handsome males like Spec Penrose and Charlie MacNeill.

The city fathers very nearly granted Joe's request, but the
word got around and immediately the town was the scene of
many mass meetings in hysterical opposition to bullfighters.
The attitude at these meetings was summarized by a *Gazette*
letter signed "A Woman":

> It can be nothing else than a blot upon the reputation of
> Our State and of El Paso County if this monstrous troupe is
> allowed to disport itself in public. We of Colorado Springs
> pride ourselves upon our interest in education, culture and
> all advancement. Then let us protest against the retrograde
> movement toward the dark ages. May we redeem ourselves
> by keeping bull fights from our borders and may we keep
> our Flower Carnival within the bounds of Refinement and
> Beauty.

Joe dropped his Flower Carnival request, but he didn't
feel badly because the bullfight was getting much free publicity and nobody could agree on a plan to stop it. All the
authorities were passing the buck. A Springs church petition
against the fight was delivered to Sheriff Bowers, who referred
it to District Attorney Harry Blackmer, who referred it to
Francis Hill, who referred it to Humane Society Secretary
Thompson in Denver, who referred it to Governor McIntire.
The Governor sent it back to Sheriff Bowers, without comment.

Thus the petition was locked in a harmless circle and Joe
was able to stage an informal carnival of his own at the

Santa Fé depot in the Springs when his bullfighters arrived
from Chihuahua on Friday morning, August 23. In the afternoon, Joe introduced his troupe to the people of Cripple
Creek by means of a gala parade down Bennett Avenue. Joe
borrowed Sally Halthusen's white horse to lead the parade,
and behind him, in individual carriages, rode the celebrities
advertised on the bullfight posters — the Great José Marrero,
the Matador; Señora Marrero, "the only lady bullfighter in
the world"; the Superb Banderilleros, Carlos Garcia and
Antonio Sentrea; and the Incomparable Picadors, Arizona
Charlie Meadows and his brother, Kid Meadows.

Nobody would have guessed from Joe's triumphant expres-
sion as he led his parade that he had struck a snag in his
arrangements. The bullfighters were supposed to bring ten
Cazaderia bulls with them from Mexico, but they informed
Joe upon arrival that the bulls had been refused entry at the
Texas border on the orders not only of Secretary of the Treas-
ury Carlisle, but also of Secretary of Agriculture Morton.
When the Cripple Creek parade was over, Joe sent Charlie
Meadows and Alonzo Welty galloping toward West Four-
Mile in search of native bulls to replace the Mexican animals.
Alonzo appealed to ranchers John Witcher, Whart Pigg, Bob
Witherspoon and the Grose boys. Before Friday night ended
they brought in seven or eight bad actors to the Welty ranch
and boxed them up ready for transfer to the Gillett arena
next morning.

The great day, Saturday, August 24, was sunny and yet
cool at Gillett in its broad valley 4000 feet below the summit
of Pikes Peak. From mid-morning, all the dusty roads out of
Cripple Creek, Victor, Altman, Elkton and Goldfield were
crowded with pilgrims headed for Señor José Wolfe's *corrida
de toros*. A special train from Denver and Colorado Springs

puffed into the Gillett station of the Midland Terminal. Around the main entrance of Joe's spidery amphitheater were five rows of gambling, saloon and bunco concessions, all managed by Soapy Smith, Denver's bunco king.

Joe made a bad mistake when he sold the concession rights to Soapy. Before the bullfight was to start at 2 P.M., Soapy fleeced many miners of everything they owned and they couldn't buy tickets. Even so three thousand people passed into the arena and watched intently when El Presidente Wolfe took his place in a special raised box with a "bugler" in a dazzling uniform at his elbow. Joe knew that a real bull-fight had to have a bugler. When he couldn't find one he hired a flute-player from the Butte Opera House.

El Presidente Wolfe wore a black Mexican sombrero, a green velvet suit dotted with many silver buttons and high patent-leather shoes. His face grew stern and proud as the flutist called the Grand National Spanish Bull Fight to order with a spirited passage from *Carmen*. Matador Marrero, his bullfighting wife, the two banderilleros and Los Picadores Meadows lined up in the bull pit facing El Presidente.

With a dramatic toss of his head, José Wolfe threw to the matador an iron peg, symbolic key to *el toril*. The first bull came charging from the pen beneath Joe's box. He was pretty mad, having had nothing to eat since leaving West Four-Mile the night before. He had had nothing to eat because Bert Carlton had refused at the last minute to deliver hay at the arena on credit.

The banderilleros plunged their darts into the neck of the bull as the big crowd of miners cheered and stamped. Garcia and Sentrea looked the part of *toreros* all right, with their long hair in queues and their crimson capes, but they weren't sure that this bull knew the classic rules of bull behavior and they spent too much time arguing with each other in excited Spanish. The picadoring Meadows boys did better with their lances, and soon the amateur bull was in a state of real professional anger. Then Matador Marrero moved to the center of the ring for the finale.

For two minutes Marrero stood motionless watching the bellowing animal, his satin costume of black and gold setting off his trim figure. The audience fell silent, caught in the peculiar mood that a fine matador could create, even on the American slopes of Pikes Peak. At last the bull focused on Marrero and charged. Marrero did not move, passing the bull around him with his cape. After several more passages, Marrero sent his barbs home with a sharp click. The bull lurched away. José Wolfe blew his silver whistle. Marrero received his rapier from Kid Meadows. The bull, very weak now, made a last charge. Marrero thrust his rapier from above to the heart and the bull fell dead.

At this moment, El Presidente felt someone tapping him on the shoulder. He turned to find Sheriff Bowers standing there. Bowers told Wolfe that he and all the bullfighters were under arrest for cruelty to animals, on the complaint of Francis Hill and the Humane Society. Joe yelled to Charlie Meadows to keep the show going. He led the Sheriff from the arena to the *toreros'* dressing room where Lou Lambert, the Gillett constable, was waiting.

The constable, a director of the Joe Wolfe Grand National Spanish Bull Fight Company, told Bowers that he could not arrest the bullfight troupe on El Paso County warrants because all of them had been in custody of the town of Gillett since morning. Bowers agreed that the constable had a prior claim to the *toreros* and he confessed off the record that he was interfering only to clear himself with the Humane Society. However, he insisted that the constable take Wolfe at once for trial before Gillett Justice of the Peace Keith, another director of the Joe Wolfe Grand National Spanish Bull Fight Company. The judge acquitted Wolfe of cruelty to animals and levied five-dollar fines on the three Mexican men, the lady bullfighter and the Meadows brothers — a total of thirty dollars. Wolfe tried to chisel the sum down to $27.50 but Judge Keith stood firm.

Having managed to put on the Saturday performance against all opposition, Joe expected another big crowd on Sunday. But he overestimated the market. Less than three hundred people turned up Sunday afternoon, and maybe it was just as well. Three of the West Four-Mile bulls refused to fight. The fourth and fifth bulls charged a few times without enthusiasm and were killed by Matador Marrero in a lackadaisical manner.

Receipts for the Sunday fight were far below expenses and Joe Wolfe canceled the Monday show. Nevertheless, he had the satisfaction of staging two complete grand National Spanish Bull Fights in which three bulls were killed strictly according to Spanish rules and against the wishes of the Secretary of Agriculture, the Secretary of the Treasury, numerous heads of the American Humane Association and leading churchmen in Colorado Springs. Members of the Cheyenne Mountain Country Club were happy and the anti-bullfight faction was torn with internal recriminations.

But Francis Hill succeeded, at last, in bringing *los toreros* before the bar of justice. On Tuesday, August 27, 1895, District Attorney Harry Blackmer filed this information with Judge Ira Harris of the District Court:

> That Joe H. Wolfe, José Marrero, Carlos Garcia, Antonio Sentrea, Charles Meadows, Kid Meadows, Sherman M. Bell

and F. W. Weinberg on the 24th day of August, 1895, in El
Paso County, did then and there unlawfully torment, tor-
ture, unnecessarily and cruelly beat and needlessly mutilate
and kill one animal, to-wit, one bull: Contrary to the form
of the statute in such case made and provided and against
the peace and dignity of the said people of the State of Colorado.

The whole bullfight company spent Wednesday, August
28, in the Springs clink which took on a gala air as dozens
of lovelorn lassies gazed through the bars at Matador Marrero
and at Charlie Meadows, a glum giant now with his long hair
held on top of his head with hairpins.

Joe Wolfe, the two Meadows boys and the financial backers,
Bell and Weinberg, were able to raise bail and were released
the next day. A week later, at the insistence of Señor Casimiro
Barela, Mexican consul in Colorado, the trials of all the
principals were held before Judge Harris. The Americans
were acquitted. Matador Marrero was fined sixty dollars,
which he paid, and departed in haste to make a bullfight date
in Chihuahua. Banderilleros Garcia and Sentrea were fined
$52.50 each. Since they had no money for fines they were
slapped back in jail, to the great satisfaction of Francis
Hill.

His satisfaction didn't last long. When he picked up the
Gazette next afternoon he read that the Cheyenne Mountain
Country Club would offer, on September 13 and 14, an
"Arizona Charlie Meadows Wild West Show," proceeds from
which would be used to pay the fines of the jailed *toreros*.
This Country Club show was doubly insulting to Hill. The
Meadows brothers included in it the inhuman bulldogging
of steers and roping of calves, both at the very top of the
Humane Society's prohibited list. As a final humiliation to

Hill, the show was a howling success — so much so that it was repeated two weeks later at the Wheel Club in Denver.

Joe Wolfe, of course, won immortality by staging the only Spanish bullfight ever to be held in the United States.[2] But that didn't save him from bankruptcy and disgrace. For a few weeks after the bullfight trial he stayed in Cripple Creek seeking to come to terms with his creditors. Then he had to flee for the second time, one jump ahead of Sheriff Bowers. He went beyond Oklahoma this time, winding up first in Florida and finally on Broadway in New York, where he operated a flashy restaurant for some years.

He was gone but not forgotten. For months the debate raged in Cripple Creek and in Colorado Springs as to whether Joe was hero or demon. A second endless debate involved the question of what constituted cruelty to animals.

Perhaps the last word on the subject was spoken by Cripple's pioneer assayer, N. B. Guyot, who concluded a spirited speech at Johnnie Nolon's with the summing-up: "Cruel to kill those bulls? Hell, yes! But there was a greater cruelty still, my friends. That cruelty was committed by Mr. Bert Carlton, the dastard hay merchant who refused to feed the starving animals on credit."

The bullfight did nothing to ease the hostility between residents of Cripple Creek and those of Colorado Springs, which had existed since the strike of '94. Eight months were to pass before a crisis occurred that brought the two communities together.

CHAPTER XIX

Purge by Fire

THE WEATHER was warm and sunshiny on Saturday morning, April 25, 1896. Residents all over Cripple were on their roofs pushing off the last of the snow that fell two weeks earlier. The wind was blowing up from Victor, but it was a pleasant soft wind. It helped dry out the boardwalks on Bennett Avenue.

Toward noon — as the gold camp learned later — a Topic bartender stopped at Levi Stobaugh's Mint Saloon near the Palace Hotel and had a glass of beer. Then he strolled east along the sunny north side of Bennett, past the flimsy false fronts of the Gold Dollar Saloon, the Turf Club, Saratoga Club, Tom Lorimer's Office Club, Ducey's Exchange, the Okay Shaving and Bath House, and the New York Chop House.

Perhaps he noticed across the street Alonzo Welty's stable, the Pueblo House, James Bald's Market, Harris Brothers clothes, and N. O. Johnson's Department Store — a branch of the fashionable larger store of the elite in Colorado Springs. The Johnson store looked out of place among so many ramshackle structures. It was built substantially of brick. Most of the others had been thrown together in a hurry during '92 and '93. They had been made of green lumber cut from nearby government land by fellows like

Sam Altman and Larry Maroney. The buildings now were in a bad state of dilapidation. The lumber in them was very dry. Cripple Creek town was a tinderbox of desiccated wood.

When the strolling bartender reached Weinberg's store at Bennett and Third he turned south and walked past Lampman's Undertaking Parlors and the Mush and Milk House to Myers Avenue. If he had looked eastward down Myers he could have seen a long line of jerry-built structures, including dance halls such as the Topic, Red Onion, the Bucket of Blood, Crapper Jack's and the Red Light. Beyond Fourth Street on Myers he could have observed a racial progression among the crib girls — first white French and Spanish, then Japanese, and finally Negro as Myers Avenue neared the M–T trestle just east of Fifth Street. Along the north side of Myers were five or six parlor houses with prim curtains. There were also thirty one-story cribs occupied by free-lance sporting ladies. On the south side of Myers near Fourth Street was the Butte Opera House which Otto Floto[1] ran for H. B. Levie, kingfish of Cripple's tenderloin.

The bartender crossed the intersection of Myers and Third to the frame building at the southeast corner, adjoining two junk shops. The Central Dance Hall was on the ground floor. He climbed the stairs to a second-floor room where his woman was ironing her frock in preparation for the afternoon's taxi-dance at the Topic. The two started to argue. He slapped her face. She came at him with a bowie knife. He grabbed her arm, and the two of them knocked over the lighted gasoline stove. Liquid flame spread over the wood floor. Three minutes later Cripple Creek residents heard Fire Chief Allen shoot off his revolver three times to call the volunteer firemen.[2]

The Central Dance Hall building burned so quickly that

some of the girls on the third floor were trapped. They came down on ropes which the firemen threw up to them. They dropped their cats, rabbits and supplies of laudanum to friends below. For thirty-five minutes the hose companies kept the blaze from spreading. But that amount of time took most of the water out of the reservoir, and the pressure failed. The warm south wind blew harder. Embers from the dance hall floated across the 68-foot width of Myers Avenue. The Topic Dance Hall caught fire. The Topic was two stories high inside, with wide galleries around the second-floor level giving access to curtained booths. The booths were empty this early in the afternoon, which was lucky, because the flames rose quickly to the galleries.

The Victor Fire Department arrived as the blaze jumped across Dance Hall alley and began to lick the backs of Bennett Avenue buildings. Firemen dynamited the shacks in a 200-foot stretch on the east side of Third Street, between Myers and Bennett. This prevented the fire from going west, but it went north and east full tilt, destroying almost everything on Bennett Avenue between Third and Fourth. Johnnie Nolon's big saloon went up, and the Cripple Creek Mining Exchange, the First National Bank and the post office.

From Bennett the fire raced north up the steep hill, wiped out thirty or forty close-ranked homes on Carr and Eaton Avenues, and swept eastward to Fifth Street, scorching the new depot of the Midland Terminal Railroad. Then the wind died down and the fire crept south, just missing the huge skeleton of the new National Hotel. The fire died about where it started, after eating up many Myers Avenue shacks between Fifth and Third — six one-girl cribs owned by Mother Jones and J. D. Bauman, Ella Holden's "The Library," Pearl Sevan's "Old Faithful," Lottie and Kittie's

Place, the big Butte Opera House with its balcony and peanut
gallery, Marie Pappalan's Abbey Saloon, and Arthur Con-
nell's Argyle Block.

The fire lasted only three hours. Though communication
with Colorado Springs was broken, people on the plains
knew that something serious had happened because they
could see the yellow haze rising back of Pikes Peak. On
that Saturday night, Mayor Hugh Steele of Cripple Creek
named a committee to find temporary quarters for 1500
homeless people. The fire had wiped out thirty of the town's
six hundred acres, and had caused a loss of $500,000, a quar-
ter of which was covered by insurance. Johnnie Nolon was
the heaviest loser. Next heaviest were Charlie Tutt and Spec
Penrose, owners of the Topic. The fire was over so quickly
that the townspeople as a whole had no time to work up a
panic.

Many of those burned out managed to get back into business very soon. Joe Finley and George Jordan, operators of
My Friend Saloon on Myers Avenue, erected a ten-by-twelve-
foot frame box on the street in front of their smoking ruin,
covered by a twelve-inch plank with oilcloth covering. They
were serving drinks by 8 P.M. Saturday. Florist F. Ziegler was
selling roses to dance-hall girls an hour later. The Cripple
Creek *Times* moved from the Argyle Block to a small job
press on Golden Avenue, and published as usual on Sunday
morning. Lumberman Larry Maroney began hauling material
for a new building to Johnnie Nolon's lot. Kittie Townley
had twenty men on the job Sunday morning throwing up new
one-girl cribs. J. C. Casey at 316 Myers had his piano player
beating out "Do You Like Tutti-Frutti?" even as the carpenters banged away at the corrugated iron enclosing his new
establishment.

By Wednesday much debris had been carted off and dumped in abandoned prospect holes. People were thanking their stars that they had escaped worse disaster. The bartender and his girl who admitted starting the blaze were released without so much as a fine. The incident was over. And then, at 1:45 P.M., Wednesday, Fire Chief Allen raised his revolver and gave the three-shot signal once more. Somebody had reported a fire in the Portland Hotel, at the southwest corner of Myers Avenue and Second. This rattletrap structure was a remnant of the old Windsor which Horace Bennett had built in '92. The fire had started in the Portland kitchen, when a maid overturned a pot of grease on the range.

A stiff wind, stiffer than the gale of the previous Saturday, was blowing up from the south. The drafty Portland burned with such fury that the roar could be heard as far as Squaw Gulch and Altman. This sound, more than the fire itself, caused a wave of fear to roll over Cripple Creek. People far from any present danger emptied their homes of possessions and tried to load them on any kind of transport — even baby carriages and wheelbarrows.

At 2:45 P.M., the Portland roof fell in with a hollow boom. Millions of embers scattered northwesterly halfway up the slopes of Mount Pisgah, and acted like incendiary bombs as they fell on houses. The Palace Drug Store and the Palace Hotel, at Bennett and Second, took fire and blazed a hundred feet in the air. The big boilers of the Palace Hotel exploded, badly injuring half a dozen fire fighters. Another shattering blast occurred at the Harder Grocery on Myers Avenue when seven hundred pounds of dynamite went off. Bennett Avenue was jammed with wagons and carts and carriages and whiskey barrels being rolled from storerooms by saloon owners. The explosions increased the nightmare as horses and burros bolted and tried to plunge out of the murk.

The wind kept blowing hard and the air was full of bits of floating fire. All the buildings on Bennett west of Third Street caught fire — ten saloons, Dave Moffat's Bi-Metallic Bank, the Monaco Restaurant, tea and grocery stores, harness and hardware shops, meat markets, laundries and stables. Only N. O. Johnson's brick store remained standing. Homes went up in smoke northwest of Bennett for nearly a half mile in West Cripple Creek, and as far north as Pikes Peak Avenue. The north-south streets swarmed with women and children climbing the hill to sanctuary around the reservoir at the top of town. Two blocks below the reservoir, fire fighters protected the Sisters of Mercy Hospital. Inside, the hospital stairways and halls were lined with injured being treated by Dr. Whiting and a dozen others.

Mrs. James D. Yambert and her daughter Florence were among the heartsick crowd at the reservoir who stared down on the destruction below. Mrs. Yambert had been in trouble for a fortnight. The April 12 snow had caved in the roof of her Carr Avenue house. Johnnie Nolon owned this house, but he had delayed fixing the roof. Now when Johnnie reached the reservoir and saw Mrs. Yambert, a grin lit up his Irish face. He shouted at her, "See how smart we were not to fix that roof!"

Just before nightfall the wind ceased. Thereafter it was easy to control the fire. But the weather turned cold as the sun sank behind Pisgah. Five thousand people were without shelter. All spare food, covering, cooking utensils and firewood had been consumed. Some men turned to looting to get food for their families. But this trend was stopped by Mayor Steele's fire committee, captains of which were Donald

Fletcher, J. Knox Burton, T. P. Airheart, and James Parker.

What helped the committee most was the fact that every-one knew real aid was on the way. As early as 3 P.M., Jimmie Burns was describing the fire by telephone to J. C. Plumb, Mayor of Colorado Springs. Gathered around the telephone at the Springs end were W. S. Stratton, Spec Penrose, Verner Z. Reed and Irving Howbert. Stratton, of course, knew every inch of Cripple Creek town. He knew from Jimmie's account that this was a critical time.

When Burns finished talking to Plumb, Stratton said, "We've got to move and move fast! No time to get money pledges. Charge everything to me. We'll divide the bills afterwards."

Thirty minutes later, Stratton and Company formed a Springs relief committee, with all duties assigned and out-lined. Stratton was chairman. He drove to the Midland depot and ordered a two-car special train. Irving Howbert hired twelve freight wagons and sent them to the Shields-Morley Wholesale Grocery. Volunteers there loaded twenty-five cases of canned beef, six cases of beans, six cases of condensed milk, twelve crates of crackers, a thousand loaves of bread. Stratton called at Giddings Store, N. O. Johnson's, and Perkins and Holbrook, cornering the local blanket supply. He sent five hundred pairs to Midland depot. Also 750 diapers. E. R. Stark, the butcher, and Alderman H. C. Mc-Creery collected 165 eight-person tents at Barnes and Sons. McCreery located a huge tabernacle tent at Colorado City.

By 5 P.M. Wednesday, Stratton's committee had delivered relief supplies for 2000 people at the depot. Fifty men loaded the stuff into the two boxcars. Two engines pulled the cars, stopping at Colorado City to pick up the tabernacle tent. At 6:15 P.M., the boxcars rattled up Ute Pass, making fifteen miles per hour, real speed for that 4 per cent grade. Sheriff Winfield Scott Boynton was in charge of the train. Spec Penrose was a volunteer brakeman, and Harry Johnson was up front helping to fire. At Divide the flyer was switched to Midland Terminal tracks for the last eighteen miles to camp.

The shivering crowd at Cripple Creek reservoir watched the eastern hills. They saw the glow of the train at Gillett, and again beyond Hoosier Pass. At 9 P.M., they whooped and whistled when the headlights appeared around Gold Hill. As the special raced down the slope it looked like Fourth of July with the fireboxes dripping coals and every wheel a circle of sparks from the grinding brake shoes. Both engineers let their whistles scream all the way down to the M–T depot at the east end of Bennett. A big crew of men with oil torches met the train. In the shadows of the torch-lights Bert Carlton had drawn up two dozen freight wagons to take supplies to the reservoir.

All that night Cripple Creekers distributed supplies from Little London's relief train. Others worked at repairing the water system, collecting firewood and organizing emergency services. Father Volpe had the pews moved out of the way at St. Peter's and the church was reserved for mothers and babies. Early Thursday morning the First National Bank of Cripple Creek opened for business in a charred ware-house. Charlie Howbert advanced pay checks to all workers at the Anchoria-Leland Mine. J. R. McKinnie did the same at the Moon-Anchor and many others followed suit. Every mine was closed so that the miners could help clear debris.

Meanwhile, Colorado Springs was almost as busy. At 2 A.M., Thursday, Stratton sent a second relief train clattering up Ute Pass. It slid into Cripple at dawn. W. S. Slocum, president of Colorado College, canceled classes Thursday morning.

The student body took to bicycles and called at North End homes for donations. Residents came across with a great variety of gifts: pots of jam, jars of vegetables and fruit, hard-boiled eggs, hams, old clothes, brandy, knives and forks, pots and pans. Stratton ordered up another dozen transfer wagons, placarded them with "Cripple Creek Relief" signs and put them to hauling to the depot the things gathered by the students.

It seemed magical that the effects of the catastrophe could be countered so quickly. Long before the ruined city ceased to smolder, everyone was fairly comfortable, the injured were recuperating. Within forty-eight hours after the second fire, 3000 homeless people had found lodging by doubling up with families throughout the mining district. Two thousand more were under tents in two relief camps and were eating two big meals a day plus a small breakfast of pork chops, hot cakes, coffee and biscuits. On Friday afternoon, Ella Holden resumed trade at her "Library." A tar-paper restaurant in the middle of Bennett Avenue advertised: "Strawberries and Pure Cream, 15 cents."

The burning of Cripple Creek brought tragic injuries to some people and financial ruin to others. But the town itself bounced back to normal quickly. Soon residents were declaring that the purge by fire was exactly what Cripple Creek needed. The burned buildings had been virtually worthless. When they were removed, immense tonnages of garbage and trash went with them. It would be possible now to enforce ordinances for a cleaner city.

A great benefit was the end of the feud between the gold camp and its well-heeled neighbor down the mountain. The generosity of Colorado Springs in shipping tens of thousands of dollars' worth of supplies to Cripple made the gold camp realize that rich people were not such unfeeling monsters after all. They were just folks like everybody else — just poor folks with money. And in the Springs nobody talked about "those terrible red-necks" or "those crazy anarchists" any more. They knew now that Cripple was composed mostly of men and women with virtues and abilities of the highest order.

Before summer had ended, businessmen in Cripple and investors elsewhere saw that the job of rebuilding the town in a solid way was a fine promotion stunt. Writers poured in to describe the transformation. As the smart brick structures with their imaginative gables rose on Bennett Avenue, people changed their attitude toward the place.

Before the fires the gold camp was regarded as a fly-by-night. An owner trying to sell his mine could give his prospect excellent geological reasons for its value. He could show to him, for instance, the splendid study, "Geology and Mining Industries of the Cripple Creek District," which Whitman Cross and Dick Penrose prepared for the United States government in '94 (Dick Penrose was able to examine the mines thoroughly because his brother, Spec, overcame the suspicions of the mine owners).

The Cross-Penrose report expressed the greatest enthusiasm for Cripple's future as a gold-producer. But there was the flimsy, disreputable look of Cripple Creek town. Why, the prospective buyer of a mine would ask, should a man sink money in a community that hadn't enough faith in itself to build a decent place to live in?

The new Cripple Creek was spectacular evidence of faith. The sprucing-up was general. The clubs, the churches, the homes, the parlor houses, the saloons, the dance halls, all went in for self-improvement. The building boom, of course, attracted new people. Once again, as in '92 and '94, the population rose rapidly — from 30,000 in May of '96 to 40,000 six months later.[3]

The growth was fine for everyone, but it brought some evil. The small underworld of professional bandits that had come with the strike of '94 became a big underworld. Feudin' and fussin' were very much on the increase. Undertaker Oscar Lampman watched the murder rate rise from one a month to two a week. Order was difficult to keep. For quite a while the police of the mining district couldn't handle the situation.

The Crumleys and Other Nice People

ONE OF THE PRODUCTION NUMBERS of *In Gay New York,*
which ran on Broadway in the last weeks of '96, was built
around a Gustave Kerker tune called "Cripple Creek
Bandits." The tune went over because it was timely. Everyone in the United States had been reading about Cripple's
bandits.

There were two rival gangs. One of them was run at
first by "General" Jack Smith, aided by such sweet-smelling
lads as the ex-convicts Jack McMahon and Ed Riley, and
the Mollie Maguire terrorist, Dynamite Shorty McLain, who
blew up the Strong Mine in '94. Another aide was Jack
Smith's brother George, manager of the Union Variety Theater in Victor.

Victor is a refined village today, but in the Nineties, when
high-stepping Jimmie Doyle of the Portland was its popular
mayor, Victor was a rough spot. Cripple Creek town had the
best gambling and the prettiest prostitutes, but Victor was
top dog in crime. It was a grand place for crooks. The Gold
Coin and Strong Mines were partly under Victor, and dozens
of other mines close by made good hideaways. The gangsters,
being also miners, knew this vast underground as you and
I know the streets of our home towns.

"General" Jack Smith got drunk in Victor one day, attacked Altman town singlehanded and freed the prisoners in the Altman jail. He was arrested in Victor on a warrant issued by Marshal Jack Kelly of Altman. After his release on bail, Smith walked to Gavin and Toohey's saloon in Altman exactly like a movie killer, his guns loose in their holsters. There, back to the bar, he waited for Kelly. Kelly arrived, *his* guns loose in their holsters. The two men drew. Smith's shot went wide, killing a member of his own gang, George Pabst. Kelly's shot struck Smith below the heart and he fell dead.

Then George Pabst's girl, a trombone-voiced giant called Hook-and-Ladder Kate, ran the Jack Smith gang for a year. Kate allegedly planned the holdup of a Wells-Fargo wagon at Grassy which was taking $16,000 from a Springs bank to the Bi-Metallic Bank in Cripple. Jim Gray and Joe Welch of the Smith gang stopped the wagon, unhitched the four horses and rode off on two of them with the swag. People admired their finesse until it developed that the Wells-Fargo driver was a Jack Smith gangster, too. Gray and Welch were arrested near Leadville, where they were living in a barn with two Myers Avenue girls, Liver-Lip Lou and Fighting Mag. They had parked the two horses near the barn and someone spotted the horses.

More bad luck depleted the Smith gang. George Smith and two others were stabbed to death during a Union Theater brawl. Hook-and-Ladder Kate committed suicide with morphine at Rose Gordon's Dance Hall. Then Henry McQuaan tried to assert the gang's dwindling authority by socking the bartender at the Green Light Saloon. Frank Lupton, the mining district's toughest cop, grabbed McQuaan, beat him to a pulp and began hauling him to the Victor jail. Seth

Ralston pushed in to free McQuaan. Lupton pulled his gun and shot. The bullet nicked McQuaan's arm, clipped off a hunk of Ralston's lip and put a hole through a Bryan campaign poster.

Lupton handcuffed Ralston to McQuaan and McQuaan to himself. A mob gathered at Victor jail to prevent Lupton from entering. He decided to take the train to Cripple Creek. The mob ran to the train and tried to uncouple his car. Lupton shot in the air and scared everybody. The train slipped around Squaw Mountain to Elkton, where another mob was waiting. Using his prisoners as a shield, Lupton held this one off. The mobsters pushed into the vestibule of Lupton's car. He shot into them, killing a man named Elmer Lumley, who was just out for a breath of fresh air. The mob dispersed in a hurry and the train moved on. Lupton delivered his prisoners to the Cripple Creek jail all right. And his feat crushed the morale of the Jack Smith gang for good.

The other gang, the Crumley gang of ex-deputies, centered around Sherman, Grant and Newt Crumley, whose father was said to be a Presbyterian minister in Georgia. The Crumleys settled in the Springs soon after the slaying of the infamous Daltons at Coffeyville, Kansas, in '92. The Crumleys may have been members of the Dalton gang. In '94 Sherman Crumley began to direct the activities of the Crumley gang in Victor. His chief aide was Bob Taylor and his best spotter was Grant Crumley. Grant, a handsome, popular man, ran saloons in Cripple Creek. He was a prominent Elk, like Spec Penrose and Jimmie Burns. Grant had a flock of girls but his favorite was Grace Carlyle, an angel-faced beauty. What Grace liked best was removing her clothes while dancing on top of Grant's bar. She was quite temperamental. When she tried to commit suicide with laudanum and a doctor saved her life, she did her best to beat him up. Once a mine owner's wife entered Grant's saloon and began talking to him. Grace stormed up. "Grant!" she shouted. "Stop scratching your behind in the presence of a lady!"

Grace worked very little for the Crumley gang. A bigger help was Bob Taylor's sister, Nell, who was married to Sherman Crumley. Another moll was Mrs. Haillie Miller. During the strike of '94, Haillie had been hired by a mine owner to go to bed with strikers and worm secrets out of them. Haillie was often too drunk to know whether she was in bed with a friend or an enemy. She got lots of information but was apt to be vague as to which side it applied.

One night while Grant was dealing faro at the Branch Saloon he noticed large sums of money flying around. He traced it to a visiting group of St. Louis businessmen who were about to leave for home. Grant sent word to Sherman. The Crumley gang stopped the midnight Florence & Cripple Creek train at the U-curve southeast of Victor. Bob Taylor handled the engine crew. Kid Wallace tied up the conductor and brakeman. A third gangster, O. C. Wilder, pushed porter Bill Watkins ahead of him through the Pullman car containing the St. Louisans. Watkins had to wake each of them and Wilder relieved them of their cash and jewelry. Sherman Crumley was the lookout.

After the holdup the gang withdrew to the Strong Mine where Taylor and Wilder were employed as guards. The jewelry was handed over to a fence, Louis Vanneck, who took it down to Soapy Smith in Denver for disposal. Louis Vanneck was a brother of the Frank Vanneck who was beaten almost to death by the strikers in '94. When Louis returned from Denver, he failed to collect what he considered to be his share of the holdup loot. He squealed, with the result that

Taylor, Wilder and Wallace went down to Canon City for a spell. Sherman Crumley was acquitted.

The gang decided to quit holding up trains and to confine themselves to more sedate forms of gangsterism like counterfeiting railroad tickets, rolling drunks and trimming tenderfeet at poker. They experimented also with the theft of mining supplies from hardware stores. Since these were hard to sell, they began using the supplies to mine ore themselves, in other people's mines. They worked up a few simple ways of selling the stolen ore and soon they realized that this high-grading was a wonderful way to make money fast.

But as their operations expanded it became impossible for them to control the racket. Miners by the hundreds took up high-grading and pretty soon most of them forgot that it was dishonest. Cripple's underground structure was the chief reason for the development of this huge illicit business which cost mine owners from one to two millions of dollars annually. Cripple's veins were innumerable. They could not be guarded. It was the easiest thing in the world for working miners to "scratch the seam," chip small pieces of ore from a rich vein and hide the high-grade in shoe tops or in secret pockets or in bags between their legs. Rich ore might contain from three to twenty dollars' worth of gold per pound. Experienced miners could haul off enough high-grade in their dinner buckets to add another dollar to their high wages of three dollars a day.

A high-grading miner didn't have to remove his stolen ore from the mine. He could park it somewhere in a drift and have it picked up by accomplices called night riders. This night-riding business was no fun. Guards might put a bullet into the rider without warning, or he might get lost for good in the labyrinth or he might stumble into a shaft and fall to his death. Harry Orchard, a labor terrorist whom we'll meet later, wrote of it:

> We had to climb down an old man-way in the Vindicator Mine — 900 feet down with the rickety ladders out in some places, and the water dripping down — and then go through old stopes and drifts 2000 or 3000 feet, find our high-grade and pack it back up that 900-foot shaft. This would take us nearly all night. I made about $500 extra money high-grading during my year at Cripple Creek.

To sell a pound of stolen ore, the high-grading miner would drop in at his favorite saloon in the evening and lay the packaged ore on the bar, receiving a claim check from the bartender. Around midnight an assayer would stop at the saloon and pick up the ticketed ore. Then he would remove the gold from the ore in his own small chlorination plant and would deliver cash to the bartender to be given to the high-grading miner the next night. The pay-off was at the rate of ten dollars an ounce, or half the official price — provided the assayer was *honest*. The remaining ten dollars went to the assayer and to the bartender.

Many high-graders were pillars of their churches and stern moralists who would rather die than commit the sin of entering a saloon. These churchmen parked their stolen ore at a haberdasher's or at a cigar store. Some miners were so fond of their good names that they passed their thefts on to their wives for disposal. The wives would give them to the laundryman when he called for the weekly bundle.

In some very rich mines where gold glittered along the walls of the stopes like jewels in Tiffany's, nearly everyone from the shift boss on down exercised the right to help himself. The skip man at the top of the hoist would aid solicitously a miner who fell down when he stepped from the hoist cage. The skip man knew perfectly well that the miner couldn't rise unaided because the stolen ore concealed in his clothes held him down.

There were infinite variations of ore theft. Leasers would pay royalty to mine owners only on low-grade ore. They would sell the high-grade secretly. Managers of samplers would adulterate the ore brought to them, by adding quantities of barren rock to it, paying for the ore on the basis of the adulterated assays. Presidents and other officers of mining companies would split the take with thieves working their own mines, thereby cheating the stockholders. Guards on boxcars transporting ore to the Tutt-Penrose-MacNeill mills at Colorado Springs or Canon City or Florence would throw off a few tons of high-grade during a stop somewhere, and recover it later. Thieves would lease a prospect hole near a bonanza and then break into the bonanza's ore bins by night. They would dump the stolen high-grade into their rented hole and haul it away next day as their own. More than once, by this accidental salting of a barren hole, the owners could sell their worthless claim at a high price.

High-grading from '95 on permeated gold camp society. Everybody seemed to be in it, from assayers to delivery boys, from bank tellers to collegians earning their winter tuition by ore theft in summer. High-grade was even dropped in collection plates at church. An odd part of the situation was that no law existed to prevent a miner from stealing ore, or an assayer from buying it. On the contrary, the law protected thieves. When Dan Styne was hauled before Judge E. C. Stimson for stealing ore from Stratton's Independence, the Judge ruled that ore was real estate and you couldn't steal real estate. High-graders could be prosecuted for the misdemeanor of trespass, but not for the crime of larceny.[1]

The Crumley boys were bad actors but they had many admirers. One of these, Miss Mary Hight, was inspired to bold action by their example. Mary was the highly respected daughter of Cripple's most respected storekeeper. One day she got a letter from a stranger, signed merely "John," asking her to meet him at 7:30 next evening in Dance Hall Alley. John proposed that they retire to his rooms close by, and next morning he would pay her ten dollars. Mary did not take the letter to the police or to her father or even to her fiancé, a bill-collector named W. S. Driver. Instead, she decided to teach "John" a lesson Crumley-fashion.

At 7:30 next night she waited for him in the shadows of Dance Hall Alley. A man approached, his head wrapped in a scarf. Mary raised a swamp-elm club and brought it whirring down, with all her strength, on the man's head. He stumbled backward and toppled into the ash pit of the Topic Dance Hall. Then he cried, "Ah, Mary, stop, stop!" It was, of course, not "John" but her innocent fiancé, W. S. Driver, who had just collected a bill in the alley. Mary never became Mrs. Driver. She learned afterward that the letter from "John" had been sent to her as a nasty joke by a Myers Avenue woman with whom she had had words in the post office.

Oscar Lampman, a Cripple Creek undertaker, was also impressed by the Crumley gang's derring-do. Oscar happened to be irked by Coroner Charles J. Hallett, who was using his position to get business for his own undertaking firm. When a Midland Restaurant dishwasher died, Lampman hauled off the body before Hallett could arrive. Hallett got a writ of replevin signed by Judge Brewster, and recaptured the dishwasher from Lampman's parlors. Lampman got an opposing writ from Judge Stimson and regained possession. Lampman took no chances this time. He hauled the corpse to Mount Pisgah Cemetery and buried it. When Coroner Hallett assembled his jury at Lampman's to view the remains, Lampman refused to divulge the new address of the dishwasher. However, he gave the jury a quart of whiskey and some glasses. After drinking the whiskey, the jury apologized to Lampman for bothering him, castigated the coroner and dismissed the case.

Cripple Creek's bandits caused plenty of excitement in the gold camp. But it was nothing compared with the excitement caused by the continuing exploits of Colorado's greatest mining king, Winfield Scott Stratton.

CHAPTER XXI

How to Make Ten Million Dollars

IT WAS NOT MERELY that the moody old man was ten times richer than the other twenty-seven Cripple Creek millionaires and near-millionaires.[1] What got everybody was his attitude toward money. It didn't mean a thing to him. As his mole-hill of gold grew into a mountain, the whole world crowded in to watch him do the expected. Maybe he would buy a Senatorship, as H. A. W. Tabor had done. Or he would buy a Countess in Paris. He would buy Russian necklaces and Arabian race horses and Italian paintings. He would buy a frosty palace at Versailles.

Stratton didn't buy a palace at Versailles. Late in '95, when he left his Wilson Creek shack and moved to Colorado Springs, he even refused a mansion in the fashionable North End. J. R. McKinnie, the cheery Santa Claus who had guided Stratton to Cripple in '91, set himself up royally at 1102 North Weber Street. Jimmie Burns bought a big place at 423 North Tejon Street, and planned a larger place on that coming street of streets, Wood Avenue. Sam Altman bought Count Pourtales' fine home.

And Stratton? He bought an unimposing frame house downtown, which he himself had built years earlier for Dr. Beverly Tucker. His return to the Springs created a

problem among the feminine arbiters of Little London society. They had known him as that morose but excellent
carpenter who had been so good at making any little thing
they wanted, such as a form to hang their corsets on, or a
secret cupboard for their matildas. How should he be treated
now? Money, naturally, could not buy a place in their
charmed circle. Certainly not! But Stratton's wealth was so
staggering that it did not seem like vulgar money. It was
more like a divine dispensation, entitling him to sit at the
head of any table.

Or so it seemed to some of the social ladies. Others said
No. As far as they were concerned, Stratton remained a
mere carpenter who smelled of whiskey just as Jimmie Burns
remained a profane plumber and Sam Strong a boorish roustabout. For a time the anxious ladies argued. A few called
at Stratton's home and found him polite but — and this
startled them — unwilling to allow them beyond the front
hall. A few asked him to tea. He did not show up. A few
condescended to speak to him on the streets. He acknowledged their greetings, but it was plain he didn't know who
they were. Then one brave soul threw caution to the winds
and invited him to the most exclusive dinner party that it
was possible to arrange. She received a stiff note of regret —
not from Stratton himself, but from his secretary, William
Ramsay.

And finally the truth dawned on the ladies. Stratton didn't
give a damn for the whole kit-and-kaboodle of them!

It was inevitable, of course, that Stratton should be drawn
into politics during one of the bitterest of presidential cam-
paigns, the McKinley-Bryan struggle of '96. Four years before,
he had supported free silver and Senator Teller. But in the
meantime he had inherited a mountain of gold. He must

realize now how foolish he had been to back silver against his own interest. Surely he would line up behind gold, McKinley and Senator Ed Wolcott.

And, Ed Wolcott thought, what a killing it would be to have Stratton in the Republican Party! As November approached, Wolcott wrote to Irving Howbert asking him to call on Stratton for a campaign contribution. Not a sensational amount — just a hundred thousand dollars or so. Irving did call. Stratton listened carefully as Irving described the virtues of the Republicans. Irving wound up with a hint that the Party would be honored to receive Stratton's financial help. Stratton said nothing, nor did he move to his desk to write that $100,000 check. But Irving was not unhappy. He was certain that he would find Stratton's check in the mail next morning.

There was no check next morning. Instead, Howbert and everybody else in Colorado read in the papers that Winfield Scott Stratton had come out for William Jennings Bryan. He not only came out for Bryan, but he placed on deposit at the First National Bank $100,000 in cash to be bet on Bryan if someone would put up $300,000 on McKinley. If Stratton lost the bet, that was that. If he won, the $300,000 would be given to the Colorado Springs Free Reading Room and Library Association.

News of this bet flashed around the world and for a week McKinley and Bryan found themselves losing much front-page space to Stratton. His bet was the largest ever offered by one man on an election. And to most people it seemed as peculiar an act as a man could commit. Why, if Bryan won and the United States resumed silver coinage at sixteen to one, Stratton's gold wealth would be cut in half!

A group of reporters arranged a press conference and

asked Stratton to explain himself. Stratton gave each reporter a slip of paper containing these words:

> I do not make the offer because of any information that I have on the election, but I have a feeling that Bryan is going to win. I am deeply interested in seeing Bryan elected. I realize that the maintenance of the gold standard would perhaps be best for me individually, but I believe that free silver is the best thing for the working masses of this country. It is because I have a great respect for the intelligence and patriotism of the working people and I believe that they will see their duty at the polls that I am willing to make such an offer.

The dignity and honesty of Stratton's statement thrilled the nation and sent a chill down the spines of the Republican managers. Up to then, McKinley's election seemed as certain as Christmas. Now the Republicans had qualms. To counteract the Stratton statement they made all sorts of motions to give the impression that they were delighted to cover Stratton's $100,000 bet. They never did cover it. Which was, of course, lucky for Stratton.

Through these years, Stratton had one friend who was utterly different from the Cripple Creekers with whom he preferred to associate. His earlier admiration for that prototype of Scott Fitzgerald, Verner Reed, increased. And he came to admire Reed not so much for his business brilliance as for his intriguing personality. Reed stopped often at Stratton's office on Pikes Peak Avenue. Stratton enjoyed talking to Reed about the Independence Mine and he told Reed secrets that nobody knew except his most trusted employees. Reed in turn told Stratton tales of the Indians of New Mexico whom he studied in his spare time with the Springs artist, Charles Craig. Stratton loved to hear Reed describe how he almost killed himself trying to sustain a four-day bear-dance with an Indian maiden.

One afternoon in '97, Reed walked into Stratton's office with a broad grin on his handsome face. He tossed Stratton a copy of his third book just off the press, *Tales of the Sun-Land.* This book was soon to be read with delighted horror throughout the country. It was the most sensational piece of sex writing that had been done in years. Stratton was deeply shocked when he read such paragraphs as this:

> She pressed her lips to mine, and seemed to drink in my very breath, and as she kissed me her form expanded into perfect womanhood. Her fair proportions, delicately moulded, were yet as strong as steel; her breast rose and fell in ecstasy, and her eyes sparkled with the light of love. The very elements seemed to grow beautiful with her; perfume floated in the air, and soft sounds, like the strains of distant music, fell upon the hearing. She twined her rounded arms about me, and from then I took no heed of time.

When Stratton finished *Tales of the Sun-Land,* he burned it in the ash pit behind his home.

Verner Reed got tired of wandering in New Mexico and began to investigate Europe. In order to do so, he opened offices for the sale of Cripple Creek mining stocks at 58 Lombard Street in London and also in Scotland. Business was slow because Europeans were interested in the gold mines of the Transvaal. But Reed did manage to sell the watery C.O.D. on behalf of Spec Penrose and Charlie Tutt to a French syndicate for $260,000. Also he helped to sell the Ingham to some Belgians and J. R. McKinnie's Moon-Anchor to an English group.

In London Reed met that American superman of the Nineties, John Hays Hammond, just after the famous engi-

neer paid a fine of $125,000 to the Boers for his part in the
Jameson Raid. Hammond had been mining for Cecil Rhodes
but he was *persona non grata* in the Rand now, and had
joined a London mine investment company, called the Venture Corporation.

Reed had a number of talks with Hammond about Cripple
Creek, and came to perceive that Hammond's elaborate show
of lack of interest in the place was faked. Bit by bit, Reed
learned that Hammond was worried about the political situation in the Transvaal and its threat to English gold mines.
What Hammond wanted was a spectacular gold mining company somewhere else, the stocks of which could be sold
readily to British investors if things went badly in South
Africa.

Hammond was a wily customer, but he could not match
Reed's subtlety. Reed began dropping in Hammond's path
nuggets of information which he alone possessed about Stratton's Independence. Hammond took notice. And before he
knew what Reed had done to him he wanted the Independence for the Venture Corporation more than anything on
earth.

When Reed got back to Colorado Springs and Cripple
Creek, he ran into T. A. Rickard, State Geologist of Colorado. Rickard had just returned from Australia, where he had
been examining the Kalgoorlie gold camp. He told Reed
that John Hays Hammond had asked him about the relative
merits of Kalgoorlie and Cripple Creek. Rickard confessed
to informing Hammond that Stratton's Independence was
the most promising mine he had ever seen.

Reed hurried to Stratton. He announced that Stratton
must sell the Independence to the Venture Corporation.
Stratton refused. Reed laid a fifty-dollar bill on Stratton's

desk. Would Stratton bet that he would not agree to sell the Independence within twenty-four hours? Stratton placed his fifty beside Reed's. Then Reed told Stratton that he could get $10,000,000 for the Independence, from the Venture Corporation, if Stratton would give him an option. Stratton felt suddenly feverish. From Reed's past performances, he knew that if Reed said $10,000,000 he would get $10,000,000. And what was $10,000,000 in the late Nineties? Income taxes did not exist. Most things cost a fifth of what they now cost. The equivalent today might be as much as $50,000,000.

When Reed left Stratton's office he had in his hand two fifty-dollar bills and an option to sell the Independence.

Reed returned to London. For many months he worked patiently on Hammond, and on officials of the Venture Corporation. The price of the Independence to them was not $10,000,000, but $11,000,000, since Reed placed a value of $1,000,000 on his services.

At first, Hammond declared himself totally uninterested in the Independence, even at a sensible price. Reed watched the approaching crisis in the Transvaal and kept after Hammond. In the fall of '98, Hammond suddenly asked Reed for a report on the Independence. Reed cabled T. A. Rickard, a man whom Hammond admired and trusted. Rickard examined the mine and reported that there was ore worth $7,000,000 just sitting around in the stopes waiting to be hauled away. And the mine was developed to a depth of only nine hundred feet! Stratton had removed from it ore valued at $3,837,360 for a net profit of $2,402,164. This profit of 63 per cent showed that the ore was incredibly rich.

Reed let the significance of Rickard's report stew in Hammond's mind through the early part of the winter. But in March of '99 Reed bore down. By then Reed and Hammond both knew that war in the Transvaal was imminent. The Rand mines were about to close. Reed told Hammond that this was his last chance to buy the Independence. Hammond bleated pathetically. Reed's price was outrageous. Hammond would buy Tom Walsh's Camp Bird Mine at Ouray, Colorado, instead. Reed knew how weak that bluff was. The Camp Bird wasn't half the mine the Independence was.[2]

And so Hammond gave in, recommending to F. W. Baker and other Venture Corporation directors that the Independence be bought for $11,000,000 — $10,000,000 to Stratton and $1,000,000 to Reed.[3]

And what about Stratton the while?

As Reed pecked away at Hammond in London, Stratton stayed home and gave no hint of what was afoot. He created the impression that the last thing he would ever do would be to sell his dream mine. When the news of Reed's sale leaked out, nobody in Cripple Creek or in the Springs would believe it. For weeks the *Colorado Springs Gazette* denied the story, even though columns on the sale had been printed elsewhere.

Early in the spring of '99 Stratton journeyed to London to sign papers with the Venture Corporation. He was feeling wretched, and he took along his doctor, David H. Rice, to treat his diabetes and liver trouble. In April he sent for his old bootmaker and manager, Bob Schwarz, to talk German for him while he underwent treatment in Carlsbad and Vienna. Then he took Schwarz to Constance, Switzerland, to visit Bob's sister and to buy her a home. He also gave her $20,000.

Stopping briefly in Paris, Stratton was bothered by reporters and by busted royalty looking for a touch, and by Springs tourists who thought he must be lonely. The J. G.

Shields family was there and the Frank Pecks and Jimmie
Burns' spinster sisters and many others, burning up Cripple
Creek profits. Stratton avoided them but he did see Verner
Reed, who, having reached the ripe old age of thirty-six, had
decided to retire with his million dollars, in Paris, and spend
the rest of his life in pleasant Bohemian pursuit of the arts.[4]

Stratton got back to the Springs in August of '99. His
health was worse than it had been when he went away.
Carlsbad and Vienna had done him no good. But what distressed him most was that the peace of mind he had enjoyed
during the first five years of his wealth was fading. He began
to have spells of black despair. The first spell descended
shortly before he set out for London. It was brought on
apparently by worry over the breakup of the lifelong friend-
ship between Jimmie Burns and Jimmie Doyle.

Money — the very thing Stratton possessed in fantastic
amounts — caused the breakup.

Stratton saw signs in '96 that the two Jimmies were on the
outs. In January of that year, Burns descended one morning
in the Anna Lee shaft of the Portland group, and inspected
stopes for two hours. He arrived at the surface, and eight
miners entered the cage from which he had stepped. As the
cage went down, the shaft caved in, killing the eight men
instantly.

Without consulting the other Portland directors, Burns
spent $100,000 recovering the eight bodies, and an even
larger sum compensating the families of the dead men. As a
result the Portland Company had to pass the March dividend.
Jimmie Doyle needed that dividend, and he expressed displeasure by hinting that Burns was negligent in letting the
eight men go down in the stope-weakened Anna Lee. Burns
staged an Irish tantrum and resigned as president of the

Portland, saying that maybe twenty-eight-year-old Doyle could do better. It took the combined diplomacy of Stratton, Frank Peck, and John Harnan to calm Burns and re-elect him president.

Eighteen months later, Burns, Peck and Harnan sided against Doyle and Stratton in an argument over the firing of a Portland super. Thereafter, Stratton seldom saw Burns and Doyle together. Burns spent his time running the Portland. Doyle concentrated on enjoying life as mayor of Victor.

The final break came in November of '98. Doyle sued Burns for $700,000 worth of alleged Portland profits which he claimed Burns had withheld from him. Since the Portland was incorporated in Iowa, Doyle sued in an Iowa court. Burns went to Judge Horace Lunt in the Springs and got an injunction restraining Doyle from going on with the suit. Doyle ignored the injunction and won a $700,000 judgment against Burns. This Iowa judgment made Doyle guilty of contempt as far as Judge Lunt was concerned. Lunt ordered Doyle to refuse the Iowa judgment or go to jail and stay there until he obeyed the Colorado court.

Stratton pleaded with Burns and with Doyle to stop the feud. He reminded them of their old days on Battle Mountain, of their struggles to get out Portland ore secretly, of the lawsuits they had won. He recalled how they had herded the three Burns sisters into their bedroom one day, pulled down the shades, and thrown on the bed $10,000 in gold pieces — the first time the girls had seen more than twenty dollars in one place.

The feud went on.

Doyle moved to Denver beyond Judge Lunt's jurisdiction. Stratton concluded that he would never return to El Paso County. But in a few weeks Doyle did return and voluntarily entered the El Paso County jail. He told newspapermen that he would rot in prison before he would give in to Jimmie Burns. And for seven months he did rot, sulking in his cell, smoking stogies and issuing blasts at Burns. In February of '99 he tried to be transferred to some other jail because smallpox turned up near this one. In March, when Stratton went to London, Doyle's loyal followers elected him for his third term as mayor of Victor. In June, jailer Lay's children found twelve nitroglycerin cartridges on the jail's cellar steps. Doyle implied that Burns was trying to blow him up. In July, Doyle accused Burns of getting illegal rebates from railroads and smelters patronized by the Portland.

Jimmie Burns said nothing at all. Finally, since neither Irishman would give in, the courts got together. The Iowa court set aside Doyle's $700,000 judgment against Burns, and the Colorado court dropped the contempt charge against Doyle. On August 3, 1899, after 209 days in jail, Jimmie Doyle was freed. He went to Victor, where he was met by the whole town and a sixteen-piece band. He was given a beer-and-pretzel reception bigger than that given William Jennings Bryan at Victor three weeks earlier.

Stratton knew that Burns and Doyle would never be friends again. Money seemed to bring only hatred and jealousy. Stratton's old lawyer of whom he had been fond, J. Maurice Finn, sued him for $28,000 damages for some imagined breach of contract. Finn was a Stratton specialist now. If anybody wanted to sue the old man, Finn was the lawyer to hire. Leslie J. Popejoy, the plasterer who had grubstaked Stratton in '91, sued him for half his property, claiming Stratton had defrauded him of his Independence interest by belittling the claim. Stratton proved that he did not know until '93 that the Independence was a bonanza. He had bought out

Popejoy in '91. Stratton could have won this suit easily, but he felt sorry for Popejoy. He paid him $40,000 to withdraw the suit.

Life, Stratton thought, was turning into an endless series of bitternesses. He couldn't even spend money to help others for fear his beneficiaries would turn around and sue him. But thank God for whiskey. It helped to take a nip every hour or so. And, now that he had ten million more dollars, it would be fun to see how fast he could get rid of it.

End of an Era

For christmas presents in '99 Stratton gave $50,000 to each of his key employees. He bought a half dozen homes for other employees. He gave $5000 to Bob Womack, whom he noticed shuffling by his office. He sent thirteen-year-old Louis Persinger to Germany to study violin (Louis became one of America's best teachers). He gave the City of Colorado Springs the ground on which the City Hall stands. He bought El Paso County Court House so that the county could build a new one. He bought the present post office block and gave it to the United States government for half its cost. He built a five-story building for the Colorado Springs Mining Exchange. He bought the rattletrap Springs streetcar system for $500,000 and made it the finest in Colorado, at a cost of $1,500,000. At the Cheyenne Mountain end of the line he built a public park with a bandstand and free concerts on Sundays. He paid his dues five years ahead as a member of the Carpenters' Union. He bought $2,000,000 worth of Denver real estate, including a $650,000 mortgage on the Brown Palace Hotel.

All told, Stratton unloaded $4,500,000 during the months following his return from London. But the poor fellow was making little headway against his mountain of money. He was barely keeping ahead of his income. He hadn't touched the $10,000,000 which he was realizing from the sale of the

Independence. What he wanted was a project on which he could really go to town.

He knew all along what that project would be — Cripple Creek again!

Ever since the publication in '95 of Dick Penrose's government report on Cripple's gold, Stratton had mused over Dick's theory that the district was created by the mushrooming of volcanic blowouts. Over the years Stratton charted the slant of Cripple's veins. He decided that these veins converged in depth. A spot existed a mile or so down, composed entirely of converging veins. That spot must contain ore a hundred times richer than the ore in his Independence.

The charts indicated that the center of this deep Pandora's box lay beneath a claim called the Plymouth Rock near the top of Ironclad Hill. Even before he sold the Independence, Stratton bought some claims near the Plymouth Rock — the American Eagles, the John A. Logan. After the Independence sale, he increased purchases until he was spending $10,000 every day. Before long, Stratton owned one hundred claims with a surface area of six hundred acres. The prices paid were pushed to dizzy heights by his own impatient buying. His total outlay came to $7,000,000. In addition he was putting out at the rate of $1,000,000 a year in development work.

Such spending had a delightful effect on the economy of El Paso County. The magic word of prosperity was Stratton, Stratton, Stratton! As a mark of appreciation, the Colorado Springs Mining Exchange gave a Stratton banquet. It was the biggest affair since the Republican spread for Irving Howbert in '94. It was held at the Hotel Antlers with a menu of bluepoints, lobster Newburg, small tenderloin à l'Independence, Champagne '93 Cazanove, Heidsieck & Company

Monopole. One hundred and sixty people came, including General Palmer, ex-Governor Adams and Mayor Robinson. Sixteen speakers made addresses praising Stratton. Thunderous applause for him went far into the night.

The only trouble was that the guest of honor failed to show up. Stratton, the *Gazette* reported, "was unable to attend, although his absence made the function resemble the play of Hamlet with Hamlet missing." Stratton's only comment afterward was: "I never dined out but once when I enjoyed it. That was on a quick trip to Mexico when my host couldn't speak English and I couldn't speak Spanish."

Stratton felt good about spending money in his own community. But part of his purpose was to keep his mind occupied, to try to stave off his despair. When the black mood came he asked himself what was the use of anything? What was the use of being rich? Had Cripple really done anybody any good? How many of those twenty-seven Cripple Creek millionaires were happy?

One day a young man hit pay dirt on Bull Hill, and was offered a good price for his claim. He wrote Stratton for advice. Should he sell or should he hang on, hoping for millions in the end? Stratton replied:

> If you get a chance to sell your property for $100,000, do it. I once gave an option on the Independence and Washington mines for $125,000, and a thousand times I have wished that the holders had taken it up. Too much money is not good for any man. I have too much and it is not good for me. A hundred thousand dollars is as much as any man should have if he wants to be happy and free from the bitterness and heartaches that come with great wealth. And I believe that a hundred thousand dollars is as much money as the man of ordinary intelligence can take care of. Large wealth has been the ruin of many a young man.

Stratton was writing from the heart. Just a week before, a tragedy occurred in Cripple Creek that saddened him as much as the Burns-Doyle breakup. Sam Strong was by no means a close friend. But Stratton was fond of Sam because Sam had been with him and McKinnie and Bill Gowdy and Burns and Doyle in those white tents on Battle Mountain. Though Sam Strong was blunt and crude and loud, he was a good fellow inside. Under ordinary circumstances he would have lived a decent life.

He could not live under ordinary circumstances. After finding the Strong Mine he sold it for $60,000 to Giddings, Lennox and Colburn. Then he bought Sam Altman's Free Coinage and other Bull Hill bonanzas. Soon Sam Strong had, as Cripple Creekers would say, "enough money to burn a wet dog with."

He had also three weaknesses. As a poor man, whiskey, women and gambling caused him no grief because he couldn't overindulge. Wealth changed that. The more gold he amassed, the more he drank and gambled and the more convinced he became of his sex appeal. Early in 1900 Sam was tangled up with so many women that he decided to marry one in self-defense — a gentle, admirable Altman girl named Regina J. Neville, aged nineteen. Sam was a burly thirty-eight.

At the close of the Neville-Strong wedding, a process server walked up to Sam and ordered him to appear in a $250,000 breach-of-promise suit brought by Miss Luella Vance of Goldfield. Luella said that $250,000 was the "sum necessary to alleviate her lacerated feelings and suffering which she sustains by the loss of Mr. Strong's companionship and to make her future life worth living."

Before Sam and Regina could leave on their honeymoon, Sam got another summons, this one on the part of Miss Nellie

Lewis of Cripple Creek. Nellie sued Sam for $200,000, declaring that he had been promising to marry her steadily since '93 — every time he had taken her to New York for a whirl, in fact. What she said next really caused a sensation. Sam, she swore, was the man who blew up the Strong Mine during the strike of '94. He had done this, she added, so that Lennox, Giddings and Colburn would feel like canceling their option on the Strong Mine.

Sam and Regina slipped off to Paris to let the hail of lawsuits abate. On their return, Sam spent a solid year getting in the clear. Nellie Lewis was awarded $50,000; Luella Vance's suit was settled out of court for $50,000. Sam stood trial for dynamiting the Strong Mine and was acquitted. Through these troubles Regina Strong supported her husband with all her strength and even kept him sober. But when he was free of the law he hit the bottle harder than ever. The suits had cost him a half million dollars. Unfortunately, he still had $750,000 left.

Sam Strong had many enemies. The most fervent of them was Grant Crumley. For a couple of years Grant ran a roulette wheel in the National Hotel, then opened his own place, the Newport Saloon, in the Mining Exchange Building, almost at the corner of Bennett Avenue and Fourth Street. Grant hated Sam in general. He hated him in particular, because Sam ran up a gambling debt of $2500 one night and paid him off with a check. Sam stopped the check next day claiming Grant's wheel was crooked. A week later he settled with Grant for $200.

Soon after, Sam went on a tour of the gambling houses. With him were his father-in-law, John Neville, and his secretary, Clarence Fitch. The trio left Johnnie Nolon's after midnight and ambled a block east to the Newport. Sam was drunk and quarrelsome. They stopped at the Newport bar. Neville pleaded with Sam to go home. Sam wanted to gamble and he moved through the bar into the gambling room where Bob Burns was running the wheel. By 5:30 A.M., when Pisgah was aglow with the rising sun, Sam was ahead $140.

Grant Crumley looked in from the bar. Sam shouted, "Whatsa matter, Grant? Running a straight wheel for a change?"

Grant withdrew. Sam staggered off to the toilet. Neville and Fitch went to the bar to talk to Crumley, who mentioned the $2500 check Sam had stopped. Sam, coming to the bar, caught the gist of the talk. He yelled at Grant, "Here, that's my daddy you're talking to!"

Grant apologized. As he did so, he removed his arm from the cigar counter on which he was leaning and put both hands in his pockets. Sam poured himself some wine. Suddenly he dropped his glass, drew his revolver and yelled, "Take your hands out of your pockets, Crumley, or I'll kill you!"

Neville and Fitch pressed in to restrain Sam. Crumley ducked behind the bar screen next the cigar counter. Then he emerged from the screen with a sawed-off shotgun which he held across the bar, two feet from Sam's head. Sam was so astonished that he dropped his revolver. The explosion of Crumley's shotgun rocked the room. The Number Four buckshot made a great hole above Sam's right eye.

Sam crumpled to the floor. Fitch knelt over him. Grant laid his shotgun across the bar. Neville ran down the deserted avenue to phone at Shockey's Drug Store. In a half hour the sheriff arrived and arrested Crumley. Doctors Crane and

Hereford came with a one-horse ambulance which carried Sam to his mother-in-law's home on Eaton Avenue. He died at 8:30 A.M.

At the jail Crumley called for a stogie and a slug of bourbon. To reporters he said, "I shot Strong because if I hadn't he would have shot me." Some months later, Grant was acquitted of murdering Strong.[1]

When Stratton heard about Strong's death he phoned Clarence Fitch and got the whole story. Then Stratton locked himself up in his downtown home on Weber Street and stayed drunk for a week. Cripple Creek gold!

The Strong tragedy hit him hard because he was worried sick already about two of his favorite young men. Stratton had been pleased as punch to see Frank and Harry Woods getting on well with their Gold Coin Mine, and their promotion of the town of Victor, and their Jack Pot and Wild Horse Mines. Nobody in camp was more honest than the pleasant Woods boys, or more generous. Frank and Harry paid top wages. They helped their men in trouble. They gave them an elaborate meeting hall in Victor, the Gold Coin Club. They built a rustic amusement center, north of Altman — Pinnacle Park — and equipped it with bear cages, a dance hall and a baseball diamond. They were exemplary citizens.

It happened that the shaft house of the Gold Coin rose right out of Victor town on Diamond Avenue.[2] As the Gold Coin went deeper, Frank and Harry had a time disposing of the dump rock. They couldn't dump the stuff in town, so they established a Gold Coin dump, 4000 feet away, in Arequa Gulch. They drove a $200,000 transportation tunnel from the Gold Coin to this dump. They built a $532,000 chlorination plant at the Arequa Gulch end of the Gold Coin tunnel, so that Gold Coin ore and dump rock could be handled in one operation. They built a $500,000 hydroelectric power system to run the electric tram cars in the Gold Coin tunnel.

Stratton watched these goings-on at first with paternal approval, then mild irritation, and at last with consternation. He realized that Frank and Harry were getting set to gobble up the camp. Nobody else was to have anything. Stratton simply couldn't recognize his boys any more. Their gentle, pious, unselfish personalities had changed completely. Two Dr. Jekylls had become Mr. Hydes. Frank and Harry had succumbed to greed.

They were buying mines in every direction. They planned to push transportation tunnels from the Arequa Gulch plant toward these mines. They increased their power supply to run all tram cars, mine hoists and interurbans, and to supply electricity for Victor and Cripple Creek. They bought from Bennett and Myers the old Grassy townsite for $180,000, and platted a new town, Cameron.

This great Woods empire sprawled from Victor east to Arequa Gulch, north over Raven, Bull and Ironclad hills for four miles and east to Bull Cliff. And it was some empire: the Wild Horse group; the Damon and W.P.H. groups; the Deadwood, Pinnacle, Bull Hill and Straub Mountain groups; the Requa, M.K. & T., Panther, May Belle and Conejos groups; the United Mines Transportation Company; the Woods Electric Company; the Economic Gold Extraction Company; Pinnacle Park; the First National Bank of Victor; and the Mount Rosa Mining Company! *And* the towns of Victor and Cameron!

Stratton saw how Frank and Harry had it figured. The tentacles of the Woods octopus were ready. Soon mine

owners near the routes of the projected Woods tram tunnels
would want to use those tunnels and use the Woods mill.
Bert Carlton's ore wagons would be obsolete. The railroads
wouldn't be needed. The mills and smelters on the plains
would lose Cripple's business. Then the camp would be so
dependent on Woods facilities that Frank and Harry could
buy what was left at their own price. Yes, even the Venture
Corporation's Independence, Burns' Portland, Moffat's Victor, A. J. Zang's Vindicator, and Stratton's six hundred acres
around Ironclad Hill!

What distressed Stratton was not fear of the Woods boys,
but deep regret at the ruin their greed was bound to bring.
Their first hard luck came in '99, when fire destroyed most
of the Victor business section.[3] In 1900 profits from the Gold
Coin Mine, on which their whole credit position rested,
began to decline seriously. Rumors of trouble at their Victor
bank forced Stratton and others to withdraw their balances.
The Cameron lots were not moving. Pinnacle Park was a
costly mistake; the income hardly kept the bears fed. The
Arequa Gulch mill was not extracting gold efficiently. Creditors and stockholders were beginning to buzz around. New
credit sources were drying up. Frank and Harry had to halt
tunneling. Their great Skaguay power dam, with its fantas-
tically expensive wooden aqueduct to their power plant, was
a failure.[4]

As 1902 began, Stratton knew that the Woods empire, supposed to be worth $30,000,000, would crash. Harry and
Frank might hang on a few more years. But in the end they
would lose everything.

Cripple Creek gold! Stratton was an invalid now. He
stayed in his curtained house on Weber Street in the Springs.
He read and slept and fretted and drank a quart or two of

whiskey each day. He had few visitors. He was not really an old man — he would be only fifty-four in July. But he looked empty, finished.

He had worked hard always. He had learned two trades, carpentry and prospecting. He had been honest and kindly. He had always behaved himself reasonably well. He had tasted every kind of living from bitter hardship to high luxury. He knew what it was like to be nobody, and he knew how it felt to be famous.

Why, then, had he never been truly happy?

He couldn't find the answer. He only knew that he had done his best. He had even managed to give most of his money back to the people by his crazy notion that billions in gold lay beneath the Plymouth Rock. Of course, that was just a hunch. It had cost him $8,000,000 but the cash went into good hands — small mine owners and many needy miners. Not one of those hundred claims showed any sign of being worth the powder to develop it.

He had never been truly happy. But in the past three years there was one thing he could think about with pleasure: that will of his. By gosh, that would make people sit up! And it wouldn't be long now.

Stratton wasted away through the spring and summer. His diseased liver did not cause him any particular pain. On Saturday, September 13, 1902, he went into a coma. Sunday evening, Bob Schwarz, his old bootmaker, sat with him in the Weber Street house that he himself had built. Stratton roused briefly and spoke to Bob. Then he died at 9:35 P.M.

On Monday, he was eulogized in newspapers across the nation. On Tuesday his body lay in state at his Mining Exchange, and 9000 people filed by. At 2 P.M., his streetcars stopped for five minutes. On Wednesday he was buried at Evergreen Cemetery on a wooded knoll facing Pikes Peak. He was the first of many Cripple Creek millionaires to wind up there.

And now the will! Stratton had some nieces and nephews besides his son by Zeurah Stratton. They would be remembered. But people believed most of his money would go to churches and schools in Cripple Creek and in the Springs. It was a thrilling prospect for the heads of these institutions.

The will was read one week after Stratton's death. A half million went to Stratton's nephews and nieces and to Zeurah's son. Then came the surprise. The will provided that the remaining $6,000,000 of Stratton's estate should be used to establish and maintain a home for poor children and old people. It would be called the Myron Stratton Home, after Winfield Scott's father.

It had been, then, the thought of this home that had sustained Stratton in his last, despairing days. It wouldn't be just another rich man's charity. The Stratton Home would have no equal for comfort and beauty and peace, anywhere in the world. Orphans would be reared with every advantage, every luxury enjoyed by children of the well-to-do. Old people would have no feeling of living in an institution. They would have their own individual cottages. Married folk would live as if they were in their own homes.

The Stratton Home with its stately buildings, its lawns and bowers, its swimming pool and tennis courts, its curving avenues of neat cottages, opened in 1914.[5] It sits on land near Cheyenne Mountain that used to be part of Count Pourtales' Broadmoor dairy farm. It cares for one hundred children and one hundred elderly people on a Stratton Estate budget of $200,000 a year. It must come very close to Stratton's happy dream of it. Many of the adults and children who have lived there must know the happiness that Stratton never quite managed for himself.

Up at Cripple, Stratton's death was a staggering blow. It was the culmination of many things. People were worried about the stability of the Woods empire. Many mines were becoming barren as they got deeper. There were no bonanzas any more. Mining was settling down to a prosaic struggle against costs.

So many depressing straws in the gold camp wind! The huge National Hotel, built by W. K. Gillett in '96, was bankrupt and half empty.[6] Johnnie Nolon, Grant Crumley and other saloon and gambling men were about to shove off to greener pastures at the new Nevada camps of Tonopah and Goldfield. Three Myers Avenue parlor houses were closing. The average age of the crib women was rising above forty — a sure sign that men couldn't afford to pay for young ones any longer. Some women were rolling drunks to make out, a disgusting breach of Myers Avenue morality.

And now Stratton was dead. The reassuring stream of his millions was shut off. Those six hundred acres of Stratton claims would not be developed properly now. No one would ever know about Pandora's box.

Stratton's death was too much, on top of everything else. Figures later showed that 1902 was the last year of peak production — $19,000,000 worth of gold. In 1903, production slumped to $13,000,000.

On September 14, 1902, Cripple's greatest days ended.

PART THREE

Carlton & Company

CHAPTER XXIII

Woman Trouble

ALBERT EUGENE CARLTON was twenty-seven years old in '93 when he helped Harry Collbran and W. K. Gillett to build the Midland Terminal Railroad by organizing the Colorado Trading and Transfer Company and hauling ore to the M–T as it advanced toward the camp. The transfer company was Bert's opening gambit. His second was to go to Pueblo, where he secured from John C. Osgood, head of the Colorado Fuel and Iron Company, the exclusive right to sell C. F. & I. coal at Cripple. Osgood controlled Colorado's best coal lands.

Coal was not a critical factor in Cripple's early years. Wood for fuel was plentiful and Bert had trouble selling enough coal to keep his monopoly. But wood grew scarce on the round hills. And, as mines got deeper, coal-fired steam hoists were installed. Then the camp's real coal-eater appeared. Spec Penrose climbed to the C.O.D. mine one day to find it full of water.

Spec wired his geologist brother, Dick Penrose, for advice. Dick told Spec to buy pumps. The pumps kept the C.O.D. fairly dry, but water appeared in other Poverty Gulch mines and it arrived in mines along Gold Hill and Raven Hill. Soon, dozens of steam-powered pumps were running twenty-four hours a day. The steam was produced by Bert's C. F. & I.

coal, the regular delivery of which was essential to all owners of watery mines. If their pumps stopped from lack of coal the water would rise quickly to ruin the pumps.

The coal agency was as good for Bert as a bonanza. More important still, it gave him influence. The M–T fellows loved him because he let them haul his coal. His own transfer company prospered because it took the coal from the cars to the mines and most of the ore from the mines to the M–T cars. Many mine owners had to love Bert because they depended on him to keep coal prices low enough so that they could run their pumps and make a profit.

Nobody was surprised in '98 when Bert bought the First National Bank of Cripple Creek from Jim Parker and J. L. Lindsay. People figured he needed a bank of his own by now to hold all his money. One year later, Bert sold the transfer company on the quiet to the Midland Terminal. After this sale Bert toted up his worth since coming to Cripple Creek six years before. The total was over $500,000.

He was thirty-three years old. He was six feet tall, and very slender. He was a friend of Penrose, Charlie Tutt and the other Socialites though he didn't try to keep up with them. He was bothered by ulcers besides his bad lung. He drank little and gambled never. Bert was a handsome man. He had the eyes and forehead of a poet; his mouth was the stern mouth of a realist. There was about him an abstracted air, like a chess champion playing thirty people at once. Business was chess to him, and the more involved, the better.

Bert hated spending money on himself; even his cigars were cheap, except the Corona Coronas Spec Penrose gave him. Bert was almost a Puritan. He idealized women, which made it odd that he should have nearly as much woman trouble in his youth as Sam Strong. Bert's intentions were

Drawing from Leslie's Weekly

1896. One of the most terrifying moments during the second Cripple Creek
fire occurred when the big boilers burst in the Palace Hotel.

Photo by H. S. Poley

1898. Lola Livingston's house on Myers Avenue (left) was never able to
achieve the distinguished clientele enjoyed by Hazel Vernon's "The Homestead." Next to Lola's were Pearl Sevan's "Old Faithful," Ella Holden's "The
Library," and Lottie and Kittie's "Sunnyrest." Beyond were cribs.

Photo courtesy of Mrs. A. E. Carlton

1901. But in the end Bert Carlton got his true love, Miss Ethel Frizzell. Lew Dockstader's minstrels serenaded the newlyweds when they returned to Cripple after their marriage in New York.

Photo courtesy of Mrs. A. E. Carlton

1900. Albert E. Carlton was almost a Puritan, which made it odd that he should have had nearly as much woman trouble in his youth as Sam Strong. Bert's intentions were above reproach. He just seemed to get into jams willy-nilly.

above reproach. He just seemed to get into jams willy-nilly. His troubles began in 1890 when he fell for a girl named Eva Stanton on a visit back home. He told Eva he was too sick to marry. Eva said she'd have him, T.B. or no T.B. They eloped and made a pact afterward to keep the marriage secret until Bert proved that he was out of the invalid class by earning a half million dollars.

Eva stayed in Illinois and Bert rejoined his parents in the Springs. He adored his mother. He didn't tell her about marrying Eva for fear she would disapprove. When Bert moved to Cripple, Mother Carlton became fond of a Springs spinster named Mary Quigley. Mother Carlton decided that Miss Quigley would make a perfect wife for her older son. Bert couldn't think of any objections. He permitted himself to become engaged.

Now he had a secret wife and a public fiancée.

In '96, W. K. Gillett threw a gala ball in Cripple Creek to mark the opening of his National Hotel. Among those coming from the Springs on the Cheyenne Mountain stage was a lovely blonde girl of seventeen, sweet-faced and demure — Ethel Frizzell. She had been invited by the Charlie Howberts and she brought her first evening dress, a flowing affair with long sleeves of white lace. At the ball she found herself a sensation, though she felt that her charms were a trifle obscured by the smothering attentions of an oldster called Bert Carlton — a fellow easily thirty years old.

Ethel escaped from Bert long enough to apply to Mrs. Howbert for advice. Mrs. Howbert warned her not to dance even once with Bert. His fiancée, Miss Quigley, was very angry about his behavior. Naturally, this thrilled Ethel, since she was the cause of it. She was glad when Bert signed himself up for every dance on her program. Since Bert was the worst dancer in town next to Spec Penrose, she passed an excruciating evening. Before it ended she was told by her ancient partner that she was now the fiancée of Albert E. Carlton.

Bert's new score: one secret wife, two fiancées.

Not, however, by Ethel's count. During the next two years she avoided Bert because she knew he was still engaged to Miss Quigley. In '99 Ethel moved to Cripple to run her father's mining office and to do stenography for Judge Edward C. Stimson. Bert kept begging her to marry him. Ethel hung back. Then the storm broke. Mrs. Eva Stanton Carlton arrived at the National Hotel. Eva had learned that her secret husband was now worth a half million dollars and in excellent health. She demanded that Bert make public that she was his wife.

The story broke in the newspapers. Bert's mother wept a while and spent two nights nursing Miss Quigley for hysterics. Bert sent Ethel Frizzell a series of mash notes. To regain his mother's love and faith he gave her a de luxe steamer passage to Europe and expenses for a year abroad. He mollified Miss Quigley by helping her to buy a large building in the Springs from which she could derive a handsome boardinghouse income. Then he obtained a divorce from Eva Stanton Carlton after paying her quite a few thousands of dollars. One of Bert's lawyers was Henry M. Blackmer.

In December, 1901, Bert and Ethel were married at the Dutch Reformed Church in New York City. On their return to Cripple they were met at the station by Lew Dockstader's minstrel band. Friends placed Ethel in a flower-bedecked carriage. Bert rode on a wagon girdled with red lanterns. The Dockstader band struck up "There'll Be a Hot Time in the Old Town Tonight," a tune which Theodore Metz was said to have written after hearing something like it along Myers Avenue.

The newlyweds were carried to the National Hotel. Well-wishers feted them until dawn, aided by thirty-seven cases of champagne. As each bottle was emptied an American beauty rose was stuck in it. Before the party ended the ballroom was a bower of roses.

Ethel and Bert began housekeeping in a long, narrow apartment above Bert's First National Bank on Bennett Avenue. For thirteen years this apartment would be the center of the gold camp's hectic financial life. Here strategies were planned in proxy battles. Here Bert bought and sold mines by the dozens, and discussed who ought to be what in the Colorado State House. Ethel got used to having twenty people for lunch — Wall Streeters, Threadneedle Streeters and members of the Paris Bourse. Her big problem was keeping cooks at an altitude of 9500 feet. The best she ever had was John Gee. One day she was discarding some Paris gowns. John asked if he could donate them to the Salvation Army. Ethel praised him for his thoughtfulness and turned over the gowns.

A week later a carriage swept by her on Bennett Avenue. In it she recognized three sporting ladies — Hazel Vernon of the Homestead, Grant Crumley's girl, Grace Carlyle, and Georgia Hayden. Each of them wore one of Ethel's Worth gowns. Ethel discovered that the girls had paid John $100 apiece for them.[1]

Those were gay years for the Upper Tens of Cripple Creek. Night after night the town was sprinkled with tail coats and silk hats and white gloves and fancy caterers from Denver, unloading wagonloads of champagne and Maine lobster. Bert and Ethel loved the merry weddings, especially Bill

Miller's to the head nurse at district hospital. Bill was a Scottish nobleman employed at the Gold Coin in Victor as a miner. Every Scot in Colorado came to the wedding, which began with a bagpipe concert and much passing of the bottle. Bill didn't handle his whiskey well and he weaved at the altar like a reed on a windswept Scottish moor. Suddenly the Gold Coin whistle blew, announcing the shift change. From force of habit Bill Miller left his bride at the altar and darted up Diamond Avenue to join his shift. He got stopped though. After being assured that this was his day off he weaved back to his bride.

Bert Carlton was an important Republican but he left tactics to his friend Danny Sullivan, Cripple's Republican postmaster. During the campaign of 1900, McKinley sent Teddy Roosevelt to Colorado to woo Silver Republicans and anti-gold-standard Democrats. Danny Sullivan arranged Teddy's visit to Cripple. The famous Rough Rider came up on the M–T and was met at Victor by an old comrade-at-arms, Sherman Bell. Teddy's bodyguards were Danny Sullivan and Cliff Newcomb, Bert's handsome cashier. Victor's miners were violently anti-McKinley. As the vice-presidential nominee stepped from the train, a swarm of Bryanites shouted insults, cussed the gold standard and waved placards, one of which read "HANG T.R." He spoke briefly at the Victor Armory. When some hecklers pressed too close, Teddy struck out to defend himself but he couldn't do much because of his weak eyes. He was rescued by Danny Sullivan, who grabbed a placard from a demonstrator and held the mob back until Bell and Newcomb could hustle him on the train.[2]

Roosevelt was received warmly in Cripple Creek town. He made a particular impression on the rolypoly lawyer, Jonah Maurice Finn, Stratton's former friend and present foe.

Roosevelt told Finn that he would return to the camp in the spring. Finn asked him to be his guest and Roosevelt accepted. The very next day Finn went to Bert Carlton and borrowed twenty or thirty thousand dollars with which to build a mansion worthy of entertaining the Vice-President of the United States.

This wonderful house rose above Cripple Creek at Placer Street and Pikes Peak Avenue, near the reservoir. It had five stories counting the basement and was surmounted by elegant turrets at the corners, and by an observatory at the top. The library and reception rooms were lined with Russian leather window seats. Around the great central stairway was a pool of flowing water, containing sportive rainbow trout. The house was lighted by one hundred electric bulbs which brought out the richness of the golden oak paneling.

Roosevelt did stop there while inspecting the Short Line Railroad, in April, 1901, and he called it "the most beautiful home in Colorado." Cripple Creekers had a blunter name, "Finn's Folly." Jonah Maurice himself, appalled by upkeep costs, referred to it as a "monument to a damned fool." After Finn moved to Denver, Finn's Folly was dismantled and re-built at Lakewood, Colorado.

At the turn of the century most gold campers regarded Bert Carlton as merely a smart youngster on the rise. Actually he was, even then, in his undercover way, almost as powerful as Stratton or Burns or the insatiable Woods boys. For six years his transfer wagons had served the camp's mines, always extending credit for coal and so on, when an owner was in trouble. Bert's bank supplemented this generous credit policy. Nobody could equal Bert's inside knowledge of the mines. That's why he won control of many fine producers like the Doctor Jack Pot and the Findley. He couldn't be beaten in the judicious application of apex suits. Some folk said his initials stood for "Apex Everybody." Apex suits were often costly and protracted affairs. Under threat of such suits many claim owners preferred to compromise.

Steadily Bert increased his mining territory. Others were expanding too, and he knew that conflict was ahead. He did not fear Stratton, for Stratton was doggedly spending his millions on a bum steer — the Pandora's box notion. He didn't fear the Woods boys; they were overexpanded. But men like Lennox and Giddings could give him trouble, and maybe the Vindicator crowd from Denver. Another opponent was John T. Milliken, that big noise from St. Louis. Milliken had paid $1,700,000 for some of Dave Moffat's best claims, including the old Anaconda and the Golden Cycle.

In the late Nineties, however, Bert's chief concern was the transportation rather than the mining front. Jimmie Burns, Irving Howbert and other mine owners were out to scalp the Midland Terminal Railroad and Bert's transfer company.

Bert got out his own tomahawk and worked up a nice edge.

CHAPTER XXIV

Tempest on the Rails

THE FIRST SLIGHT HINT of competition to Bert's transfer company appeared in December of '97. L. D. Ross, a Springs real estate man, built the High Line, an interurban service six miles long. It ran from Cripple Creek town up the hills in twists to Hoosier Pass, southward along Bull Hill past Windy Point, at 10,400 feet, then down Battle Mountain to Victor. It had fantastic grades of 7½ per cent. Ross' generator produced only 175 horsepower, so one electric car always coasted downgrade as the other groaned up. The car wheels had three-inch treads and the brake shoes wore out in a month. The lighted cars at night looked like Peter Pan's Tinker Bell as they flitted along the dark heights.

Tinker Bell notwithstanding, Bert did not like the High Line. It was strictly passenger but it *could* carry freight. It was such a success that Ross went on to build the Low Line from Victor northward around the base of the hills. In Cripple Creek town Ross got a permit to run his track in a big loop from Fifth Street to Bennett to Second to Myers and back to Fifth. Ross knew that Bert would hit the roof when he found that the tracks would pass by his transfer company at Bennett and Fifth. Bert needed the whole street there for backing and loading.

Ross arranged to lay the Fifth Street tracks on a Sunday

when Bert would be unable to appeal to the courts. Bert saw the crew laying track and he hurried to a phone. Soon he had a dozen transfer wagons parked in the path of the track-layers. His men shoveled tons of coal into the midde of Fifth Street. Jesse Waters, the Midland Terminal super, arrived with a case of whiskey. The M–T, of course, always backed Bert. Ross men put down their picks to sample Waters' whiskey. That ended track-laying for the day. On Monday Bert got an injunction against Ross, who gave up Fifth Street and laid his tracks along Third Street instead.

In '99, Ross pushed the Low Line from Victor northward through Goldfield to Independence. Bert and Jesse Waters were suspicious of this extension. Their fears were justified some weeks later when Ross sold the High and Low Lines to a syndicate of mine owners — Stratton, Irving Howbert, Jimmie Burns, Bill Lennox, Ed Giddings, J. R. McKinnie, the Bernard boys and W. S. Jackson. The electric lines were standard-gauge. In explaining the purchase, Irving Howbert announced that the syndicate would build a new railroad direct from the Springs to compete with the Midland Terminal. The new road would use a good deal of High and Low Line track to get about the camp. A new transfer company would be formed. A new mill would go up in Colorado City.

Bert knew who was the ringleader in all this. Jimmie Burns had been complaining about M–T freight rates for a long time — four dollars a ton from Cripple to the Springs as against one dollar a ton for nearly twice that distance, from the Springs to Denver. Jimmie didn't like Bert's transfer company rates, either. And Jimmie deplored treatment rates charged by Tutt, Penrose and MacNeill at their chlorination mill in Colorado City. The three mill men were treating half of Cripple's low-grade ore. They planned to build or buy other plants at Colorado City, Canon City, and Florence, which would take most of Cripple's output.

With the power of the Portland Mine behind him, Jimmie Burns was able to line up strong backing for the proposed Short Line Railroad. He agreed to erect a rival mill in Colorado City to force down treatment rates. Irving Howbert accepted the job of Short Line president and raised $3,500,-000 for construction. He turned the first shovel of dirt on January 4, 1900.

It was some job. Dauntless Irving had to build forty-five miles of roadbed hacked out of the pink Pikes Peak granite from the Springs, up past St. Peter's Dome and Rosemont to Cameron (Grassy) in the gold camp. Near Cameron the Short Line met the electric lines, one fork descending to Cripple Creek town, the other dipping south to Victor. It was no shoestring affair, as the M–T and the Florence & Cripple Creek had been. The Short Line expressed the financial power of the mine owners at the very peak of their prosperity. Its hundred-ton locomotives, its heavy rails, its ten thrilling tunnels, its elegant club cars, its two hundred gorgeous yellow boxcars stamped it as one of the finest mountain carriers on earth.

The scenic beauty along the Short Line far exceeded that of the other two roads. From start to finish it was breathtaking. Near Rosemont, almost a mile above the Springs, passengers could gaze south to the Spanish Peaks and Raton Pass, east to the Kansas line, west to the Big Divide. When Vice-President Roosevelt made the trip in the spring of '01, he shouted "Bully!" He added: "This is the ride that bankrupts the English language!"

On the surface it didn't seem as though the M–T crowd

and Bert Carlton could possibly fight such a splendid competitor. But they did fight — and successfully. Bert made the
rounds of mine owners who owed him money or who had
ever owed him money, and urged them to stick by the M–T.
Jesse Waters slashed M–T freight rates and ran spur tracks
to every mine producing as much as a shirttail-full of ore.
He handed out hundreds of passes and granted the countless
favors in the power of a railroad, from letting little Joe ride
the cab to rushing emergency hospital cases by special to
Denver.

When the Short Line started running, Irving Howbert
and Jimmie Burns got less ore than they had expected. But
they felt they could make up the difference by passenger
traffic. And they did, for a time. The scenic glories of the
Short Line caught on. Jesse Waters noticed that hardly anyone rode the M–T any more. That gave him an idea. He had
to run passenger trains anyhow, so he had nothing to lose
by lowering fares. He reduced the M–T's round-trip rate
from $2.25 to $2, then to $1.50 and $1. The Short Line had
to meet these reductions. Waters made it fifty cents for the
round trip of three hours each way — a rate that caused
hotel men to complain that they were losing trade because
tourists slept on the M–T.

The rate war continued through the winter of 1902. In
April Waters let people ride the M–T to Cripple for two bits,
forty cents round trip. He hauled any kind of freight in any
quantity for the sum of a nickel per hundred pounds. Then
Irving Howbert offered the round trip on the Short Line for
twenty-five cents. So many excursionists turned up that ticket
agents couldn't handle them before train time. People piled
into the coaches and rode free.

That was too much for both sides. Three days later Howbert and Waters called a truce. They promised that the Short Line and the M–T in the future would try to cut each other's throats by subtler and less expensive means.

While Waters slugged it out with the Short Line, Bert Carlton battled against the new transfer company. Its head was J. B. Cunningham, a Victor lumber merchant. Many of Bert's old customers were loyal to him and they did not object to signing transfer contracts on an annual rather than on a month-to-month basis. Bert had a big stick: his C. F. & I. coal agency. But he didn't want to wield it unless he had to. In the case of Bill Lennox he had to. Bill, part-owner of the Strong and Gold King Mines, was a big backer of the Short Line and of the new Cunningham transfer company. He refused to sign a year's transfer contract with Bert. But he told Bert to get him two cars of coal in a hurry for his mine pumps. Lennox instructed him to hand the coal over to Cunningham for hauling, upon its arrival in camp.

Bert agreed. He wired Denver and the two cars of coal came down on the Colorado Midland. At Divide the cars were switched to the M–T tracks. Lennox, who had received hourly reports of their progress, told Cunningham to get his wagons ready.

The two cars didn't arrive in camp. Lennox tried to trace them. They had vanished into thin air. Lennox slowed his pumps to conserve his diminishing coal supply. The water in the Gold King rose a little. Cunningham rushed to Denver to see Harry Collbran, now no longer with the M–T but still general manager of the Colorado Midland.[1] The conversation:

CUNNINGHAM: Where in hell is Lennox' coal?

COLLBRAN: Haven't you been in the lumber business, Mr. Cunningham?

CUNNINGHAM: It's two weeks since that coal left Denver!
COLLBRAN: Lately, you entered the transfer business. You
            know we've backed Mr. Carlton since '93.
CUNNINGHAM: We'll sue the lot of you!
COLLBRAN: Why don't you go back to the lumber busi-
            ness?

The two cars of coal stood so long on a hidden M–T siding
that "they got flat spots on their wheels," as Jesse Waters put
it. The water rose higher in the Gold King. Bill Lennox had
to capitulate. He signed Bert's transfer contract. Within an
hour he had his coal.

Cunningham fought Bert a while longer in the transfer
business, but then he gave up as Collbran had suggested
and returned to selling lumber.

The beautiful Short Line was a testimonial to the courage
of Jimmie Burns and Irving Howbert. But, for two reasons,
it never had a chance as a business enterprise. First, it was
run by amateurs pitted against a top-rank professional rail-
roader, Jesse Waters, with Bert Carlton putting in more
body blows. In the background was a financial wizard, Henry
M. Blackmer,[2] who controlled both the M–T and the Florence & Cripple Creek through his holding company, the
Cripple Creek Central Railroad.

Second, Stratton's death and the decline in gold profits
made it hard for even one railroad to survive. In 1905, Howbert had to sell the Short Line to the Colorado & Southern
Railroad to escape receivership. The C. & S. leased it promptly
to the M–T. Jesse Waters restored passenger and freight rates
to the highest bearable levels. Then Bert Carlton, Spec Penrose, and Charlie MacNeill bought large amounts of M–T
stock. Thus the Short Line wound up in the hands of the
very fellows whose powers it had been built to curb.[3]

Bert Carlton was pleased at the ease with which he had weathered the Short Line attack. He was pleased because he needed his strength for a far more serious attack, not only against him but against Cripple Creek as a whole.

After the strike of '94, Cripple had enjoyed a long period of labor peace. The Western Federation of Miners under Ed Boyce became the strongest industrial union in the United States, with headquarters in Denver. In 1902, Charles Moyer became W.F.M. president. The real boss was the executive secretary, an implacable socialist named Big Bill Haywood. Big Bill wanted to wipe capitalism off the earth. He decided to test his power at Cripple Creek because Cripple Creek was the biggest W.F.M. camp in the West.

He began by persuading Cripple's W.F.M. members to let local officers act without membership vote. Then, working through these local officers, Haywood dictated hiring and firing. He told miners what papers to read. He prepared scab lists and made sure that Teller County officials were friends of the W.F.M. He moved in on Colorado City to unionize the mill workers. Charlie MacNeill opposed him bitterly there.[4] Charlie allowed his Standard Mill men to join the W.F.M., but refused to meet Big Bill's other demands.

On August 10, 1903, Haywood called the mill workers out of the Standard. To make sure that MacNeill had no ore to mill even if he got scabs, Haywood ordered 3500 Cripple Creek union men to quit in fifty mines.

The Black Time

BERT CARLTON was too fair a man to be sanctimonious about Big Bill Haywood and the W.F.M. Bert knew that the mine owners had loaded the political dice in the election of Governor Peabody in 1902. And they had defeated an eight-hour-day act which most people wanted. These were sins. But they didn't compare in Bert's mind with Haywood's sins. Haywood didn't like any part of the world as it was, and he intended to smash it. He and the W.F.M. had to be beaten.

To this end, Bert and others reorganized and strengthened the Mine Owners' Association, which originally had been formed to go after the high-graders. Clarence Hamlin, Verner Reed's former partner, became secretary. Hamlin worked for Penrose, Tutt and MacNeill, who had recently bought the Granite and Gold Coin and Ajax Mines. Secretary Hamlin's job was to issue work permits to all miners who would quit the W.F.M. He and Bert arranged the opening with scab labor of several mines, including Bert's Findley, the Bernard boys' El Paso, the Ajax, Milliken's Golden Cycle, Zang's Vindicator, Lennox' Strong, the Tornado, the Elkton and the Thompson.

Local W.F.M. officers retaliated with sporadic acts of terrorism. Governor Peabody sent Adjutant General Sherman Bell and the state militia. Bell, who had been one of Teddy

Roosevelt's favorite Rough Riders, roared into Cripple like Teddy charging up San Juan Hill. Bell shouted, "I'm here to do up this damned anarchistic Western Federation." He spotted troops everywhere, put searchlights atop the hills and tossed four W.F.M. officers into a bull pen at Goldfield.

Bell decided to close the Victor *Record,* the local W.F.M. mouthpiece. He assigned forty-five militiamen armed to the teeth to the task of invading the offices and hauling off editor George Kyner and four employees. A beautiful linotypist named Emma Langdon, Cripple's own Barbara Frietchie, barricaded the doors against a second militia platoon and defied the soldiers to invade the privacy of a lone woman. Then Emma spent the rest of the night setting up the paper. She had it ready in the morning, carrying the banner: SOMEWHAT DISFIGURED BUT STILL IN THE RING! Mrs. Langdon took her papers to the Goldfield bull pen and handed them around to the soldiers who had captured the *Record's* staff. Later she wrote a book about the strike.

The gold camp was not under martial law. General Bell had no legal right to hold men in a bull pen. Judge William Seeds issued writs of habeas corpus ordering Bell to produce the four imprisoned W.F.M. officers in Cripple Creek court. Bell assembled a large militia guard, placed his prisoners in the center of it and the whole troop marched grimly from Goldfield to Cripple. Everyone in town jammed Bennett Avenue to watch Bell set up a Gatling gun outside the court. He posted a detail of sharpshooters on the roof of the National Hotel across the way.

Judge Seeds never batted an eye at all this show of force. He heard the case, reprimanded General Bell and ordered the four W.F.M. officers released. Bell rattled his sword a day or so and then did release the four.

The strike would have ended there if ordinary Cripple Creekers had had any say. But they were caught in the struggle between Hamlin, Bert Carlton and other leaders of the Mine Owners' Association on one side, and Big Bill Haywood on the other. By November of 1903 Hamlin had so depleted the W.F.M.'s membership by his work permit system that local W.F.M. officers resumed terrorism, trying to wreck trains and blow up scabs.

An ex-cheesemaker from Canada, Harry Orchard, took on one murder assignment which he thought would help the W.F.M. Harry had been high-grading for months in the Vindicator and he knew where a carload of dynamite was stored. He moved some of it to what he thought was the Vindicator's seventh level. Actually it was the sixth level. He rigged up a pistol near the dynamite at the cage opening. If a man stepped from the cage at that level the pistol would go off, exploding the dynamite. Orchard knew that the cage carried fifteen scabs down the main Vindicator shaft to work on the seventh level. He figured that the explosion would kill them all.

Nothing happened for days. Then, on November 21, Charles McCormick, the Vindicator super, and Melvin Beck, shift boss, were blown up at the *sixth* level. Because of Orchard's confusion about levels he had failed to kill any scabs. Instead he had murdered two harmless bosses.

The outrage brought back General Bell and the State militia. This time the mine owners agreed to loan the State enough money to pay the militia's expenses.[1] And Cripple was placed under martial law so that Bell could destroy the W.F.M. without any nonsense about civil rights. Bell deposed local cops and filled the Goldfield bull pen with W.F.M. men. He intimidated the courts and made strikers surrender their arms. He forbade street meetings.

Big Bill Haywood spent $100,000 publicizing Bell's tyranny. Just when he was going well a train-wrecking terrorist at Cripple confessed to Bell that he acted under orders of local W.F.M. officers, and that these officers were controlled by Haywood. Public opinion shifted in Bell's favor. Clarence Hamlin's list of nonunion miners lengthened. More mines opened. The W.F.M. went under cover. Violence almost ceased. On February 2, 1904, Governor Peabody ended martial law. By April all the State militia had returned to Denver except for a token force in Victor Armory. The strike was still on theoretically, but the power of the W.F.M. seemed broken.

The annual convention of the Western Federation of Miners began in Denver during the last week of May, 1904. Everybody was cross and argumentative. Big Bill Haywood was in serious trouble because he had spent $500,000 trying to win the strike at Cripple, and now the majority felt that it had been a mistake. Harry Orchard, the terrorist, who had never been caught for killing McCormick and Beck, attended the convention. He brooded and plotted and then he left and returned to Cripple. His idea was to kill some more people, so that Bell and the State militia would come back to camp. This would fuse sentiment within the W.F.M. and save Haywood from getting booted out of his job.

Orchard went to the village of Independence, on Bull Hill between Altman and Victor. He asked for help to blow up scabs, had no luck and walked through Altman to Midway. He got his help from a terrorist named Steve Adams. Orchard bought two boxes of dynamite and some giant caps in Altman and hid them in an empty cabin near the Independence depot of the F. & C. C. Railroad. He bought a team, a wagon and a saddle. On Sunday afternoon, June 5, he loaded his wagon with camping supplies and set off down the Cheyenne Mountain stage road as though on a fishing trip. With him was a barkeep, Johnnie Neville, and Johnnie's child, Charlie. The three camped for the night near Clyde. After supper, Harry Orchard and little Charlie had a game of mumblypeg. Charlie cut himself, and Harry, who couldn't stand the sight of blood, almost fainted. Then Harry Orchard saddled a horse and rode back to a point on the F. & C. C. between Victor Mine and Midway. He hid his horse in the bushes and joined Steve Adams at the Independence cabin where the two boxes of dynamite were stored.

It was 10 P.M. For an hour the two men worked on a wooden tilt-up that would explode dynamite by spilling acid on giant caps. When all was quiet in Independence, Orchard and Adams carried the dynamite to the F. & C. C. depot. The depot was on the downslope south of the tracks which ran above Independence near the Findley, Delmonico, Pikes Peak, Orpha May and Lucky Guss Mines. Orchard put the dynamite boxes on the ground under the platform. He placed the giant caps on the boxes and adjusted the tilt-up. He removed the corks from his acid vials, nearly spilling one in the process. He stretched the wire from the tilt-up across the tracks toward the Delmonico ore-house, and tied the wire's end to an old chair rung. Then Orchard and Adams waited in the shadow of the ore-house for the 2:15 A.M. train.

The train was bringing the nonunion crew for the graveyard shift on Bert Carlton's Findley Mine.

At 2 A.M., miners coming off the Findley's night shift began collecting on the depot platform. It was crowded as the train ground up the hill from Victor. The engineer blew his whistle 150 yards from the depot. By the light of a small moon the crouching terrorists could see a dozen miners running to catch the train. Then Orchard and Adams stepped from their shadow and yanked the chair-rung.

Two terrific explosions shattered the depot platform and almost derailed the approaching train. Of the twenty-seven miners on the platform, thirteen were killed instantly. Their dismembered bodies were blown 150 feet up the hillside as far as the Delmonico Mine. Most of the others on the platform were badly injured. The lives of six of them were saved later by the amputation of arms and legs.

Miners on the unharmed train laid out the injured men beside the tracks in the glare of the locomotive's headlight. Someone phoned Bert Carlton. At 3 A.M. Bert, James Murphy, the Findley manager, and Sheriff Henry Robertson left Cripple Creek town on a switch engine with doctors and nurses. When daylight came the horrible news spread and hundreds hurried to Independence. Men with dinner buckets combed the area for pieces of flesh. Bert Carlton found a leg with the boot still on.

Nobody went to work that Monday morning. Deputy sheriffs and bloodhounds tried to trace the murderers but Orchard and Adams had soaked their shoes in turpentine. They had gone up the F. & C. C. track, separating near the Victor Mine. Orchard rode his horse back to the camp on the Cheyenne Mountain stage road. Charlie Neville woke up and Orchard gave him a piece of stick candy. Next morning the three continued on down to the Springs and northward to Denver and Wyoming.

Neither Orchard nor Adams were ever caught for the crime.[2] Most Cripple Creekers blamed it on the W.F.M. Clarence Hamlin, of the Mine Owners' Association, called a mass meeting at 3 P.M. Monday. As early as noon, gold camp residents began converging on Victor. Hamlin and others persuaded Sheriff Robertson, a W.F.M. sympathizer, to resign. Their persuasion was the threat to hang him. Ed Bell became sheriff. At 3 p.m. a tense crowd packed in an empty Victor lot below the Gold Coin shaft house. It was composed mainly of nonunion miners, but some union men were there, too. More W.F.M. members watched from the second story of Union Hall, across the street. Lots of fellows carried guns. Soon Bert Carlton and Clarence Hamlin arrived. One of Bert's transfer wagons was moved to the edge of the lot.

Hamlin scrambled up on the wagon and faced the crowd. He was a little man, so small that once in his salad days he hid in a grandfather's clock to escape the ire of a rival to a lady's affections. But Clarence wasn't really afraid of anyone. On the wagon, he began a passionate tirade. He urged the frenzied people to take their guns and clean up the gold camp. He yelled, "Chase these W.F.M. scoundrels out of the district. Make them leave for good and all. Chase them so far that they will never come back. The time has now come for every man to take this matter in his own hands."

When Hamlin yelled the word "hands" a heckler asked a question. A man next to the heckler swung at his face and a fight started. Someone fired a gun. Then there was a fusillade of shots. The transfer wagon horses bolted and Hamlin toppled from the wagon. The crowd thought he had been shot. People trampled one another in the rush to get out of the line of fire. Some of this fire seemed to come from Union Hall windows. The platoon of militiamen ran up and cleared the vacant lot. Five men lay on the ground, two of them dead.

The militiamen surrounded Union Hall. Sheriff Ed Bell

and Postmaster Danny Sullivan entered the club rooms and told the W.F.M. members to come out. They refused. The militiamen aimed their rifles and poured volley after volley into the rooms, wounding four men. The rest surrendered and were led off by the militia. Berserk civilians rushed into Union Hall, wrecked the walls, smashed furniture, ripped curtains, and destroyed membership ledgers. Afterwards, this gang and other gangs roamed the gold camp for W.F.M. members and wrecked every union hall and union store. About two hundred men were imprisoned.

On Tuesday, June 7, General Bell arrived back in Cripple. He conferred with Carlton and Hamlin and named seven residents to examine union members and deport those who refused to renounce the union. Deportation, Bell said, was permitted under a law for dispersal of a mob.

Twenty-five W.F.M. members said good-by to their families that same afternoon and were loaded on an F. & C. C. train headed south. On Friday, June 10, seventy-two more miners were deported. They were carried under guard on the M–T and Santa Fé lines to a desolate spot on the prairie two hundred miles east of Cripple and marched across the State line into Kansas. Here they were abandoned. Another large group was dumped on a cedar-and-piñon wasteland of New Mexico. Altogether 225 union miners were deported from Cripple Creek by the militia.

The dynamiting of Independence depot was the ghastly event that made it possible for the mine owners to drive the W.F.M. out of Cripple and out of Colorado for good. It ruined the W.F.M. career of Big Bill Haywood. In 1905 he became a founder of the I.W.W. and for fifteen years he waged his crazy, pitiful war against the United States. He brought many industrial wrongs to light but he never received honor for them in his own country. He fled to Russia finally, where he died a minor Red hero.

Times change. Bill Bill Haywood could not behave today as he did at Cripple in '03–'04. Neither could Governor Peabody, Sherman Bell, Clarence Hamlin, or Bert Carlton. The strike was not a matter of justice against injustice. The miners liked their pay and working conditions, which were far better than pay and conditions in any other mining camp. The miners didn't want to strike.

The strike was simply a battle for power. Haywood started it and made clear that he would not follow the Marquess of Queensberry rules. Carlton & Company accepted the challenge and went in swinging.

There was one little drama on the side.

You may recall that Jimmie Burns had always been a friend of the W.F.M. The Portland Mine did not close a single day up to the Independence depot outrage.[3] Then General Bell closed the Portland by a proclamation which read in part:

> WHEREAS, the Portland Mine, situated in said county is, and for a long time has been, engaged in employing and harboring large numbers of dangerous, lawless men, who have aided, encouraged, and given comfort and assistance to those who have been guilty of said crimes and outrages, so that said mine has become and now is a menace to the welfare and safety of the good people of said county and a hindrance to the restoration of peace and good order:
>
> Now, by the power conferred on me as commander of the military force in Teller County, and as a military necessity, it is ordered that the said mine be at once closed and all men found therein or thereabouts who are dangerous to the community be arrested and held until further orders.

Burns sued Governor Peabody, Bell, Hamlin, and the Mine Owners' Association for $100,000 damages. But the other Portland directors voted Jimmie out of office. They withdrew his suit and opened the Portland with nonunion men. Irving Howbert was elected president of the Portland.

Jimmie was unhappy for a while to be no longer head of the Portland but he soon found compensations. Life had done well by the little plumber since that cold January day in '92 when Doyle staked the Portland. Burns was a very rich man now. He had found a truly beautiful woman to be his wife — Olivia Belle Parker of St. Joe, Missouri. He had a stately home in the Springs on Wood Avenue, along those three blocks which were pointed out to tourists as "Millionaires' Row." He dressed almost as beautifully as Spec Penrose and he was the equal even of Charlie MacNeill as a connoisseur of fine whiskey. He had the best butler, the best chauffeur and the best cook in Little London. Jimmie Burns had arrived.

One of his old Cripple Creek friends had reached quite a different destination. Fortune had not been good to Bob Womack.

CHAPTER XXVI

Good-by, Bob

Miss LIDA WOMACK, Bob's ever-loving sister, had a definite plan in mind late in '93 when she had urged Bob to leave Cripple. She wanted his help in starting a boardinghouse. She was too old to manage Sunview Ranch any longer. She couldn't care for Sam Womack properly out there. Poor old Sam was very, very frail. He hadn't much longer to live.[1] Boardinghouses, Miss Lida had learned from Irving Howbert, who knew everything, were profitable in the Springs. That was because more and more people were coming from the East to spend a year or two in the Colorado sun to convalesce from T.B.

Bob was enthusiastic about Miss Lida's plan. So she finished selling Sunview and opened a boardinghouse at 703 North Cascade Avenue. Bob didn't settle down all at once to the new business. He went away often on prospecting trips — to the San Juans, and to the dozens of small camps that sprang up weekly throughout the West Pikes Peak country around Cripple Creek. But all the while, Bob was growing fond of boardinghouses. He bought some big white aprons and became Miss Lida's Number Two cook. He washed dishes, baked biscuits and kept the range supplied with kindling. He whistled while he worked. His whistling penetrated across the street to the workroom of his old friend, Hiram Rogers, the *Gazette* reporter who had let Bob's discovery pass in 1890. Now and then Hiram would stick his head into Bob's kitchen. "Found any more Cripple Creeks lately?" Hiram would say. Bob would reply, "No use telling you, Hiram. You wouldn't even put it in the paper."

Occasionally, Bob got drunk and revisited Cripple for some weeks. But his association with invalids in the boarding-house made him consider his own health more. One day he approached Miss Lida and asked timidly if she would advance one more grubstake. The patient lady burst into tears and asked Bob if his search for gold had not brought him enough unhappiness. Bob smiled. This grubstake, he said, would be spent on the Keeley cure.

Dr. Leslie E. Keeley had invented a cure for alcoholism involving the squirting of bichloride of gold into the veins and drinking raw carrot juice. Keeley Institutes operated all over the United States, and thousands of people gave up alcohol, not because of the gold or the carrots, but because of the helpful atmosphere. Keeley's principle was a lot like that of Alcoholics Anonymous. Bob went to Denver and took his Keeley cure. He never drank whiskey again.

Miss Lida did so well with her boardinghouse that she became ambitious. In '98 she took over the Garland Hotel, across from the Antlers Hotel. She and Bob were helped in this venture by Theodore Lowe and by Bob's brother, William, who was running the Antlers Livery Stable. William steered tourists to the Garland. Soon the Antlers burned down, which placed a burden of extra business on the town's remaining six hotels. Miss Lida decided to sell the Garland while the selling was good. She received a high price. With some of the money she bought a large boardinghouse at 432 North Nevada Avenue and the smaller home behind it, 121 East St. Vrain.

Bob's kitchen work was arranged so that he could deliver packages part-time for Charlie Zobrist, who ran the drugstore at Tejon and Pikes Peak Avenues. Jimmie Burns met Bob with his arms full of parcels on the street one day. He told Bob it was a disgrace for the discoverer of Cripple Creek to have to do such chores. A little later the papers announced that Burns and other mine owners were going to raise $50,000 to keep Bob in comfort for the rest of his life. But Bob never saw the $50,000.

In the spring of '02 Bob got a letter from the '91 Club of Cripple Creek, asking him to be guest of honor at the gold camp's Fourth of July celebration. On July 3 Bob took out his black alpaca suit from Miss Lida's cedar closet. He had worn it last in '99, when Margaret Womack married Theodore Lowe. Bob put the suit on over a striped silk shirt, with gold cuff links, a high stiff collar and a black tie with a glass stickpin. Across his vest stretched his heavy gold watch chain. He wore a high-crowned black derby on his gray head. William Womack drove him to the Short Line depot. At Cripple he was met by an Elks Club guard of honor.

The Big Fourth of July parade assembled at 10:30 A.M., in Old Town on Main Street. Old Town was that part of Hayden Placer where the pioneers had squatted in '91. D. C. Williams led the parade, as marshal of the day. Behind him were Police Chief J. Knox Burton and his police force in brilliant blue. When Bob saw the big police squad he shook his head in wonder, remembering how Pete Eales used to police the whole camp alone. To a reporter he murmured, "How things have changed! Why, you have a great city now!"

The Teller County band followed the policemen and then came a six-horse flowered carriage with top-hatted coachmen.

Bob sat stiffly in this carriage all alone. He was scared to death and very happy. A dozen aging men walked behind the carriage — all that remained of the '91 Club. After them came the burros and miners and businessmen and the fellows who would compete in the rock-drilling contests.

The Bennett Avenue crowd raised a great racket as Bob passed. He removed his derby and bowed this way and that way like celebrities he had seen. He found the whole ordeal terribly tiring. When the parade ended he slipped off to the Short Line depot below Warren Avenue to wait for the first train home.

He told Miss Lida later that he had had a nice time, but it had made him sad, too. All those gaps. Sam Strong murdered. Tim Hussey gone crazy. Alonzo Welty and his wife killed in a carriage accident. Johnnie Harnan drinking up his Portland fortune.[2] Fred Frisbee broke and planning a move to California.

Bob visited Cripple just once more, on July 28, 1904. He wanted a last look at his Poverty Gulch shack. He had a slight cold. On the train ride back he sat next to an open window, with his left arm resting on the sill. When he got home he found that he couldn't move his left arm. It was a paralytic stroke which spread through the left side of his body. After some weeks Miss Lida sent him to Pueblo for treatment in the mineral baths. The baths didn't help him.

Now Miss Lida had two invalids to care for. Old Sam was so blind that he could hardly see the nasturtiums he loved to raise around the front porch. Bob could not move by himself. In order to give him all her time, Miss Lida stopped serving meals at 432 North Nevada. She built a little downstairs bedroom for Bob in the house at 121 East St. Vrain. He was an uncomplaining invalid. None of his old prospecting pals called on him because they were either dead or had moved away. Miss Lida didn't like to talk about Bob's condition to outsiders for fear people would think she was inviting charity.

And so Bob lay there on his bed in the little room for years. He did not seem unhappy. His greatest joy was when one of William Womack's daughters came to read to him. They came often, especially Dorsey Womack. She was a beautiful girl, warmhearted and unselfish. Dorsey enjoyed seeing Bob's face light up when she came in to see him.

Early in February, 1908, Dorsey happened to talk casually about Bob for a few minutes to Charles T. Wilder, the editor of the *Gazette*. Out of curiosity Wilder phoned Bob's doctor, who mentioned that Glockner Hospital was trying out a new treatment for paralytics. The treatment was expensive but it might help Bob. Next, Wilder talked with Clarence P. Dodge, owner of the *Gazette*. On February 9, 1908, Wilder announced in the *Gazette* the Bob Womack Relief Fund to raise $5000.

For a month Wilder published daily stories about Bob's Cripple Creek career. He showed what Bob's discovery of the El Paso Lode had meant to Colorado Springs. At least twenty-eight residents had become millionaires. Springs bank deposits had quadrupled. The population had trebled. So had real estate values. Every important building in town had been built with Cripple Creek gold. The Colorado Springs Mining Exchange was a big money-maker. The Colorado City mills employed hundreds of men and paid out a million dollars each month. If Bob hadn't found Cripple's treasure, the Springs would have remained what it was in 1890, a small summer resort which slept through the other nine months.

Each week Wilder published in large type on the *Gazette's* front page the progress of his effort to raise $5000 for the Bob Womack Relief Fund. The total at the end of the first week was $402. After a month the Womack Relief Fund reached $812. Then Wilder called off the campaign and turned the money over to Miss Lida.

It was enough to pay for several months of treatments, but they didn't do Bob any good. In January of 1909 he was depressed by the death of Charlie Tutt at only forty-five. Charlie had done many nice things for Bob. In March, Dorsey Womack read to him long accounts of the death of General Palmer. Dorsey read other things, too — novels and poetry. Her voice was musical and it always soothed him. Sometimes Dorsey told Bob about her boy friends and asked him how to handle them. There was a great deal of sympathy between the old prospector and the sixteen-year-old high school girl.

Early in July of 1909 Dorsey went visiting in Pueblo. The visit was a round of parties. She began running a fever but she was having too much fun to pay any attention to it. One night in the middle of charades she collapsed. Ten days later she died of typhoid fever.

Dorsey's death was the end for Bob. His disintegration raced along now. After Dorsey's funeral, Miss Lida moved Bob temporarily from 131 East St. Vrain to 117 South Limit Street. This was the home of Margaret Womack and her second husband, Jack Edwards. Jack had been ordered to New Mexico on an extended tour to promote Singer sewing machines among the Indians. Jack and Margaret gave their house to Miss Lida, rent free, so that she could rent her own place to tourists.

Bob didn't care where he was. He lay in bed with his face

to the wall. He rarely spoke, not even to Miss Lida. The final coma began during the first week of August. On August 10, 1909, at 6:30 A.M., Bob died. He was sixty-six. Miss Lida and Sam were with him. The funeral was held next day at Fairley and Law's.

Bob was buried at the foot of Dorsey's fresh grave in Evergreen Cemetery. Miss Lida chose the pallbearers. There wasn't a mining man among them.

Bert's Tunnel and Aladdin's Cave

CRIPPLE CREEK is a 10,000-acre bowl of volcanic rock with impermeable granite sides which extend upward to an altitude of 9200 feet. In the Nineties, when water ran into the bowl, it couldn't get out below that 9200-foot altitude. The average surface altitude of Cripple Creek mines was 10,000 feet. Mine owners, therefore, ran into water when their shafts reached an average depth of eight hundred feet.

Pumps were used to keep mines dry for ten years after Dick Penrose recommended them in the C.O.D. As a coal dealer, Bert Carlton liked pumps because they ate up coal. But as a mine owner Bert thought pumps were too costly. He felt that drainage tunnels were cheaper in the long run. He encouraged the construction of a dozen experimental drainage tunnels, the largest of which was the mile-long El Paso. This tunnel was completed in 1904 at a cost of $80,000 — fourteen dollars a foot. It punctured the granite rim of the Cripple Creek bowl at 8800 feet. It released the water in the bowl above that level into Cripple Creek stream three miles below Cripple Creek town.

Bert contributed $5000 to help build the El Paso Tunnel, since it would drain his Doctor Jack Pot Mine. And yet, the tunnel wasn't nearly as deep or as large as he had wanted it to be. He favored a $500,000 tunnel. The other big mine owners threw up their hands when they heard this $500,000 figure and said Bert was crazy.

The El Paso Tunnel ran through the fourth level of the El Paso Mine — the Beacon Hill El Paso, not Bob Womack's. Men could work in the El Paso Mine quite a bit below the fourth level, because of pumps. It snowed heavily during the winter of '06. As the snow on Pikes Peak melted, a lot of water poured down into Cripple's volcanic bowl. One March day the El Paso Mine sprang a terrible leak below the fourth level. The men got out just in time.

When Bert Carlton arrived to have a look, the water was roaring into the El Paso shaft at the rate of 5000 gallons a minute. The small-bore El Paso Tunnel couldn't handle it. In a few hours water rose six hundred feet in the mine, submerging two thirds of it. The water ruined $40,000 worth of pumps. The stock-market value of the El Paso Mine dropped $540,000. Stock prices of a dozen other mines in and around Beacon Hill dropped in sympathy. Bert almost enjoyed reminding the owners of these mines that they had said he was crazy for wanting a $500,000 drainage tunnel. If they had built it in the first place, instead of the inadequate El Paso Tunnel, they would now be ahead at least $5,000,000.

The mine owners decided, better late than never. They met and palavered for months to reach agreement as to who should pay how much for a real tunnel. On March 7, 1907, they subscribed $400,000 for the job. A contractor promised to get it done in two years at twenty-one dollars a foot, ten feet a day. It was named the Roosevelt Deep Drainage Tunnel and work started May 1, 1907, down Cripple Creek stream at Gatch Park.

1902. When Bob Womack, discoverer of Cripple Creek, returned as guest of honor at the Independence Day Celebration, he recalled the tiny group of men who had constituted the gold camp in April, 1891. "How things have changed!" he murmured. "Why, you have a great city now!"

1899. Verner Z. Reed, a Scott Fitzgerald character twenty-five years ahead of the *Jazz Age*, was only thirty-six when he got a million-dollar commission for selling the Independence Mine. He took the million to Paris and spent the next dozen years in happy pursuit of Bohemian outdoor and indoor sports.

1908. Gold, like sex, is something men have yearned for since the days of Adam and Eve without knowing precisely why. The results of that yearning were strikingly evident in Cripple's main producing area during the burst of confidence caused by Bert Carlton's work on the Roosevelt Drainage Tunnel.

1914. Dick Roelofs, "the miracle miner," poked his head through a hole in the Cresson Mine and found himself looking at gold worth $1,200,000. A little later he retired and became, during the next thirty years, one of New York's most colorful *boulevardiers*.

Right off, the contractor was in trouble. The rock at Gatch Park was a hard and seamless granite. After eight months the tunnel was in only 1200 feet instead of the expected 2400 feet. At that rate the tunnel would cost twice the estimate. The mine owners had a heated session in January, 1908. The majority favored dropping the whole thing. They had the jitters anyhow because of the financial panic of October, 1907. Among those at the session were Sherman Aldrich and Ed De LaVergne of the Elkton, John T. Milliken of the Golden Cycle, Frank Peck of the Portland, Frank Castello of the Mary McKinney, Bill Lennox of the Strong, F. L. Sigel of the Vindicator and Clarence Hamlin of the Granite.

Bert Carlton rose and made a speech. He had prepared it well. He had in his hand a sheaf of estimates and other mine data. If, he said, the Roosevelt Tunnel wasn't pushed through to puncture the granite bowl at 8000 feet altitude, Cripple Creek would be finished in three years. Mines and mining machinery worth many millions would be valueless. Bert declared that gold ore worth $317,500,000 lay in the undrained 800-foot area of the mines between the El Paso Tunnel and the proposed Roosevelt Tunnel. Bert said he knew a man who could drive the Roosevelt Tunnel at the rate of eight feet a day for twenty-eight dollars a foot, no matter how hard the granite was around Gatch Park.

Sherman Aldrich, chairman of the tunnel committee, asked who this tunnel genius might be.

Bert said modestly, "A. E. Carlton."

The mine owners thought he was kidding. They had known Bert as a coal dealer, transfer man, banker and promoter, never as any kind of tunneler. To make his offer seem more ridiculous Bert named his assistants to accomplish one of the world's most difficult drainage projects. The drill boss would be a pint-sized Scotsman, James A. McIlwee, whose sole claim to fame was that he had mined coal in the old country with Harry Lauder. McIlwee was just an ordinary miner with just average knowledge of how to handle dynamite. Bert's choice for chief engineer was T. R. Countryman. As far as anybody knew, Countryman was merely another mining man.

The mine owners argued over Bert's proposition for several hours. Nothing about it impressed them except the fact that Bert had made it. They knew that if Bert Carlton agreed to do something he always did it. Someone called for votes. Sherman Aldrich cast the first one with the remark, "I favor handing Mr. Carlton this lemon." The rest supported Aldrich.

Bert had his contract. He started work on the Roosevelt Tunnel February 1, 1908. For three years he kept at it, displaying a physical stamina that would have been surprising even in a man with two good lungs. Each day he drove his big Winton down the bumpy lane along Cripple Creek to Gatch Park. Then he walked up the tunnel, or rode a tiny tram. Around his lean lanky figure he wore a dusty tan coat with velvet collar. A miner's lamp was usually attached to his gray cap. Later on he reached the tunnel heading by descending construction shafts in wobbly buckets with water dripping all around. At the heading he would go over the day's work with McIlwee and Countryman. McIlwee's Scottish burr was so thick that Bert often asked Countryman to interpret for him.

During 1908 Bert built 3434 feet of tunnel. In 1909 he built 7079 feet for a total of 11,951 (his predecessor had built 1438 feet). He added 3786 feet during 1910. This brought the tunnel to 15,737 feet — not quite three miles. It punctured the granite rim of the golden bowl, and drainage started at 8500 gallons a minute. Other contractors would extend the tunnel in the next seven years to 4.6 miles at a total cost of $815,000. But it was Bert Carlton's first three miles ($530,000) that restored confidence in the mines and delayed the big decline in gold production that came in 1919.

The Roosevelt Tunnel was put through by Bert where others had failed because of his ability to handle men and to pick the right man for the right job. The unimposing little Scot, McIlwee, developed into one of the nation's most sought-after drill bosses. Countryman's engineering brought the tunnel's two headings together with an error of less than a quarter-inch. The beneficial effect of the tunnel was felt at once. Water receded below the 8800-foot level of the old El Paso Tunnel at the rate of 110 feet a year. The drainage promised to permit mining in vast new parts of the Portland, Vindicator, El Paso, Granite, Elkton, Gold Dollar and many other old-timers. Hope blossomed in the camp.

Cripple Creekers realized that everything depended on these new areas in old bonanzas. The discovery of new bonanzas was out of the question. In twenty years Cripple's 10,000 acres had been more thoroughly explored than any other spot on earth. Engineers estimated that $300,000,000 had been spent hunting gold at Cripple — almost as much as the value of gold ore recovered. No more bonanzas could exist.

Some people kept hunting anyhow, human nature being what it is. Among them were two Chicago insurance men, J. R. and Eugene Harbeck. They had been fooling with a dud mine, the Cresson, since '94. The legend was that they got drunk in a Loop bucket shop and woke up owning the Cresson. The Harbecks had no money to develop it. But whenever good news came out of Cripple on the Associated Press wire they would sell a few shares of Cresson stock to suckers around Chicago. They would spend the proceeds on the Cresson.

They did some leasing, too. One of the leasers, Frank Ish, one-time owner of the *Cripple Creek Crusher,* sank a 600-foot shaft on the Cresson before he went broke and lit out for Goldfield, Nevada. Ish didn't find a single ounce of gold. You would think that the Harbecks could have taken that hint. And still they dribbled along. Nobody understood why they didn't forget the Cresson and put their money in something comparatively solid, like horse racing. The Cresson wasn't only barren; it was badly located above the Elkton in the gulch between Raven and Bull Hills. The spot was so rough that Jesse Waters refused to run an M–T spur there. When Waters refused to run a spur you knew the mine was hopeless. The Harbecks spent half their money coping with transportation up that wild gulch.

Charles Waldron, a big German from Stuttgart, was managing the Cresson at the time Bert Carlton started the Roosevelt Tunnel. Waldron ran the Chicken Hawk, too. He didn't want to run two mines so he gave up the punk one — the Cresson, of course. The Harbecks had some cash right then and asked Bert Carlton for another manager. Bert recommended a round-faced, ruddy, stocky fellow in his thirties named Dick Roelofs. Dick's record as a mine manager was even less impressive than McIlwee's record as a tunnel builder. Dick had sunk a shaft or two for Bert, and he was said to have got a degree in Pennsylvania as some sort of civil engineer. Ed De LaVergne, manager of the Elkton, took a shine to Dick and taught him assaying. But Dick was often idle. Things got so bad once that he took a job clerking at the Green Bee Grocery on Second Street.

The Harbecks hired Roelofs, who went to work on what appeared to be a worthless 600-foot hole overhung by an $80,000 debt. He signed up a small crew under a monosyllabic Vermonter, Luke Shepherd. Then a news black-out descended on the Cresson. It lasted three years, at the end of which fantastic rumors began to fly.

Dick Roelofs, so said the rumors, had struck acres of low-grade $15 ore. He was making the low-grade pay by superb management. He was using the pillar system — driving laterals every twenty feet or so from the main drift. His stoping was something: he stoped out holes big enough to dump Finn's Folly into. The Cresson underground was full of Dick's gadgets to speed mining. He invented a safety trip which stopped the cage from running out the top and killing men. He solved the transportation problem by erecting an aerial tram from the Cresson a mile down the gulch to Elkton. He got tagged with a nickname, "the miracle miner."

The Harbecks never issued earnings statements but people heard that "the miracle miner" made the dud Cresson pay $60,000 in 1910. Next year the barren mine was debt-free with presumed earnings of $100,000, reflecting some unwatering by the Roosevelt Tunnel. In '12 and '13 newspaper reporters claimed that the Cresson earned $150,000 annually. But Cripple Creekers wouldn't believe this one. At this late date the Cresson couldn't be a bonanza like the Portland or the Independence or the Golden Cycle. The Harbecks must be slipping an occasional tip to the reporters to write such tall tales.

Everyone admitted though that Roelofs was making some

money because the Harbecks had to hire a tax expert, a young Springs lawyer named Hildreth Frost. Late one afternoon, November 24, 1914, Frost answered his office phone in the Springs. It was Dick Roelofs and he was in a terrible state. His voice was hushed and strained. He told Hildreth, for God's sake, to catch the evening train and go to Dick's rooms in Cripple.

Hildreth reached Cripple on the Short Line at 10 P.M. He walked up Second Street to the Palace Block at the corner of Bennett and climbed the stairs to Dick's second-floor rooms. He could hear Dick's typewriter clicking faintly. But when he reached the landing the typing had stopped. Hildreth banged twice on Dick's door. No answer. Then he yelled through the keyhole.

Dick opened the door. He yanked Hildreth in, closed the door and locked it. Dick's round face was pale. He parked Hildreth in a chair, drew another close up and whispered that something unmentionable had happened that afternoon on the twelfth level of the Cresson. It was so big a thing that Dick couldn't take the responsibility alone. Two witnesses must go down into the Cresson with him in the morning. Dick told Hildreth to be a witness and to ask Ed De LaVergne to be the second witness. Hildreth phoned Ed at the Elkton and made a date.

Dick Roelofs and Frost rode the Low Line to Elkton at seven next morning. Then, with De LaVergne, they walked up the gully to the Cresson where Luke Shepherd gave them magnesium flares. They descended the cage to the twelfth level. Dick walked them around a half mile down there, so they wouldn't know exactly where they were. They turned off the drift into a lateral and brought up against a double steel door. Dick banged a signal against the door and it

opened. Behind it were three guards armed with six revolvers. Beyond the guards at one side of the lateral was a
sort of ladder-platform beneath a large hole in the wall five
feet wide. Dick motioned to Ed and Hildreth to climb on
the platform and stand in the hole. When the three men
were lined up there Dick struck a kitchen match and lighted
the magnesium flares. Ed thrust his flare through the hole
into the darkness.

What the three men saw stunned them as a child is stunned
by his first Christmas tree. It was a cave of sparkling jewels.
The brightness blinded them at first but then they made out
that the jewels were millions of gold crystals — sylvanite and
calaverite. Spattered everywhere among the crystals were
glowing flakes of pure gold as big as thumbnails. The cave
was forty feet high, twenty feet long and fifteen feet wide.
Small boulders glittered on the rough floor. Piles of white
quartz sand glowed like spun glass.

This was an Arabian Nights scene in the twentieth century.
When the magnesium flares sputtered out Ed De LaVergne
muttered, "This is a high-grader's dream!" The three stepped
down from the platform. The guards gathered around and
Ed gave a little talk. The cave, he explained, was called a
"vug." Technically it was a geode — a hollow, rounded
nodule of rock lined with gold crystals. Ed had never seen
or heard of a vug approaching the size of this one. He
praised Dick for posting armed guards and installing steel
doors in the dead-ending lateral. This vug was richer than
any room in Tiffany's. The crystals imbedded in the walls
might be worth as much as $100,000!

Ed was a little off there.

During the next month Dick Roelofs' crew scraped 1400
sacks of crystals and flakes from the walls of the vug and sold

them for $378,000. A thousand more sacks of lower-grade ore brought $90,637. Before Christmas, the crew stoped out the vug to a depth of several yards. This outer section realized some $700,000. Altogether, the Cresson vug produced $1,200,-000 in four weeks.

In November the Harbecks had pleased the Chicago suckers who had bought Cresson stock by declaring a $200,000 dividend. After Christmas the suckers received an extra dividend of $1,000,000. That extra dividend gave most stockholders ten times the amount that each had paid originally for his sucker shares.

The name of Dick Roelofs, "the miracle miner," flashed around the world as Stratton's had done in '99. Cresson stockholders couldn't do enough for him. Among other things they bought him a $4500 White motorcar. Oddly enough the man who managed all the complicated machinery of the Cresson couldn't learn to drive that White. Dick sold it finally. In '16 he became a leading Cresson stockholder himself. Three years later, at the advanced age of fifty, he retired and spent the next thirty years as one of New York City's gayest blades. The Cresson, the great bonanza that escaped notice for twenty years, continues to produce, with a record to date of $45,000,000.

No Cripple Creeker enjoyed Dick Roelofs' success more than Bert Carlton. He had always admired Dick and had been happy to recommend him to the Harbecks. Furthermore, the Cresson vug dramatized the usefulness of Bert's Roosevelt Tunnel. The vug was situated in territory which the tunnel had drained. It strengthened Bert's conviction that the drained area contained as much ore as he had claimed at the tunnel meeting in 1908.

There was plenty of life in the old camp yet! Bert could

go to work now on plans that had occupied him off and on for many years. The principal mines should come under a single management and should be integrated with transportation and milling facilities. The Woods boys had tried integration at the turn of the century and had fallen on their faces. Their trouble had been overoptimism and failure to stymie their competitors before getting out on a limb.

Bert intended to make no such mistakes. But before he could bear down on integration, Bert took time out with everyone else in Cripple for a brief interlude of rage and laughter. The interlude concerned the visit of an eminent writer, Mr. Julian Street.

CHAPTER XXVIII

Mr. Street Goes to Town

JULIAN STREET was not quite thirty-five when he visited the Pikes Peak Region. He was already one of the most successful of young American writers. He could write anything — fiction, verse, plays, travel articles. His writing had warmth and humor and often it achieved a real dramatic effect.

The great man arrived late one cold March evening, in 1914, at the Antlers Hotel, with Wallace Morgan, the illustrator. Street was collecting material for his seventh book, a series of essays on the American scene to be called *Abroad at Home*. The thirteenth chapter was to be about Colorado Springs. All the chapters were to be published also as articles in *Collier's Weekly*. Street woke up next morning and found that Springs society was going to give him the full treatment. He didn't mind. He was accustomed to being lionized because he was a famous author and because he was an elegant young man with vast charm.

But he hadn't anticipated the extent of the lionizing. Spec Penrose's Pierce Arrow transported him to Jimmie Burns' beautiful new theater, to Glockner Hospital, the Garden of the Gods, and Seven Falls. He and Wallace Morgan were feted at luncheon at the Cheyenne Mountain Country Club. In the afternoon, Eugene Shove, president of the Elkton Mine, took them on a tour of Springs palaces,

winding up at the $250,000 wedding-cake mansion of the
Charles Baldwins. Then they attended a cocktail party in
their honor at the El Paso Club. Afterwards they were wined
and dined until midnight by the Cooking Club. It was quite
a day.

Cripple Creek was not on Street's schedule but his curiosity was aroused by the tales which Shove, Penrose, Charlie
MacNeill and other Cooking Club members told him about
the place. Street perceived that the plushness of the Springs
— its profusion of clubs, fine homes, first-class hotels and
expensive shops — derived from the gold which Springs residents had found on the other side of Pikes Peak. He expressed a desire to see Cripple. Somebody offered him a car
and he accepted. Even Street lost his poise for a moment
when he realized that the "car" was a private railroad car
complete with butler.

The private car was coupled to the Short Line train the
next afternoon. Street and Morgan climbed aboard by themselves; apparently their hosts of the previous night had bad
hangovers. The heavy private car slowed down the train.
On steep grades the engineer had to stop the train altogether
to get up steam. Consequently the train reached Cripple
behind schedule, which meant that Street and Morgan had
only fifty minutes before the train would start back.

If Shove had arranged for them to be met at Cripple,
the arrangements fell through. As the train pulled into the
Short Line depot, Morgan fell into deep slumber and refused to wake up. Street stepped from the private car. There
was no one in sight. It was very cold. Street didn't know
where he was or where to go or what to see. The altitude
made his heart beat like sixty. His head ached.

Street walked north to Warren Avenue, jogged a block,

and north again, up Third. At Myers Avenue he was panting
so hard that he couldn't climb higher. He turned east on
Myers and plodded a block. On the north side of Myers,
beyond Fourth, he stopped before a crib. He got into a long
and intimate conversation with an aging prostitute. She took
him into her crib and showed him around. Then he looked
at his watch. It was almost train-time. He hurried back to
the depot and gratefully boarded the private car. Cripple
Creek never saw him again. In fact, Cripple hadn't seen him
this time — except, of course, one prostitute.

Before Street left the Springs for Salt Lake City next day,
he told Eugene Shove that Cripple had intrigued him. He
would do a separate piece on its glories. When Cripple
Creekers heard this news they were delighted. Julian Street
was a wonderful fellow. His article on Cripple in *Collier's
Weekly* would bring a flood of tourists.

The article appeared in the *Collier's* issue of November 21,
1914. Street titled it "Colorado Springs and Cripple Creek."
It was a fine piece of travel-writing. Springs residents loved it.
It described the Springs as the only civilized spot between
Chicago and San Francisco. It stressed the cosmopolitan
atmosphere of the city and the sophistication of the people.
It called the Burns Theater "a model of what a theater
should be." The Antlers Hotel "would do credit to the
shores of Lake Lucerne." The El Paso Club and Cheyenne
Mountain Country Club would be "very good clubs any-
where."

This was Street at his best. He made the Springs seem
one of the most glamorous, most artistic, most admirable
places in all the world. Then came a thrilling paragraph
about the Short Line, bringing the article to 4200 words.
Street had 800 words left to cover Cripple Creek.

The opening sentence of his gold camp section contained two errors of fact: he wrote that Cripple was above timber line and above the "cat line." Then he described Myers Avenue, asserting that each crib carried the first name of the occupant on the door — a practice which had been discontinued ten years earlier. He wrote that the aging prostitute whom he met at the corner of Myers and Fourth was named Madame Leo; she wore a blouse, white skirt and spectacles and she smelled of "strong, brutal perfume." Street glanced in her crib and noticed a chair, an iron bed, an oak dresser and a colored print "showing Cupid kissing a filmily draped Psyche."

Madame Leo's conversation formed the body of the piece. She informed Street that business was very bad in Cripple, that she wished they'd open a dance hall, that she earned only two or three dollars a day. She asked Street to send her "some nice boys" from Colorado Springs and she closed the talk by admonishing him not to forget her. Street said he wouldn't and he ended the article with the words, "And I never, never shall."

In spite of errors and some distortion, those eight hundred words told much about the gold camp as it was in 1914. Madame Leo was a true symbol of its decline. But, to Cripple Creekers, the article was a jagged spear plunged into a wound. It wasn't merely that Street eulogized Colorado Springs at length and then, almost as an afterthought, described in the most gruesome terms the community to which the Springs owed most of its blessings. Worse still, the article forced Cripple Creekers to face the fact that their beloved camp was disintegrating. Production, true enough, was holding up — over $12,000,000 annually. But production alone doesn't make a gold camp. In '98 Cripple Creek town had a population of 25,000. Homes covered the hills for miles around. Ore was easy to extract. Profits ran as high as 80 per cent of gross. As much money was poured into new mines as came out of old ones. Everyone was gay, prosperous and spurred on by the infinite promise of an infinite future.

Then Stratton died, costs rose, profits fell, capital dried up. People moved away — first the gamblers, then speculators, prospectors, dance hall girls, real estaters, assayers, lawyers, railroaders, mule-skinners, young miners. Who remained? Only those who really loved the place, who loved the encircling mountains and the blue heavens and the wonderful freedom of spirit up so high.

When Julian Street's article appeared in *Collier's,* Cripple Creek town had less than 5000 people left. It had the wasted aspect of a body that had lost four fifths of its substance. It wasn't the exciting capital of a world-famous gold camp any longer. It was just a dilapidated town working for a handful of bosses like Bert Carlton and John T. Milliken. It was a settlement of workers employed by a few unromantic corporations.

But Cripple Creek's loyal citizens sprang to its defense with the fury of the farmers at Lexington. The churches called protest meetings. Hundreds of letters of rebuke were mailed to *Collier's Weekly.* Every boarder at the National Hotel signed a petition castigating Julian Street. Mayor Jimmie Hanley wired Mark Sullivan, editor of *Collier's,* demanding that he publish a refutation of the article. Local sentiment followed that of an editorial in the *Cripple Creek Times,* which referred to Street as "a phantom-brained murderer of the truth." The editorial added:

> We are not in a position to state whether the author wrote deliberately. He may not be wholly to blame for the appear-

ance of such a disgraceful piece of literature for it is possible
that — as he admits — the rarefied air of this district affected
his mentality. Then, too, Mr. Street visited here before state-
wide prohibition became an acknowledged fact in Colorado,
and judging from the source from whence he obtained his
information, we might logically infer that the restricted district of the city did a thriving business during his brief stay
here.

In New York, editor Mark Sullivan withstood for weeks
a barrage of wires from Mayor Hanley and raging letters not
only from present Cripple Creekers but from thousands of
former residents living in all parts of the country. Julian
Street's critics simply refused to drop the matter, even though
distracted mightily by the Cresson vug excitement. At last,
Mark Sullivan broke silence and wrote Mayor Hanley offering to publish a refutation of Street's article, provided it met
Collier's editorial standards. The proviso seemed a little
cynical. At any rate it didn't fool anybody at Cripple. Nevertheless, Mayor Hanley held a contest, offering $25 first prize
for a piece to submit to *Collier's*. Dr. Thomas A. McIntyre
won, and his article was sent to Mark Sullivan in January,
1915. It was turned down.

When the rejected manuscript came back to Cripple a
meeting of townfolk was held at the Elks Club. The discus-
sion was serious. Suggestions were made for action against
Julian Street by Governor's proclamation or in the Colorado
legislature, or even in the United States Senate. Suddenly,
someone said something. A small laugh went up. Then a
loud laugh. Then the whole club roared. The meeting ended
in a torrent of mirth.

Mayor Hanley and his four aldermen met that same night.
Hanley made a proposal. It passed. Hanley phoned the Asso-

ciated Press. The AP man laughed. Ten minutes later the message was flying over the nation on the AP wire:

TONIGHT THE CITY COUNCIL OF CRIPPLE CREEK COLO-
RADO APPROVED UNANIMOUSLY CHANGING THE NAME OF
MYERS AVENUE TO JULIAN STREET.

King Bert

THE RICH ORE WAS GONE from many Cripple Creek mines by 1915. But enough was left in the camp so that Albert Eugene Carlton could triumph at last.

We haven't written much about John T. Milliken because he was an absentee landlord, though an active one. From the start Bert regarded him as his worst enemy. Milliken moved in on Cripple in 1900 by paying $600,000 for some of Dave Moffat's mines, including the Golden Cycle. He was forty-seven years old, an autocratic, driving little man who had made millions as a chemist in St. Louis. He built a gold reduction mill at Florence, didn't like the way it worked and sold it in '03 to Charlie Tutt, Spec Penrose and Charlie MacNeill.

Three years later he built the Golden Cycle Mill at Colorado City. By that time, Tutt, Penrose and MacNeill had sold their gold mills to the Guggenheim family. Milliken's Golden Cycle was the most modern cyanide mill in the world. Within five years the Golden Cycle drove the Guggenheim mills out of business.

In 1908, Milliken bought at a bargain price the United Gold Mines Company, that huge consolidation of more than one hundred Cripple Creek mines which the Woods boys had been forced to sell. Milliken made these mines a part of the

Golden Cycle Mill company. Their function was to provide the mill with ore. He bought large lignite coal mines near the Springs to protect the mill's fuel supply. He had a cute way of keeping the M–T Railroad from charging too much for hauling ore to his mill. Every so often he issued plans for an aerial tramway which would stalk down the mountain thirty miles from the Golden Cycle Mine near Victor all the way to the Golden Cycle Mill in Colorado City.

Though Bert Carlton was very important in Cripple after Stratton's death, his power was restricted because he was not immensely wealthy. His dazzling financial skill allowed him to hold his own against minor millionaires, with the help of his First National Bank on Bennett Avenue. But he couldn't handle a temperamental tycoon like Milliken. Through the years, Bert came to believe that the gold camp was too small for two men as set in their ways as Milliken and himself. Bert thought that he would have to get out in the end. Milliken's millions would win hands down.

But Bert changed his mind. It was while he was working on the Roosevelt Tunnel. He was talking one day with his old friend Spec Penrose about his interminable proxy fights with Milliken and how Milliken cramped his style. Penrose declared that Milliken wanted to get control of the Penrose-Tutt mine, the Ajax. Bert said he wished to God there was a way to get Milliken out of Cripple. But, he added, it couldn't be done unless somebody bought him out. And nobody had *that* much money.

Penrose said, "Is that so?" Then he told Bert what he and Charlie MacNeill had been up to for the past five years.

This book is about gold, but we can shift to copper for a moment, because gold led MacNeill and Penrose into the copper business. In 1902, MacNeill hired a metallurgist,

Daniel C. Jackling, for the Tutt-Penrose-MacNeill mill at Canon City. Jackling had worked for MacNeill at Cripple earlier, and then went to Utah for some years to experiment with a vast deposit of low-grade copper ore at Bingham Canyon. When he got back with MacNeill, Jackling displayed an obsession about Utah copper and the money he could make if he had a half million dollars to build a new type of copper mill. After a bit, Spec Penrose joined MacNeill in listening to Jackling. Spec asked his geologist brother, Dick, what he thought. Dick okayed Jackling's idea.[1]

The half million dollars for Jackling's mill was raised mainly by MacNeill, Spec Penrose and Charlie Tutt. These three had done well at Cripple, but they were not nabobs then by any means and it wasn't easy for them to put up such a chunk of capital. But they got it together all right, with minor help from both of Spec's brothers, Dick and Senator Boies Penrose. And so, in 1904, the Utah Copper Company was born at Bingham, Utah. Soon Charlie Tutt pulled out because he had a copper mine in Oregon he liked better. Spec bought the Tutt interest. Jackling built his mill while Charlie MacNeill and Spec sweated it out. Before Jackling got the mill running right, the two Cripple Creekers were scraping the bottom of their personal barrels to maintain Jackling's grubstake. If Jackling's mill didn't do what it was supposed to do, the Cripple Creek profits of Penrose and MacNeill would be lost.

It did what it was supposed to do — and then some. The results were so sensational that Jackling's mill was hailed throughout the industry as a revolutionary achievement. It recovered copper so cheaply that Jackling himself had to revise his estimates. He had told MacNeill and Penrose that 37,000,000 tons of 2 per cent copper ore was available at

Bingham. In a short time, the Jackling mill was making profits on 1 per cent ore. Naturally, this increased the ore reserves. Jackling raised his estimate to 100,000,000 tons. Actually, Utah Copper has treated more than 460,000,000 tons of ore. It has produced copper worth $1,500,000,000, and has paid dividends of $500,000,000. Some mining people consider it to be the most productive metal mine in the whole world.

But we are concerned with what Spec Penrose told Bert Carlton in 1910, the sixth year of Utah Copper's life. In the previous year Penrose had brought the Guggenheims into the Utah Copper picture, obtaining many millions from them for a vast expansion of Jackling's mill and for a railroad from mine to mill. Spec disclosed to Bert that copper profits had expanded in proportion, with the result that he and Charlie MacNeill were drowning in money. Charlie's income was $100,000 a month. Spec, Utah Copper's biggest stockholder, got twice as much. And these immense profits would probably continue through their lifetimes and longer. Buy out John T. Milliken? At the rate they were going, they could buy the State of Colorado in time, unless some Texas oil man got there first!

Penrose asked Bert if Cripple were still a good investment. Bert explained about the benefits of the Roosevelt Tunnel and about economies that could be achieved if Milliken were out and he, Bert, ran the principal mines, the Golden Cycle Mill and the M–T Railroad. Since the mines were connected underground, dozens of shafts and costly hoisting machinery could be abandoned. Stock prices could be stabilized. Production could be regulated to fit the capacity of the mill.

That was enough for Penrose, who had a talk with MacNeill. The two of them decided to back Bert. He was

not to take any more guff from Milliken. Instead he was
to let Milliken understand that he could match him dollar
for dollar, or better. As soon as the Roosevelt Tunnel proved
its worth, Bert was to fight Milliken openly for control of
everything Milliken owned in Cripple and in Colorado City.

It was a corporation battle royal. Carlton and Milliken
owned considerable stock in each other's companies and in
companies controlled by other groups. The result was a series
of explosive directors' and stockholders' meetings, of complicated legal maneuvers, of skirmishes on the political and
every other front.

Even on the social front. Here Bert won some splendid
victories. For instance, he served as marriage broker when
an old friend of his, Colonel T. B. Burbridge, wooed the
widow of one of the great Vindicator Mine's owners. The
Colonel got his girl and the Vindicator moved over to Bert's
side. Right away the Vindicator started a million-dollar suit
against Milliken on the grounds that the Golden Cycle had
encroached that much on Vindicator ore.

Bert Carlton, the hick general, was certainly outflanking
the Napoleon from St. Louis. However, few people believed
Bert could win until, unexpectedly, Milliken abandoned the
field. This occurred a few weeks after the Cresson vug excitement and the uproar over Julian Street. Milliken had good
reasons to surrender, in addition to the fact that Carlton had
outmaneuvered him. He had found huge old riches in Oklahoma. Because of them, his Cripple Creek defeat didn't
worry him.

The Milliken-Carlton deal was announced late in February, 1915. It had two parts. First, Milliken's Golden Cycle
Mine at Cripple was detached from the Golden Cycle Mill
at Colorado City, and was sold to the Vindicator for $1,500,-

ooo. Second, Bert Carlton, Spencer Penrose and Eugene Shove (Julian Street's tour guide) paid Milliken $4,500,000 for the Golden Cycle Mill and associated properties, including the United Gold Mines, the lignite coal mines, $500,000 in cash, and $1,500,000 proceeds from the sale of the Golden Cycle Mine to the Vindicator. President Carlton promptly issued Golden Cycle Mill stock at a dollar a share. Two months later he declared a dollar dividend, just to show folks what kind of president he was.

Of course the Cresson Mine was a brand-new competitor now, but, with Milliken out of Cripple Creek, Bert held the balance of power. In addition, he had a friend at the Cresson, manager Dick Roelofs. Bert approached the Cresson's owners and they slapped a price on the mine — $3,900,000, or $3.25 a share. Bert formed a syndicate — Spec Penrose, MacNeill, Shove, Roelofs, Adolph Zang of the Vindicator, Leslie Carlton, Colonel T. B. Burbridge and Claude Boettcher, the Denver financier. They bought the Cresson and Bert took it over, issuing Cresson stock at $3 a share. Almost at once Bert declared a regular *monthly* dividend of ten cents — $1.20 a year, or 40 per cent profit on the investment. In 1919 Cresson stock hit $13.80 a share.

During these consolidations, Bert and Ethel left their Cripple Creek apartment over Bert's bank and moved to the Springs. Their first Springs home was, properly, on Millionaire's Row (Wood Avenue), across from Jimmie Burns. Ethel signalized her residency by giving a bandstand to Monument Valley Park where Spec Penrose had just given a swimming pool.

Cripple Creekers were used to people deserting them, and often they resented it. But they didn't resent Bert and Ethel. Bert had stuck by them through hell and — literally

— high water for twenty-two years; Ethel for seventeen years. And, anyhow, they knew that Bert would remain their man. After the Cresson deal he just got in deeper and deeper. He bought back the Colorado Trading and Transfer Company from the Midland Terminal. He slipped off to Paris and, backed by Penrose and MacNeill, bought enough stock to get the M–T away from Henry Blackmer. He bought the Colorado Midland and junked all but the Ute Pass part; that part went to the M–T. He bought the Vindicator Mine in '22. Only the Portland and the Strong escaped him, though the Portland did become a United Gold Mines property in '33.

By 1930, Bert Carlton was head of Cripple Creek mines having total production records of $227,000,000.

He was a simple man, except in business. Ethel induced him to build a fine home north of the Springs at Pine Valley, but Bert took no interest in it. He preferred their apartment at the Broadmoor Hotel. When Ethel had a few rooms finished at Pine Valley she drove Bert out for the week-end. He fell ill and died there a few days later of uremic poisoning, at the age of sixty-five. The date was September 7, 1931.

Even after death Bert has led Cripple. His brother, Leslie, carried on his policies ably until he died, in '38. Then Ethel stepped in, the same Ethel whose feet Bert tramped on so lovingly at the National Hotel dance in '96. Ethel didn't know much about mining but she knew what Bert wanted for Cripple. In the late '30s, the mines were having water trouble again. Ethel demanded and got the famous Carlton Drainage Tunnel, 1136 feet below Bert's Roosevelt Tunnel. The Carlton Tunnel was finished in '41 at a cost of $1,250,-000. It is six and a quarter miles long, and it drains Cripple down to 6900 feet above sea level.

When World War II came, Cripple Creek had to shut down. Afterward, inflation set in and the mines couldn't be worked unless operating costs could be cut. Ethel went at it again. The Midland Terminal Railroad and the Golden Cycle Mill in Colorado City were dismantled. The splendid Carlton Mill — a $2,000,000 cyanide mill — was built at Cripple just below the Elkton and Cresson Mines. This mill can treat ore at a base cost of about $3 a ton. Because of it, Cripple Creek mining has resumed.

The valiant spirit of the man who, back in 1891, expected to be dead of T.B. in six months, lives on in the clanking corridors of the Carlton Mill, in scores of Carlton mines, in the damp depth of Carlton Tunnel. Recently Harry Gehm, one of the wisest of Cripple's old-timers, summed up what Bert meant to the camp. Harry said, "Bob Womack discovered the place. Stratton was its beacon light in the boom days. A. E. Carlton was its heartbeat."

What are we to think of Cripple in the end?

Colorado is a happy land. It is also a wealthy land. The wealth gives its people health, good education, leisure and a serene optimism about life. The wealth traces back to two great and equal events: the discovery in 1878 of Leadville, the world's greatest silver camp, and the discovery in 1890 of Cripple Creek, the world's greatest gold camp.

The effects of Cripple Creek gold are on display everywhere. Verner Reed and Henry M. Blackmer used their gold to make Denver the oil capital of the Rockies. Dave Moffat won at Cripple a third of the money which built the Moffat Road and resulted in the Moffat Tunnel. Bert Carlton spent his gold to organize and develop the Holly Sugar Corporation, second largest beet sugar producer in the United States.

J. R. McKinnie created industries from Garden City to Grand Junction. The Bernard boys spent their gold improving Colorado horses and cattle.

But Cripple conferred its greatest blessings on Colorado Springs. Every foot of that pleasant place bears Cripple's stamp. On a wooded knoll, southwest of town, is the Myron Stratton Home, perhaps the most beautiful haven for human beings on earth. Beyond the Home is the Broadmoor Hotel. Spec Penrose and Charlie MacNeill built it out of copper profits but they were Cripple Creekers first, last and always. Furthermore, Cripple's gold formed the ante which won for them their copper jackpot. The Broadmoor is really Spec's creation, though MacNeill backed him. After MacNeill's death, Spec owned the Broadmoor alone, expanding its facilities to embrace a zoo, a golf course, ice palace, a stadium seating ten thousand, stables, museum, funicular, cog railroad up Pikes Peak, trout lake and a mountain 10,400 feet high with honeymoon lodge on top. Spec, a man of Oriental splendor, died in 1939. His estate, El Pomar Foundation, gives away almost a million dollars a year, largely to the people of Colorado Springs.

Down in town a movie marquee mars the white façade of Jimmie Burns' theater, but it is still a handsome structure. Nearby is the Exchange National Bank Building which Cripple's gold created. Stratton's Mining Exchange is a block beyond. To the north is the Giddings block; to the south the Carlton Building. Other real estate in the area belongs to the Stratton Estate or to relatives of Cripple Creekers like Irving Howbert or Charlie Tutt or Bill Lennox. North on Cascade and Nevada Avenues and lower Wood Avenue are the rambling mansions of Cripple Creek millionaires, mostly apartment houses now. They were a godsend in World War

II, absorbing the population increase that came with Camp Carson. Further north is Glockner-Penrose Hospital. The altar in the lovely chapel at Glockner-Penrose was donated by Jimmie Burns and his sisters.

Cripple's future? As a gold producer, good. Geologists say the mining district will be producing gold in moderate amounts a century hence. But Cripple was the last of the great nineteenth-century camps with their frenzied activity, big populations and rampant individualism. Modern machinery and social security have seen to that. When a man is out of work today he doesn't head for the hills. He is more apt to stay at home and wait for another job to turn up.

But Cripple has a bright future of another kind. Summer tourists.

When World War II ended, a couple of GIs, Wayne and Dorothy Mackin, took the Imperial Hotel on Third Street and began staging hilarious melodramas in the downstairs bar. They became so popular that you couldn't get a seat for love or money, except days ahead. Thousands of tourists have descended the 700-foot shaft of the Mollie Kathleen, above Poverty Gulch, to see a real gold mine. Lately Margaret Giddings, granddaughter of Ed Giddings, and Blevins Davis, of Ballet Theater, bought the Cripple Creek newspaper, the old Midland Terminal Depot and other properties for tourist promotion.

Tourists have always come up, and they'll keep coming up. The ramshackle old town has special charm for us these days. We get bored at times with our antiseptic lives, our caution, our mania to be insured against everything. None of that stuff on Bennett Avenue. It is falling to pieces, but the romance remains. As we look up the swayback, past Johnnie Nolon's, we feel giddy, free.

Of course it might be the altitude. But why not ghosts, inspiring us with their own careless love of life? Joe Wolfe under his great sombrero planning a flimflam. Sally Halthusen, all aglow as she stalks a Socialite. Grant Crumley carrying a tray of oysters and champagne to the Carlton apartment. Dick Roelofs, blinded by the golden brilliance of the Cresson vug . . .

Why not Cripple Creek ghosts?

Appendices

TABLE I

Cripple Creek Gross Gold Production, 1890–1951

SOURCE: **U. S.** Bureau of Mines *Minerals Yearbooks*

Year	Production	Total to Date	Shipping Mines	Comment
1890	$ 0	$ 0	0	Womack Discovery
1891	200,000	200,000	3	
1892	557,851	757,851	50	
1893	2,025,518	2,783,369	150	Golden Era starts
1894	2,634,349	5,417,718	175	
1895	6,210,622	11,628,340	250	
1896	7,456,763	19,085,103	350	
1897	10,167,782	29,252,885	400	
1898	13,547,350	42,800,235	450	
1899	16,107,943	58,908,178	475	
1900	18,199,736	77,107,914	475	
1901	17,288,030	94,395,944	475	
1902	16,965,689	111,361,633	475	Stratton dies
1903	11,862,739	126,224,372	325	Big business takes over
1904	14,484,270	137,708,642	225	
1905	15,676,494	153,385,136	200	
1906	13,976,727	167,361,863	160	Acute water trouble
1907	10,404,360	177,766,223	155	
1908	13,059,620	190,825,843	150	
1909	11,499,093	202,325,936	150	
1910	11,031,555	213,356,491	145	
1911	10,593,278	223,949,769	145	Roosevelt Tunnel
1912	11,049,024	234,998,793	144	drainage starts
1913	10,948,008	245,946,801	140	
1914	12,045,364	257,992,165	140	Cresson vug found
1915	13,727,992	271,720,157	140	King Bert
1916	12,172,061	283,892,218	140	
1917	10,448,051	294,340,269	135	
1918	8,170,412	302,510,681	75	Golden Era ends
1919	5,867,511	308,378,192	41	
1920	4,360,960	312,739,152	41	

TABLE I *(Continued)*

Year	Production	Total to Date	Shipping Mines	Comment
1921	$4,329,218	$317,068,370	47	
1922	4,062,044	321,130,414	55	
1923	4,065,545	325,195,959	48	
1924	4,960,716	330,156,675	43	
1925	4,608,604	334,765,279	40	
1926	4,451,992	339,217,271	36	
1927	3,321,875	342,539,146	50	
1928	3,070,203	345,609,349	49	
1929	2,644,961	348,254,310	41	
1930	2,535,378	350,786,638	63	
1931	2,385,769	353,175,457	41	
1932	2,200,724	355,376,181	52	
1933	2,273,878	357,650,059	111	
1934	4,479,966	362,130,025	135	Gold up to $35 an ounce
1935	4,300,891	366,430,916	130	
1936	4,956,287	371,387,203	135	
1937	5,089,899	376,477,102	136	
1938	5,092,556	381,569,658	134	
1939	4,702,125	386,271,783	110	
1940	4,533,831	390,805,614	105	
1941	4,686,810	395,492,424	99	Carlton Tunnel opens
1942	3,667,061	399,159,485	42	
1943	1,584,039	402,327,563	22	
1944	1,084,289	403,411,852	20	
1945	999,049	404,410,901	19	
1946	1,673,489	406,084,390	25	
1947	2,041,738	408,126,128	37	
1948	1,874,915	410,001,043	28	
1949	473,805	410,474,848	13	Railroad, mill dismantled
1950 (est)	500,000	410,974,848	15	
1951 (est)	2,000,000	412,974,848*	30	Carlton Mill running

* Ben Hill, Harry Gehm and other Cripple Creek old-timers estimate that to the official Bureau of Mines total production of $412,974,848 should be added at least $20,000,000 of high-graded gold that never went to mint or mill. This figure would raise the grand total production for 61 years to $432,974,848.

NOTE: Above figures include ½ of 1 per cent silver value.

TABLE II

Great Gold Camps of the World
Estimated Value of Production

Discovery Year	Gold Camp	Estimated Production	Comment
1884	Witwatersrand, South Africa	$9,714,900,000	A region: supplies half of world total
1910	Porcupine, Ontario, Canada	981,951,959	Passed Cripple late 1930s
1911	Kirkland Lake, Ontario	551,547,959	Passed Cripple late 1930s
1876	Homestake, South Dakota	494,113,151	Single mine: passed Cripple late 1930s
1890	Cripple Creek, Colorado	432,974,848	99½ per cent gold, 475 mines
1888	Kalgoorlie, Western Australia	425,000,000	In decline
1851	Bendigo, Victoria, Australia	425,000,000	Almost exhausted
1846	Lena District, Siberia	412,620,000	A region: To 1926
1859	Virginia City, Nevada (Comstock)	380,000,000	⅔ silver, ⅓ gold: done

SOURCES: Witwatersrand (Rand) figure from *Journal of the Chemical and Metallurgy and Mining Society of South Africa,* Vol. 49,#10, April 1949.

Ontario Estimates from Ontario Department of Mines, Toronto.

Colorado Estimates from Charles W. Henderson, *Professional Paper 138; Mining in Colorado,* U. S. Geological Survey, and from *Colorado State Year-Book, 1949–50.*

Other United States and Alaska Estimates from U. S. Bureau of Mines *Minerals Yearbooks,* 1900–1950.

All other estimates from William Harvey Emmons, *Gold Deposits of the World* (McGraw-Hill).

TABLE II *(Continued)*

Discovery Year	Gold Camp	Estimated Production	Comment
1882	Yenisei Region, USSR	$371,120,000	To 1923
1882	Kolar, British India	300,000,000	The single Champion Lode
1849	Mother Lode, California	270,000,000	A region: exhausted
1873	San Juan Mountains, Colorado	200,000,000	A region
1896	Klondike, Yukon Territory	186,030,000	In decline
1859	Central City, Colorado	170,000,000	In decline
1902	Goldfield, Nevada	100,000,000	Includes much silver
1900	Fairbanks, Alaska	85,000,000	In decline
1898	Nome, Alaska	80,000,000	In decline

TABLE III

Cripple Creek Mining District Population, 1890–1950

Year	Population	Year	Population	Year	Population
1890	15	1896	36,850	1905	28,050
1891	450	1897	39,304	1910	13,117
1892	2,500	1898	42,615	1920	5,682
1893	12,500	1899	43,003	1930	3,447
1894	19,603	1900	50,111	1940	5,137
1895	29,401	1901	44,201	1950	1,980
		1902	43,237		

SOURCES: Annual *Cripple Creek District Directory* to 1905. U. S. Census thereafter.

TABLE IV

Cripple Creek District Towns
Platting Dates and Population, 1900

Town	Platting Date	Population, 1900
Cripple Creek:		
Fremont	Nov. 4, 1891	25,000
Hayden Placer	Feb. 15, 1892	
First Fremont Addition	Feb. 1, 1892	
Freeman Placer Addition	May 17, 1895	
Victor: (includes Hollywood, Lawrence, Portland Station, Strong's Camp)	Nov. 6, 1893	12,000
Goldfield	Jan. 8, 1895	3,500
Elkton (includes Arequa, Beacon, Eclipse)	Never platted	2,500
Altman (includes Midway)	Sept 25, 1893	1,500
Independence (includes Hull City)	Nov. 12, 1894	1,500
Anaconda (consolidation of Mound City, Barry, Squaw Gulch)	1894	1,000
Gillett	Jan. 19, 1894	700
Cameron: as "Cripple Creek"	Feb. 27, 1892	700
as "Grassy"	Oct. 29, 1894	
as "Cameron"	Apr. 7, 1900	
Beaver Park (Love)	Mar. 11, 1892	75
Arequa (Bob Womack homestead)	Feb. 17, 1892	*See Elkton*
Lawrence	Jan. 4, 1892	*See Victor*

TABLE V

Leading Cripple Creek Mines: Gross Production, Surface Altitude, and Depth

Mine	Gross Production to 1951	Surface Altitude, Feet Above Sea Level	Depth in Feet
Portland	$60,000,000	10,240	3,200
Cresson	49,000,000	10,003	2,400
Independence	28,000,000	9,840	1,420
Vindicator	27,200,000	10,210	2,150
Golden Cycle	22,510,000	10,060	2,170
Ajax	20,700,000	10,100	2,600
Elkton	16,200,000	9,730	1,700
Granite	15,828,000	10,080	1,000
Isabella Group	15,700,000	10,460	1,150
Strong	13,000,000	9,750	950
El Paso (Beacon Hill)	10,800,000	9,360	1,300
Mary McKinney	10,700,000	9,530	1,400
Last Dollar	7,500,000	10,270	1,600
Dr. Jack Pot	7,126,000	9,751	1,000
Hull City	5,010,000	10,280	1,200
Jerry Johnson	5,000,000	10,320	900
Findley	3,137,000	10,490	1,400
Anchoria Leland	3,000,000	10,130	1,300
Gold King (Womack's El Paso Lode)	3,000,000	9,850	1,000

Notes

CHAPTER I: Kentucky Goes West

1. Bob's full name was Robert Miller Womack. Miller was a friend in the neighborhood.

2. They were. Poor Sam had only fifty-two more years to live.

3. Irving Howbert; born Columbus, Ind., 1846, son of a Methodist minister, reared in Quincy, Iowa; to Colorado in 1860; clerk of El Paso County 1869–1879; cashier First National Bank of Colorado Springs, 1878; made silver fortune at Leadville, in 1880s; served Pikes Peak region thereafter as its greatest pioneer next to General William Jackson Palmer, founder of the Denver & Rio Grande Railroad. Howbert died in 1934.

CHAPTER II: They Called It a Cripple

1. Before 1871, Cripple Creek valley was called Pisgah Park.

2. F. V. Hayden, father of the United States Geological Survey, spent several summers surveying the West. Hostile Sioux Indians once captured him and found only a bag of rocks and fossils on him. They concluded he was insane and let him go. After that they called him The-Man-Who-Picks-Up-Rocks-Running.

3. If Cripple's gold had been found in '74 instead of '90, Colorado Springs, instead of Denver, might be capital of the Rocky Mountain empire today. Denver in '74 had no very good reason for existing at all. What made it was the Leadville boom after 1878.

CHAPTER III: Hoax at "Mount Pisgah"

1. Old Mose had roamed the West Pikes Peak country since 1860. He ate at least two men and unnumbered cattle. He weighed

a thousand pounds and stood ten feet high. He was killed in 1904 by an expert bear hunter from Indiana, J. W. Anthony.

2. Chicken Bill Lovell got his name when he was caught in a blizzard while freighting chickens to Leadville. Rescuers found him three weeks later, fat and sassy and almost buried in feathers of the chickens he had consumed. He salted and sold many barren Leadville mines. But one, the Chrysolite, backfired. H. A. W. Tabor bought it and took out a half million dollars in silver.

CHAPTER IV: Cow Path to Golconda

1. Bob and William Womack sold their homesteads long before their patents came through. William's homestead patent was issued December 20, 1884; Bob's April 29, 1889 (El Paso County Records, Book 45, pages 122 and 201).

CHAPTER VI: Little London and Ed De LaVergne

1. General Palmer, actually, was a very great man, but his place with the top American Western heroes has been obscured because of his own modesty and because nothing has ever been printed about him indicating that he chewed tobacco, spat, made love, or otherwise behaved like a human being. He was born in Delaware, brought up a Philadelphia Quaker, started railroading for the Pennsylvania and joined the Union Army in '61. He missed Shiloh, but was at Antietam, where he got captured as a spy, by a hair escaped being shot, and was jailed for three months in Richmond. After his exchange he recruited the Fifteenth Pennsylvania Cavalry, picking his recruits "mainly from educated, middle-class families." His outfit served with honor all over Tennessee and almost captured Jeff Davis in Georgia. Then the General built the Denver & Rio Grande railroad to populate the empty Colorado Rockies, surely one of the boldest projects in railroad history.

2. Midland freight trains had no air brakes and often ran wild on the awful slope down Ute Pass from Hayden Divide (now Divide). An upgrade siding was built halfway down with a switchman always on duty. If the freight was out of control, the switchman turned the runaway into the steep upgrade to halt it.

CHAPTER VII: Bob Lands in the Clink

1. A list of early Cripple Creek claims follows, taken from the records at El Paso County Court House:

Lone Tree Prospect Tunnel, located Sept. 17, 1874, by H. T. Wood, Ben Requa and others.

Grand View Lode, located Oct. 13, 1886, by Robert M. Womack.

Greenwood Lode, located Aug. 26, 1887, by Edwin Wallace and Theodore Lowe.

Hematite Lode, located Nov. 1, 1887, by Edwin Wallace.

El Paso Discovery Lode, located Oct. 20, 1890, by Robert M. Womack and John Grannis.

Blanche Lode, located Feb. 20, 1891, by George Carr and others.

Hobo Lode, located Feb. 20, 1891, by George Carr and others.

Blue Bell Lode, located Feb. 20, 1891, by George Carr and others.

El Dorado Lode, located Feb. 26, 1891, by Ed De LaVergne, Harry Seldomridge, Fred Frisbee, and E. A. Colburn.

Old Mortality Lode, located Feb. 28, 1891, by Ed De LaVergne and others.

Grouse Lode, located March 2, 1891, by W. B. Pullin and others.

Wilson Placer, located March 16, 1891, by C. L. Wilson, J. C. Wilson, John Wilson, H. A. Wilson, W. H. Grose, and T. Grose.

Sheriff Lode, located March 22, 1891, by Matt France, Len Jackson and others.

Sangre de Cristo Tunnel, located March 26, 1891, by Ed De LaVergne and others.

Lillian Leland, located March 30, 1891, by C. L. Wilson and others.

Womack Placer, located March 31, 1891, by Robert M. Womack and Thomas J. Bryan.

Hayden Placer, located April 4, 1891, by Ed De LaVergne, J. C. Plumb, Frank Howbert, H. C. McCreery, Fred Frisbee, Sam Kinsley, and Harry Seldomridge.

Cripple Creek Placer, located April 4, 1891, by Ed De LaVergne, Fred Frisbee, George Carr and others.

Conundrum Lode, located April 4, 1891, by C. L. Wilson and others.

Lone Star #1, located April 5, 1891, by E. B. Kelley and others.

Pride of the Rockies, located April 15, 1891, by Matt Sterrett.

South Park Lode, located May 11, 1891, by Tom Houghton and Frank Castello.

Gold King Lode, located May 16, 1891, by J. R. McKinnie and W. H. Gowdy.

Mayflower Lode, located May 27, 1891, by Tom Houghton and
Frank Castello.

Mary McKinney Lode, located May 27, 1891, by John Houghton
and others. (Named after the wife of one of the Houghton
boys; no connection with J. R. McKinnie.)

Deer Horn Lode, located May 28, 1891, by Matt Sterrett.

No Name Placer, located June 6, 1891, by W. S. Stratton, Fred
Trautman, L. W. Popejoy, and August House.

CHAPTER IX: Count Pourtales to the Rescue

1. Tom Parrish was the father of Anne Parrish, the novelist.

CHAPTER X: A Town Is Born

1. The postmaster of this "Fremont" post office on Hayden
Placer ground was Bill Gowdy, whom we saw last on Battle Mountain with Stratton, McKinnie, Sam Strong and Jimmie Burns. The
post-office job paid eighteen dollars a week, so naturally Bill
Gowdy quit prospecting. This post office consisted of a crackerbox
with twelve partitions, in a corner of Gowdy's log cabin. It handled mail bearing various address-names. "Fremont" was the most
popular because John Charles Frémont, who had died the year
before, was a great hero in the Rockies.

One day Bill Gowdy received word from postal authorities that
"the request of the residents of Fremont, Colorado, to change
the name of their town to Moorland, Colorado, is hereby granted
by the U. S. Post Office." It was news to Bill that anyone at
Cripple had made such a request, but orders were orders,
so he told the tenderfeet that "Fremont" was out as a postal
address and the mysterious "Moorland" was in. And then another
order came from postal authorities: "Through a clerical error the
U. S. Post Office directed you to change the name of Fremont,
Colorado, to Moorland, Colorado. The community making the
original request for a change of name was not Fremont, Colorado,
but Fremont, Kansas, which will be known henceforth as Moorland, Kansas. Moorland, Colorado, is hereby cancelled in favor of
the former designation, Fremont, Colorado." The bureaucrats
were with us even then.

2. To cross up the Hayden Placer group in its use of "Cripple
Creek" as its townsite name, Bennett platted the distant Allen

Gullion homestead of Grassy into a townsite also called "Cripple Creek" — at least on the records. Nevertheless, Hayden Placer was incorporated officially as the town of "Cripple Creek" on June 9, 1892. In 1894, Bennett gave in and changed the name of his ghostly "Cripple Creek" back to "Grassy." Later, in 1900, "Grassy" became "Cameron."

3. Bennett died in 1941 near Denver, at Wolhurst, perhaps the most famous country estate in Colorado before its destruction by fire in 1951. It was built by Senator Ed Wolcott. It was owned later, before Bennett, by Thomas F. Walsh, the San Juan gold king and father of Evalyn Walsh McLean. Bennett paid $150,000 for Wolhurst.

CHAPTER XI: Happy Days!

1. Fred Stone was the first of many Cripple Creek residents who would win fame elsewhere. Another in the pioneer period was a huge youngster of twenty-two, Bernard Baruch, who passed some time as a pick-and-shovel miner on Bull Hill. To prove he wasn't just another soft Eastern dude, Baruch had to fight a man who claimed to be the boxing champion of Altman. Baruch beat the tar out of him in two brisk rounds. His genius for mathematics showed up one night at the Branch Saloon, when he almost broke the bank by hitting the right combination at roulette twelve times running.

The late Ralph Carr (no relation to George Carr) reached camp in '94, attended school there and worked on the *Cripple Creek Times*. He was Governor of Colorado from 1939 to 1943, one of the best the State has had. The most loyal of all Cripple Creekers is Lowell Thomas, who grew up in Victor. He has helped the camp often in recent years. His first job, on the *Victor Record*, was to tramp all over town hunting for "the red type." He went to Sunday School at Anaconda several times, drawn by the music of an organist named Texas Guinan. Texas entertained well too and soon her Sunday School was as popular as her speakeasy would be in her days of glory as New York's "Hello, sucker!" girl.

Aspen boasts of its native, Harold Ross, late founder of *The New Yorker*. Cripple has its *New Yorker* editor too, Robert Coates, the art critic, who lived in Victor as a boy. Tour guides mention many others as Cripple Creekers, but most of them were just in and out. Ford Frick, today's baseball commissioner, covered Cripple Creek stories for the *Colorado Springs Telegraph.* Jack Dempsey mucked briefly in the Portland Mine and boxed once or twice at the Gold Coin Club. Later Dempsey became a close friend of Spec Penrose. He trained for one of the Tunney fights at Spec's Broadmoor Hotel.

2. For readers fascinated by "firsts" here is a bunch of them: Cripple Creek's first lady claim locator was Mrs. Mollie Kathleen Gortner, who staked the Mollie Kathleen in September, '91; first shipping mine, Womack's El Paso (later called Gold King), November, '91; first physician, Dr. A. Hayes; first banker, James Parker of the Bank of Cripple Creek (later the First National); first wedding, Miss C. O. Rowe, married O. E. Ayres, February 2, 1892; first electric lights, April, 1892; first English sparrows, September, 1892; first school superintendent, David Shields; first high school graduates, Miss Florence Yambert and Miss Alma Moore Simpkins, class of '97; first newspaper, *Cripple Creek Crusher,* E. C. Gard, editor (the first issue, December 7, '91, used gold ink). Second paper, *The Prospector,* W. R. McCrea, editor (the first issue was published a few hours after the *Crusher*).

CHAPTER XII: First He Was a Carpenter

1. This James Renwick McKinnie had fought with the Union in the Civil War until it was discovered that he was under age. For years thereafter he hunted buffalo and mined in the San Juans. Then he taught school near Steubenville, Ohio, married the teacher in the next school, and took up farming near Bird City, Kansas. The wind, hail and grasshoppers there were bad but worse still were the long visits of Presbyterian ministers who adopted McKinnie's farm as a way-station West. In 1890 McKinnie loaded his wife and six children into a covered wagon and reached the Springs on Thanksgiving Day. When spring came he started hauling supplies to Cripple Creek. Ten years later he would be a leading Rocky Mountain tycoon.

CHAPTER XIII: The Luck of the Irish

1. David H. Moffat was born in up-State New York in 1839, and started West in '55. He reached Denver in '61, opened a sta-

tionery store and in '67 was named cashier of the First National Bank of Denver. Thereafter, Moffat developed more than a hundred gold and silver mines in Colorado. During the 1900s he spent his personal fortune of $11,000,000 in a heroic effort to breach the Colorado Rockies directly west of Denver with a railroad. Harriman opposed it. Moffat died in 1911, but others took up his railroad dream, the Moffat Tunnel was driven under James Peak in 1927, and today the main line of the Denver & Rio Grande goes due west to Salt Lake City from Denver through the Moffat Tunnel. Though Dave's influence at Cripple was great between 1892 and 1900, he rarely if ever visited the gold camp.

2. Many mining camps have grocer success stories (H. A. W. Tabor of Leadville was a grocer). Sam and George Bernard each had small groceries in the Springs. A Fountain schoolteacher, Van E. Rouse, clerked for Sam in the summer. In '92, Sam Bernard and Rouse took over from William Shemwell a half interest in the Elkton claim for canceling Shemwell's $36.50 grocery bill. George Bernard paid Smith Gee, the colored ash-hauler, $50 for Gee's eighth interest. George financed development work for two years until he was just about broke and the Elkton was to be abandoned. Then the Bernards found pay dirt — $40,000 worth in the first week. Eventually the Elkton produced gold worth $16,-000,000. Later, Sam Bernard got control of another rich mine, the Beacon Hill El Paso (not Womack's) — a $11,000,000 producer. The Bernard boys took their millions and more or less retired from mining in 1902. George bought a huge ranch north of the Springs and raised blooded cattle. Sam went in for trotting horses. But George died practically penniless in 1933. Sam died in '37, an indigent patient at Colorado State Hospital.

CHAPTER XIV: Preface to a Nightmare

1. Altman was the highest incorporated town in North America, and one of the highest in the world, being surpassed only by a few places in the Andes and the Himalayas.

2. Calderwood's early career resembled that of the C.I.O.'s Philip Murray who, like Calderwood, was born in Scotland, worked in the mines there as a child, came to the Pennsylvania mines in his teens, was a good Catholic and was strongly influenced by Pope Leo XIII.

CHAPTER XV: The Battle of Bull Hill

1. This cannon sits near the entrance of Spencer Penrose's Broadmoor Hotel.

CHAPTER XVI: The "Tar" in Tarsney

1. When Waite was voted out of office, Tarsney went back to Durango, Colorado. He reappeared in the headlines briefly during the Spanish-American War, when he was a sutler on a ship to Manila and was accused of racketeering. After that he dropped from sight.

CHAPTER XVII: Boom, Cripple!

1. The pious Woods boys opened the Woods Investment Company office in their new town of Victor on a Saturday. On Sunday morning they conducted Victor's first Sunday School in that office.

2. It was General Palmer who first applied the English narrow-gauge idea on a large scale in the United States. He built the Denver & Rio Grande with tracks a yard apart instead of the standard-gauge width of four feet, eight and one-half inches. A narrow-gauge road is 37 per cent cheaper to build than standard gauge. In mountain country narrow-gauge grade can't be changed to standard gauge because its curves are too sharp, and its grades too steep.

3. The F. & C. C. grand entry was a flop. The last car of the first passenger train jumped the track at Anaconda, fell forty feet down the bank, and killed W. G. Milner.

4. The F. & C. C. was forty miles long, from Florence to Cripple Creek town, climbing from 5187 feet to 10,300 feet. The grades were so bad that only eight loaded freight cars could be hauled up Eight-Mile Canyon at one time. Nevertheless, the line kept running until the disastrous washout of 1912. In 1916, the right of way was transformed into the beautiful Phantom Canyon Auto Highway.

By way of contrast to the F. & C. C., the Midland Terminal was only eighteen miles long from Divide (altitude 9183 feet) to Cripple Creek town (altitude 9500 feet). Its up-and-down range was about 2000 feet (the F. & C. C.'s range was over 5000 feet).

The M–T had a solid bed and it was seldom out of commission. The longest idle period was from January 27 to April 14, 1899, due to a record snowfall.

5. The building still stands there.

6. Harry Gehm, who lost his shirt investing in mills at Cripple, declares that Charlie MacNeill's chlorination mill at Lawrence was one of two successful mills out of forty-two built up there between 1892 and 1915. The other was Tom Kavanaugh's at the Jo Dandy dump. Chemical treatment of Cripple's ores required great skill because of the variety of ores.

CHAPTER XVIII: A Lot of Bull

1. Joe Wolfe was accompanied by George Carr on this Oklahoma trip. The former foreman of the Broken Box Ranch liked Oklahoma and he never returned to Cripple Creek to live.

2. Many people have tried to stage bullfights in this country, but there is no record that any of them actually killed bulls in the classical Spanish fashion.

CHAPTER XIX: Purge by Fire

1. This is the Otto Floto who later became sports editor of the *Denver Post*. According to Gene Fowler in *Timber Line,* the owners of the *Post,* Tammen and Bonfils, decided to start a circus, which they called "Floto Dog and Pony Show." Later they christened their larger circus "The Sells-Floto Circus." Otto Floto had nothing to do with either enterprise. Tammen just liked his name.

2. Cripple Creek town had had only one fire before this. On April 16, 1892, seven buildings burned down on the south side of Bennett Avenue. A dance-hall girl, Miss Lutie Cook, was the heroine of this fire, handing down the two small Pennington children from the second-floor window of the Arcade Restaurant.

3. But many pioneers were not seen in Cripple after the fires of '96. Theodore Lowe, for example, took to prospecting in Nevada, where he died in 1902, while on a trip with William Womack. Dr. John Grannis lost his El Paso Lode profits in unwise mining ventures in Arizona and Mexico. He returned to dentistry in the Springs, dying in 1911. Although Count Pourtales

sold his Buena Vista holdings at the wrong time, he made a million or so in an Arizona gold mine, the Commonwealth, which Dick Penrose promoted. He returned happily to his feudal Silesian domain, Glumbowitz, where he died in 1908. James J. Hagerman lost his health and $3,000,000 in a huge irrigation project in the Pecos Valley of New Mexico. He died at Milan, Italy, in 1909, a disillusioned and almost poor man.

CHAPTER XX: The Crumleys and Other Nice People

1. Another boon to high-grading occurred in March of '99, when gold camp residents broke away from El Paso County and set up their own Teller County, named for the Silver Republican, Senator Henry M. Teller. This action gave them their own court, sheriff and juries, the latter being composed of miners who wouldn't think of convicting a fellow miner for high-grading.

By '99, the Western Federation of Miners was an out-and-out Socialist union. Big Bill Haywood and other officers in Denver taught Cripple Creek members that they had a right to steal gold because the nation's wealth belonged to the men who produced it. This attitude inspired some mine owners to form the Cripple Creek Mine Owners' Association, to police the mines and the assayers. It didn't work at first. The ore stealers organized the High-Graders' Association to combat the Mine Owners' Association. When the mine owners began hauling assayers' account books into court, the assayers doctored their books, listing as their customers the names of members of the Mine Owners' Association. One mine owner got proof that an assayer was buying ore stolen from his mine. He had the assayer's gold impounded at the First National Bank. The assayer sued for the gold and when it was returned to him he sued again for a dollar to pay the bank's storage charges. And he collected!

Actually, the early Mine Owners' Association didn't care too much about stopping high-grading because some of its leading members were financing crooked assayers and crooked sampling firms. But things got so bad in the 1900s that several assayers were driven from the district. At some mines change rooms were set up, where miners were compelled to change clothes at shift time. Later the Mine Owners' Association got legislation through which required assayers and everyone else to declare the source of their gold when handing it over to the Denver mint or to reduction plants. And so, during World War I, high-grading ceased. But perhaps it wasn't legal measures that ended high-grading. What really stopped it was that Cripple ran out of high-grade.

CHAPTER XXI: How to Make Ten Million Dollars

1. Twenty-seven millionaires (besides Stratton) is a low estimate. Here is an incomplete list, with previous professions, and ages in '99:

Sam Altman, lumberman	54
John Harnan, prospector	39
J. R. McKinnie, lather	53
Ed De LaVergne, engineer	53
Charles MacNeill, millman	28
George Bernard, grocer	48
Sam Bernard, grocer	40
Jimmie Burns, plumber	49
Jimmie Doyle, handyman	31
Frank Castello, storekeeper	44
Ed Giddings, department store owner	51
Judge E. A. Colburn, lawyer	56
W. S. Montgomery, lawyer	41
A. D. Jones, druggist	39
John K. Miller, druggist	40
James W. Miller, druggist	35
William Lennox, coal dealer	49
Frank G. Peck, cigar store keeper	37
Albert E. Carlton, no profession	33
Verner Z. Reed, promoter	36
Charles Tutt, real estate	35
Spencer Penrose, real estate	34
Frank Woods, real estate	38
Harry Woods, real estate	41
Sam Strong, roustabout	37
Ed Stark, butcher	49
Van E. Rouse, schoolteacher	36

The average age of this group of millionaires or near-millionaires was forty-two!

2. Not at that time, at least. Tom Walsh started developing the Camp Bird in '96. T. A. Rickard appraised it at $6,000,000 in 1900. Hammond bought it at that price from Walsh in 1902. Walsh had taken out gold ore worth $1,500,000 of which $750,000

was profit. The Camp Bird's production up to 1916 was $27,-
209,768; of this, $17,731,788 was pure profit. Thus, the Camp Bird
turned out to be a richer mine than the Independence, the total
production and profits of which are given in the next note.

3. Hammond paid far too much for the Independence. He
expected gross production in the first year of $7,000,000, with a
profit of $4,500,000. Instead he got $3,387,657 gross, only $2,-
000,000 profit, even though he gutted the mine frantically to boost
stock prices. So Hammond rushed to Cripple Creek to investigate.
He showed up at the Independence at 9 A.M., on May 10, 1900,
wearing the highest and shiniest boots, and carrying the longest
candlestick ever seen in the gold camp. He emerged to state that
the Independence had been grossly overvalued by somebody,
which meant T. A. Rickard. But a few weeks later the Australian
super and his aide, both of whom had been hired by Hammond,
were fired. Hammond had found out that these two had been
stealing Independence ore by the dozens of carloads.

The Independence never paid its English owners. In 1915 they
sold the mine to the Portland Gold Mining Company for
$325,000. The owners had given Stratton and Reed $11,000,000
for the mine. Their total dividends to 1915 came to only $5,-
237,739 on a gross production of $19,583,060. To have received a
modest 10 per cent annual return on their investment, the Englishmen should have received $27,175,000 in dividends over the
fifteen-year period. So all in all they took a $21,000,000 beating.

4. Reed stayed in Paris for thirteen lively years, during which
he made world news by driving an underslung Panhard across
the Sahara Desert (Scott Fitzgerald was later partial to underslung Panhards, too) . But then, Reed got his living expenses up
so high that his paltry million wouldn't suffice. Therefore, he
went to Denver to make thirty or forty million more in Wyoming
oil and banking. He went to Denver, they say, instead of back to
Colorado Springs, because Little London society kept reminding
him that his father had run a livery stable on Cucharras Street.

CHAPTER XXII: End of an Era

1. Grant had a good case but even if he hadn't he would probably have gotten off because he was a popular man. And he had
influential friends since he was a charter member of Cripple
Creek Lodge No. 316, B. P. O. E. Other leading Elks were Jimmie

Doyle, Oscar Lampman, Bert Carlton, J. Maurice Finn, Peter McCourt (Baby Doe Tabor's brother), Spencer Penrose, and Danny Sullivan.

2. The Gold Coin wasn't the only mine right in a town. Cripple Creek had one, too, just south of Bennett Avenue, near Fourth Street, Don Hanley's mine. But it never produced anything.

3. This Victor fire in August, 1899, started in Jennie Thompson's "999" dance hall. It destroyed the business section from First to Fifth Street and from Portland Avenue to Granite Avenue, including two railroad stations, the Gold Coin shaft house and the Gold Coin Club. The Woods boys lost a dozen properties, most of which they rebuilt more expensively than before.

4. It was this hydroelectric power scheme more than anything that finished the Woods boys. To keep it going they had to sell more power and that is why they tried to enter the electric street-car business in Pueblo, Colorado. The Thatcher family, who had been running Pueblo since territorial days, objected to the intrusion and helped knock down the credit props that were holding Frank and Harry up. By 1910 the Woods Investment Company was done, and the Woods boys moved away. Harry recouped some of his losses, dying in 1928 at Laguna Beach, California, in modestly comfortable circumstances. Poor Frank, an appealing man in many ways, suffered personal tragedies in the deaths of his son (in a mine cave-in), his daughter, and two wives. Frank died in Los Angeles, in 1932, so poor that his friends raised money to bury him.

5. It took twelve years for the lawyers of the Stratton Estate to get things straightened out enough to open the Home. The lawyer who finished the job was a youngster named David P. Strickler, who remains today in charge of all the Stratton interests. It was Strickler who successfully fought the claims of twelve women who said they were Stratton's widows. He settled also the final suit of Leslie J. Popejoy, Stratton's original grubstaker, for three thousand-odd dollars. Perhaps the toughest problem was fighting off the State of Colorado. Time after time politicians tried to get control of the Stratton Estate because Stratton's will contained a paragraph asking the State to take over if the trustees were incompetent. But Strickler has always been the opposite of incompetent. The politicians haven't got to first base.

There is one moot point about Myron Stratton Home. Stratton's will gives preference to residents of El Paso County. The will is dated August 5, 1901, more than two years after Teller County (Cripple Creek) was carved out of the western end of El Paso County. As a result, Cripple Creek miners are not eligible to enter the Home in their old age. And yet it seems unlikely that Stratton intended to ban his old miner friends. However, David Strickler feels that he must interpret the will literally even though he has reason to believe that the will, dated August 5, 1901, is almost an exact copy of a will made by Stratton in late '98 or early '99, before Teller County was created out of El Paso County. The implication is that Stratton neglected to amend the 1901 will so that Teller County residents would be eligible to enter the Home.

6. The National was quite a place. It contained 150 guest rooms, a huge bar, dining room, elevators, steam heat, private baths. It was five stories high, and built of brick. It was torn down just after World War I. You can see the empty lot where it stood at Bennett Avenue and Fourth Street.

CHAPTER XXIII: Woman Trouble

1. Hazel Vernon, the best known of Cripple's madams, was always regarded with suspicion by wives whose husbands had spent bachelor days in the gold camp. Not long ago an octogenarian wife decided to find out for sure whether her husband had known Hazel in the old days. While dining in a hotel with her husband, she had a note delivered to him which read, "How wonderful to see you, Jack dear! I am waiting in the bar! As always, Hazel V." The old fellow read the note, blushed, mumbled "My broker's on the phone" and scurried off, eyes alight and looking thirty years younger.

2. Lowell Thomas told this anecdote on his news broadcast while visiting Victor, his home town, in 1949. An excellent long version by Ralph Carr appears in the May 23, 1952, issue of the *Cripple Creek Gold Rush*.

CHAPTER XXIV: Tempest on the Rails

1. Harry Collbran was eased out of the M–T, which he himself had created, by his old partner, W. K. Gillett. Collbran's friend, Jesse Waters, stepped into Collbran's shoes as operating

head of the road. Collbran stayed in Denver awhile, with the Colorado Midland Railroad, and then went to Korea to build a line of railroads for the Korean government. Jesse Waters bought his steamship passage to Korea because he was penniless at the time. Waters, a really fine person, was killed in 1914, while making a safety inspection trip on the M–T wye in Poverty Gulch.

2. Blackmer came to Colorado Springs from Massachusetts, in 1885. He was elected county attorney in '92, district attorney in '94, and he turned out to be one of the most brilliant, and surely the sharpest, of all the Cripple Creek crowd. He gave up his Cripple Creek interests around 1912, to invest in Wyoming oil with Verner Reed and others. In 1924 he fled to France to escape testifying in the Teapot Dome scandal in which his friends were involved. During the next quarter century, he became one of the world's most famous fugitives from justice. In September, 1949, at the age of eighty, he returned to the United States, pleaded guilty to four charges of income tax evasion, paid fines of $20,000 and reached an agreement with the Justice Department which dismissed several perjury and evasion charges. He is still a multimillionaire, although he has paid the government millions in various income tax fines.

3. In 1916 the Midland Terminal group didn't even want the Short Line on lease any longer, and it went into receivership in 1919. W. D. Corley bought it for $370,000 in October, 1922, and sold off the rolling stock to circuses and lumber companies. He transformed the grade into the glorious Corley auto road. The Midland Terminal kept plugging along until 1949, though it ceased paying dividends in 1918 and passenger traffic was abandoned in 1932. The High and Low Electric Lines stopped running in 1922.

4. Among Haywood's minor complaints against the owners of the Standard Mill were the facts that MacNeill owned a $12,000 Rachet-Schneider car, Penrose had circled the globe in '99 and Charlie Tutt owned a 42-foot cabin cruiser at his summer place in Oregon.

CHAPTER XXV: The Black Time

1. The loan prompted the *Army and Navy Journal* to comment: "The arrangement virtually placed the troops for the time being in the relation of hired men to the mine operators and

morally suspended their function of State military guardians of the public peace. It was a rank perversion of the whole theory and purpose of the National Guard, and more likely to incite disorder than prevent it."

2. After leaving Cripple, according to his later confession, Harry Orchard tried to murder various people, including Governor Peabody, Charlie MacNeill, Judge Gabbert of Denver, and Sherman Bell. Finally, on December 30, 1905, he set a bomb which killed the antiunion ex-governor of Idaho, Frank Steunenberg. Idaho officials caught Orchard and kidnapped Haywood and other I.W.W. officers in Denver, and brought them to Boise to stand trial for allegedly master-minding the bombing. Harry Orchard turned State's evidence and was exposed by Haywood's counsel, Clarence Darrow, as a psychopathic perjurer. In spite of prosecution by District Attorney William Borah, Darrow won acquittals for Haywood and his fellow officers. Orchard went to the Idaho penitentiary for life.

A letter to the author, dated March 6, 1951, from the Idaho State penitentiary, reads:

Re: Harry Orchard
ISP #1406

DEAR SIR:

In reply to your letter of March 2, 1951, I advise that Harry Orchard is still alive and still incarcerated in this institution. He is about 84 years old, but is still sound for a man of his age. He naturally has slowed down but is not yet feeble.

He has for years been an outside trusty and during all his years of incarceration, his conduct has been above reproach.

Very truly yours,

L. E. CLAPP, WARDEN

3. Jimmie Burns' daughter, Mrs. Will Nicholson, of Denver, permitted me to copy this touching letter which Jimmie received from his employees right in the middle of the strike trouble:

Victor, Colorado
Jan. 28, 1904

Hon. James F. Burns, Pres.
The Portland Gold Mining Co.
Colorado Springs, Colo.
DEAR SIR:

The undersigned address you as a Committee of Employees of the Portland Mine appointed for the purpose of selecting and presenting our employer a fitting token of appreciation and esteem. Something fashioned of the fine gold from Colorado's greatest gold mine and a gift that may always be kept and treasured by yourself as a memento of regard from Five Hundred Mine Employees.

We would be unfeeling and ungrateful indeed did we not appreciate the heroic stand you have taken during the past few months in our behalf and against powerful odds. But we hope and believe that you have the Good Will and God Speed of all liberty-loving people.

We hereby present to you a watch and chain made of gold taken by our labor from the mine inseparably identified with your fortunes and prominently associated in the struggle you have made for justice and human liberty. The photographs on the watch dial are of those who are most dear to you and have been placed there with the hope that they may be a constant reminder of the good will and happiness that the givers wish you and yours.

Sincerely,
Employees of the Portland Mine

CHAPTER XXVI: Good-by, Bob

1. Only twenty-six years. Sam died finally on June 8, 1919, age ninety-nine years and seven months.

2. When he was broke, in the 1930s, Harnan wrote the Portland Company, from Nevada, for a job. The Portland super, who had never heard of him, replied that he had no work for him, because he could only use men familiar with the Portland mine.

CHAPTER XXIX: King Bert

1. Throughout his life, Spec Penrose gave full credit to Dick Penrose for Dick's guidance in mining matters. Not long ago a mining engineer named Herbert Hoover stated that Dick Penrose was one of the greatest mining men that America has produced.

Bibliography

Books

Anonymous. *Biographical Colorado*. Chicago. Chapman Publishing Co., 1899. Contains Alonzo Welty's account of how Cripple was named.

Atwood, Wallace W. *The Rocky Mountains*. New York. Vanguard Press, 1945. Colorado geology.

Bennett, Horace W. *Bright Yellow Gold*. New York. John C. Winston Co., 1935. Recollections.

Bennett, Horace W. *Silver Crown of Glory*. New York. John C. Winston Co., 1936. More recollections.

Brissenden, Paul Frederick. *History of the I.W.W*. New York. Columbia University Press, 1920.

Collier, William Ross, and Westrate, Edwin Victor. *The Reign of Soapy Smith*. New York. Doubleday, Doran & Co., Inc., 1935. Tells why Soapy never reached Cripple Creek town and gives one version of Denver "City Hall War."

Commons, John R. and Associates. *History of Labour in the United States*. New York. The Macmillan Co., 1918.

Crane, W. R. *A Treatise on Gold and Silver*. New York. John Wiley & Sons, 1908.

Fisher, John S. *A Builder of the West: The Life of William Jackson Palmer*. Caldwell, Idaho. Caxton Printers, 1939.

Garland, Hamlin. *Hesper*. New York. Harper & Brothers, 1903. A novel based on Strike of 1894. Garland's "Sky-town" is Altman; "Robert Raymond" is "General" Johnson; "Jack Munro" is Jack Smith; "Bozle" is Cripple Creek town; "Matt Kelly" is Emil W. Pfeiffer; the "Red Star Mill" is the Strong Mine.

Garland, Hamlin. *Money Magic*. New York. Harper & Brothers, 1907. A novel about Cripple Creek and Colorado Springs.

Holmes, Julia Archibald. *A Bloomer Girl on Pikes Peak, 1858.* Denver. Denver Public Library, 1949. The first lady to reach the summit writes a delightful account of her trip.

Horner, John Willard. *Silver Town.* Caldwell, Idaho. Caxton Press, 1950. About the Idaho Springs area when the Womacks began mining there.

Howbert, Irving. *Memories of a Lifetime in the Pikes Peak Region.* New York. G. P. Putnam's Sons, 1925. Perhaps the best account of pioneer days in the area.

Langdon, Emma F. *The Cripple Creek Strike, 1904.* Denver. Great Western Publishing Co., 1904. Official account of the Western Federation of Miners.

Lavender, David. *The Big Divide.* New York. Doubleday & Co., 1948.

Madison, Charles A. *American Labor Leaders.* New York. Harper & Brothers, 1950. Good material on Big Bill Haywood.

Morrell, W. F. *The Gold Rushes.* New York. The Macmillan Co., 1940.

Newton, Harry J. *Yellow Gold of Cripple Creek.* Denver. Nelson Publishing Co., 1928. Colorful yarns.

Orchard, Harry (Albert E. Horsley). *The Confessions and Autobiography of Harry Orchard.* New York. The McClure Co., 1907.

Ormes, Manly and Eleanor. *The Book of Colorado Springs.* Colorado Springs. Dentan Printing Co., 1933. Local history.

Perlman, Selig. *History of Trade Unionism in the United States.* New York. The Macmillan Co., 1929.

Peterson, Florence. *American Labor Unions.* New York. Harper & Brothers, 1945. Background on Western Federation of Miners.

Quiett, Glenn Chesney. *Pay Dirt.* New York. D. Appleton-Century, Inc., 1936.

Rickard, T. A. *A History of American Mining.* New York. McGraw-Hill Book Co., 1932.

Rickard, T. A. *The Romance of Mining.* Toronto. The Macmillan Co. of Canada, Ltd., 1945. Fine chapter on Cripple Creek.

Ruxton, George Frederick. *Life in the Far West.* Edinburgh and London. W. Blackwood & Sons, 1849. Earliest description of Ute Pass area.

Stone, Fred. *Rolling Stone.* New York. Whittlesey House, 1945. Contains chapter on Stone's Cripple Creek stay in 1892.

Street, Julian. *Abroad at Home.* New York. The Century Co., 1914. Contains the controversial Collier's article, "Colorado Springs and Cripple Creek."

Vanderwilt, John W. *Mineral Resources of Colorado.* Denver. Colorado Mineral Resources Board, 1947.

Waters, Frank. *Midas of the Rockies.* New York. Covici Friede, 1937. One of the best of all books on Colorado. The subject is Winfield Scott Stratton.

Williams, Albert N. *Rocky Mountain Country.* New York. Duell, Sloan and Pearce, 1950.

Willison, George F. *Here They Dug the Gold.* New York. Reynal and Hitchcock, 1946. On Colorado mining camps.

Wolcott, Frances M. *Heritage of Years.* New York. Minton, Balch & Co., 1932. Engaging gossip about Colorado Springs society in the Eighties by the wife of the late Senator Edward O. Wolcott.

Wolle, Muriel Sibell. *Stampede to Timberline.* Boulder, Colo. University of Colorado Press, 1949. Splendid survey of Colorado ghost towns.

Yellen, Samuel. *American Labor Struggles.* New York. Harcourt Brace & Co., 1936.

Articles in Periodicals

Anonymous. "The Shepherds of Colorado," *Harper's Monthly,* Sept., 1879. Early farming around Colorado Springs.

Anonymous. "The Roosevelt Drainage Tunnel," *The Mining Investor,* Colorado Springs, March 8, 1915.

Arnold, Frazer. "Sam Hartsel," *Colorado Magazine,* May, 1942. Origins of South Park Round-Up District.

Bird, Leah M. "Minor Political Parties in Colorado," *Colorado Magazine,* Nov., 1942. Populism and Governor Waite.

Fuller, Leon W. "A Populist Newspaper of the Nineties," *Colorado Magazine,* May, 1932. Populism and Governor Waite.

Guyot, N. E. "Cripple Creek: An Inside Story," *Engineering and Mining Journal-Press,* Dec. 13 and Dec. 20, 1924. A vivid picture of pioneer days at Cripple by the first assayer at Squaw Gulch.

Jackson, William S. "James Pourtales — Fifteen Western Years," *The Westerners Brand Book,* Denver, 1949. This fine paper was read before the Denver Westerners, a group of Rocky

Mountain historians, and later included in the annual publications.

McMechen, Edgar C. "The Founding of Cripple Creek," *Colorado Magazine,* Jan., 1935. Valuable report of an interview with Horace W. Bennett just before his death.

Pfeiffer, Emil W. "The Kingdom of Bull Hill," *Colorado Magazine,* Sept., 1935. Eye-witness account of the Strike of '94.

Rose, Marc A. "The Carlton Drainage Tunnel," *Forbes Magazine,* Oct. 15, 1941.

Thompson, Attie Long. "Our Home In the Petrified Forest," *Colorado Magazine,* May, 1934. Origins of Florissant.

Warman, Cy. "The Story of Cripple Creek," *Review of Reviews,* Feb., 1896.

Westermeier, Clifford P. "Cowboy Sports and the Humane Society," *Colorado Magazine,* Oct., 1949. More material about Arizona Charlie Meadows.

Pamphlets and Manuscripts

Anonymous. "History of Cripple Creek, 1894." Published in Cripple Creek. Includes directory.

Anonymous. "History of Cripple Creek," *Cripple Creek Sunday Herald,* Jan. 1, 1895.

Anonymous. "History of Cripple Creek District," *Cripple Creek Times,* Jan. 1, 1903.

Anonymous. "The Story of the World's Greatest Gold Camp," *Cripple Creek Times,* Aug. 1, 1904.

Anonymous. "Men of Note in the Cripple Creek Mining District," *The Mining Investor,* Colorado Springs, 1905.

Anonymous. "Golden Jubilee, St. Peter's Parish, 1892–1947," published by the Catholic Church in Cripple Creek, 1948.

Anonymous. "Criminal Record of the Western Federation of Miners, 1894–1904," compiled by the Colorado Mine Operators' Association, Denver, 1904.

Gehm, Harry J. "Mills of the Cripple Creek District," unpublished manuscript, 1949.

Hagerman, Percy. "The Cheyenne Mountain Country Club, 1891–1916," published privately by Raymond W. Lewis, Colorado Springs, 1947. Amusing stories of Charlie Tutt, Spencer Penrose, Count Pourtales and other early Cripple Creekers.

Hartzell, Charles. "A Short and Truthful History of Colorado During the Turbulent Reign of Davis the First," *C. J. Kelly Printers,* Denver, 1894. Anti-Waite propaganda.

Manning, J. F. "Visions of Victor," no publisher or date listed but probably published in Victor about 1896.

Rastall, Benjamin McKie. "The Labor History of the Cripple Creek District; a study in industrial evolution," *University of Wisconsin Press,* Bulletin No. 198, 1908. This excellent study for a Ph.D. thesis says almost everything there is to say of the labor troubles of 1894 and 1903–1904.

Rinker, Catherine. "History of Cripple Creek," unpublished M.A. thesis, University of Colorado, 1932.

Rogers, Hiram. "The Story of Cripple Creek," *Sargent and Rohrabacher,* Colorado Springs, 1900. By far the best of existing accounts of early Cripple Creek. The pamphlet as a whole is titled "The Fortunes of a Decade."

Reports and Directories

Colorado. *Biennial Message of the Governor,* January 4, 1895. Davis H. Waite's version of the Strike of '94.

Colorado Mining Association. *New Light on the Geology of the Cripple Creek District,* by A. H. Koschmann, Denver, 1941.

Colorado Scientific Society. *Geology and Ore Deposits of the Cripple Creek District,* by G. F. Loughlin and A. H. Koschmann, Denver, 1935.

Colorado Springs City Directories, 1888–1910.

Cripple Creek Town Directories, 1894, 1896, 1900, 1902.

Cripple Creek. *Compiled Ordinances,* 1902. Lists all officials from 1892.

Hills, Fred. *Official Manual of Cripple Creek, 1900.* Published by the author in Colorado Springs. Lists business records of 475 mining companies.

Myron Stratton Home. *Winfield Scott Stratton and the Myron Stratton Home,* by David P. Strickler, president of the Home, Colorado Springs, 1942.

Myron Stratton Home. *Triennial Report,* 1946–1948. Centennial Issue compiled by the Home's officers. Presents financial statements, principal events and records of admissions since Home opened in 1913. Also rules for admission and detailed balance sheets for 1946–1948.

United Gold Mines Company. *Annual Report,* 1904. This report, issued by the Woods brothers, gives a description of their properties at their fullest extent.

United States Government. *Geology and Mining Industries of the Cripple Creek District, Colorado,* by Whitman Cross and R. A. F. Penrose, Jr. Government Printing Office, Washington, D.C., 1895. So good it remains standard today.

United States Government. *Geology and Ore Deposits of the Cripple Creek District,* by G. F. Loughlin and A. H. Koschmann, a U.S. Geological Survey paper, Government Printing Office, Washington, D.C., 1950.

United States Government. *Seventh Annual Report of the United States Geological and Geographic Survey of the Territories,* 1873, by Ferdinand V. Hayden, Government Printing Office, Washington, D.C., 1874.

Newspapers

Colorado Springs Gazette (a daily)	1888–1918
Cripple Creek Crusher	1891–1894
Cripple Creek Gold Rush	1952
Cripple Creek Mail	1895–1896
Cripple Creek Prospector	1892–1893
Cripple Creek Sunday Herald	1895
Cripple Creek Times	1895–1918
Cripple Creek Weekly Journal	1893–1894

IMPORTANT WOMACK ARTICLES IN *Colorado Springs Gazette:*

July 5, 1902. "Cripple Creek News Notes." Contains interview with Bob Womack.

July 28, 1904. "Bob Womack May Recover." Front-page account of Bob's paralysis.

Feb. 9, 1908. "A Relief Fund for Bob Womack. Father of Cripple Creek Now Destitute. Is a Helpless Paralytic. Entirely Dependent on Care of Faithful Sister." Front-page opening of Relief Fund.

Aug. 11, 1909. "Discoverer of Great Gold Camp Dies Penniless. Bob Womack, the Father of Cripple Creek, Succumbs to Paralysis. Grief Hastens Death." Front-page obituary.

Jan. 12, 1919. "Father of Gold Camp Discoverer Nears Hundredth Year of Adventurous Career." Interview with Sam Womack.

June 9, 1919. "Samuel Womack, 99, Dead at His Home." Sam Womack obituary, front page.

Dec. 18, 1927. "Sister of Founder of Cripple Creek Dies at Home Here." Obituary, Miss Lida Womack, front page.

April 20, 1931. "William Womack, Region Pioneer, Dies at Home." Obituary, Bob's brother, front page.

Jan. 23, 1938. "Last of Womacks of Cripple Creek Fame, Mrs. Ida V. Womack." By C. S. Dudley, feature interview.

Sept. 6, 1940. "Mrs. Ida V. Womack Dies. Brother-in-law Discovered First Gold at Cripple Creek."

Acknowledgments

In writing this book I am deeply grateful to the following for giving me countless hours of their time: Harry J. Gehm, a Cripple Creeker from 1895 to 1916; the late Miss Florence Yambert, who spent most of her life in the Cripple Creek post office; the late Charles Howbert (brother of Irving), who lived in Cripple from 1893 to 1923; Mrs. Albert E. Carlton; the late Percy Hagerman, son of James J. Hagerman; and Ben Hill, dean of Cripple Creek engineers.

I wish to thank also Mrs. Spencer Penrose; Charles Tutt, Jr.; Miss Louise Kampf, Mrs. Helen Waring and Miss Laura Tait of the Coburn Library, Colorado College; Miss Margaretta M. Boas, Mrs. Margaret Reid, Mrs. Lora Light and Miss Edith Kearney of the Colorado Springs Public Library; Miss Dorothy Smith of the Pioneer Museum, Colorado Springs; Mrs. Alys Freeze and Mrs. Opal Harber of the Western Collection, Denver Public Library; Edgar C. McMechen and Miss Frances Shea of the State Museum; Raymond G. Colwell of the Historical Society of the Pikes Peak Region; Mrs. Mary Myrtle Thompson, Mrs. Kathleen Leonard and Mrs. Camille Densmore of the El Paso County Clerk's office; Mrs. Hazel Pickett and Fred Bochmann of Evergreen Cemetery, Colorado Springs; David P. Strickler, president of Myron Stratton Home; and Hildreth Frost, for indispensable records of claims and other real estate.

Also Mrs. Jack Edwards and Mrs. Roberta Davis of Colorado Springs, nieces of Bob Womack; Homer Davis of Manitou, Bob's grandnephew; Mrs. Elizabeth V. Hite of Colorado Springs, William Womack's sister-in-law and former secretary of Irving Howbert; John Robert Witherspoon and Alfred B. Dell of Guffey, old ranchers who rode with Bob Womack in the Eighties.

Also Jimmie Doyle, who, when interviewed in '49, was still spry and full of Irish fun as chief clerk in the Land Office, State Capitol, Denver; Virgil Mann, former secretary to A. E. Carlton; Mrs. Will Nicholson (Gladys Burns), daughter of Jimmie Burns; Melvin Sowle, half brother of Horace W. Bennett; Richard Roelofs, Jr., of New York City; Mrs. Ralph Giddings, daughter-in-law of Ed Giddings; Louis Castello, son of Frank Castello; George Frank Welty, son of George Welty; E. W. Faulkner, son of Annie Welty; Mrs. Avis Beagles, granddaughter of Frank Welty; Mrs. Roy Welty, daughter-in-law of Frank Welty; William Bowers, grandson of Professor Henry Lamb; Thomas Gough, husband of Sally Halthusen; Arthur Perkins, whose father was Uncle Ben Requa's partner at Fountain; Fred Steck, Jimmie Burns' chauffeur.

Also Miss Louise Trautman, daughter of Fred Trautman; Mrs. Madeline Nolon McKinnie, daughter of Johnnie Nolon and daughter-in-law of J. R. McKinnie; William I. Howbert, son of Irving Howbert; William M. Arkins, an old-time Cripple Creek reporter now married to Harry Woods' widow; Vernon Peiffer, Cripple Creek postmaster; Mrs. Hazal Conrad of Four-Mile, granddaughter of David Shields, pioneer Cripple Creek teacher; P. H. Nichols and L. H. (Pix) Nichols, miners at Cripple since '92; Mrs. A. W. Oliver of the Teller County Welfare Office; the late Mrs. Martha Nash of Altman and Cripple Creek; Grover Severs, for years the postman on Myers Avenue; Eugene Moffet, former Independence assayer; Mrs. Luther A. Jenks and Mrs. L. W. Rogers of Independence; Mr. and Mrs. William Peterie of Four-Mile; Mr. and Mrs. Troy Wade of Cripple Creek; and Ed Zell, former assayer at the Anaconda.

Also Margaret and Kenneth Geddes, who owned the *Cripple Creek Times-Record;* Mrs. Hazel Bunker and the Malcolm Andersons of the new *Cripple Creek Gold Rush* (formerly the *Times-Record*); Lowell Thomas, Victor's most famous former resident; Mrs. Lloyd R. Jackson of Columbus, Ohio, an ardent student of Cripple Creek; Mrs. Dorothy Erb, Mrs. William C. Allen and Clyde Allen of Florissant; Mrs. Mae Mayo of Four-Mile; Judge Philip L. Rice and Miss Ethel M. Damon of Lihue, Hawaii, for data on the De LaVergne family; Merrill Shoup, president of the various Carlton companies; Max Bowen and Miss Hazel Bates of the Golden Cycle Corporation; W. D. Corley, Jr., whose father bought the Short Line for a scenic highway; James Hill for data on Smith Gee; John J. Lipsey of the Denver Westerners; Tom Rolofson of Cripple Creek; Albert S. Konselman, who operates the Jo Dandy and other Cripple Creek mines; and Mrs. Evelyn Schwab, who loaned me for many months an invaluable map of Cripple Creek town.

Index

Index

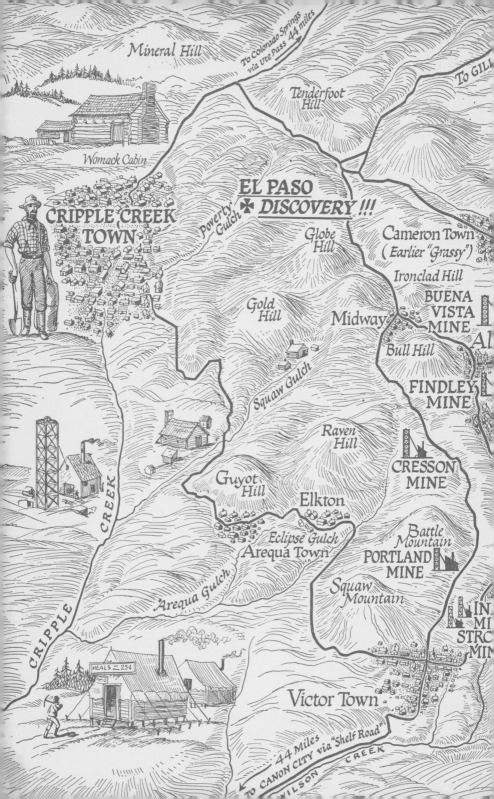

Mineral Hill

Womack Cabin

To Colorado Springs
via Ute Pass 44 miles

Tenderfoot
Hill

To GILL

EL PASO ✠ DISCOVERY !!!

Poverty Gulch

**CRIPPLE CREEK
TOWN**

Globe
Hill

Cameron Town
(Earlier "Grassy")

Ironclad Hill

Gold
Hill

Midway

**BUENA
VISTA
MINE**

Al

Bull Hill

Squaw Gulch

**FINDLEY
MINE**

Raven
Hill

**CRESSON
MINE**

Guyot
Hill

Elkton

Eclipse Gulch
Arequa Town

Battle
Mountain

**PORTLAND
MINE**

CREEK

Squaw
Mountain

IN
MI
STRC
MIN

Arequa Gulch

CRIPPLE

MEALS 25¢

Victor Town

44 Miles
To CANON CITY via "Shelf Road"

WILSON CREEK